02/11

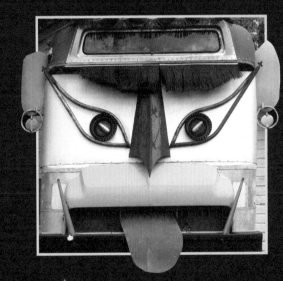

WEIRD
COLORADO

WEiRD COLORADO

Your Travel Guide to Colorado's Local Legends and Best Kept Secrets

By Charmaine Ortega Getz

Mark Sceurman and Mark Moran, Executive Editors

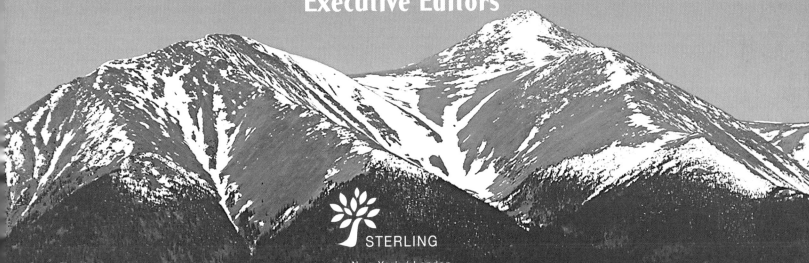

STERLING

New York / London
www.sterlingpublishing.com

021411

WEIRD COLORADO

STERLING and the distinctive Sterling logo are registered trademarks of Sterling Publishing Co., Inc.

Published by Sterling Publishing Co., Inc.
387 Park Avenue South, New York, NY 10016

Distributed in Canada by Sterling Publishing
c/o Canadian Manda Group, 165 Dufferin Street
Toronto, Ontario, Canada M6K 3H6
Distributed in the United Kingdom by GMC Distribution Services,
Castle Place, 166 High Street, Lewes, East Sussex, England BN7 1XU
Distributed in Australia by Capricorn Link (Australia) Pty. Ltd.
P.O. Box 704, Windsor, NSW 2756, Australia

10 9 8 7 6 5 4 3 2 1

Manufactured in China.
All rights reserved.

Photography and illustration credits are found on page 271 and constitute an extension of this copyright page.

Sterling ISBN-13: 978-1-4027-5463-0

For information about custom editions, special sales, premium and corporate purchases, please contact Sterling Special Sales Department at 800-805-5489 or specialsales@sterlingpub.com.

Layout and production by bobsteimle.com

DEDICATION

To the love of my life, my husband, Steve Winograd, who stoked my sanity whenever it seemed in danger of slipping away.

CONTENTS

Our weird journey began a long, long time ago in a far-off land called New Jersey. Once a year or so we'd compile a homespun newsletter to hand out to our friends called *Weird N.J.* The pamphlet was a collection of odd news clippings, bizarre facts, little-known historical anecdotes, and anomalous encounters from our home state. The newsletter also focused on the kind of very localized legends that were often whispered around a particular town but seldom heard outside the boundaries of the community where they first originated.

We had started the publication with the simple theory that every town in the state had at least one good tale to tell. *Weird N.J.* soon became a full-fledged magazine and we made the decision to actually do all of our own investigating and see if we couldn't track down just where all of these seemingly unbelievable stories were coming from. Was there, we wondered, any factual basis for these fantastic local legends that people were telling us? Armed with not much more than a camera and notepad, we set off on a mystical journey of discovery. Much to our surprise and amazement, much of what we had initially presumed to be nothing more than urban legend actually turned out to be real, or at least contained a grain of truth that had originally sparked the lore.

After about a dozen years of documenting the bizarre, we were asked to write a book about our adventures, and so *Weird N.J.: Your Travel Guide to New Jersey's Local Legends and Best Kept Secrets* was published in 2003. Soon people from all over the country began writing to us, telling us strange tales from their home states. As it turned out, what we had first perceived to be a very local-interest genre was actually just a small part of a much larger and more universal phenomenon.

People from all over the United States had strange tales to tell that they believed to be true, and they all wanted somebody to tell them to.

When our publisher asked us what we wanted to do next, for us the choice was simple: "We'd like to do a book called *Weird U.S.*, in which we could document the local legends and strangest stories from all over the entire country," we told them. So for the next twelve months we set out in search of weirdness wherever it could be found in these fifty states.

In 2004, after *Weird U.S.* was published, our publisher asked us once more where we wanted to go next. In the year that it had taken us to put together *Weird U.S.,* we had come to the conclusion that this country had more great tales waiting to be told than could be contained in just one book. We had discovered—somewhat to our surprise—that every state we researched seemed to have more fascinating stories to offer than we actually had pages to accommodate. Everywhere we looked we found unwritten folklore, creepy cemeteries, cursed locations, and outlandish roadside oddities. With this in mind, we told our publisher that we wanted to document it *all*, and to do it in a series of books, each focusing on the peculiarities of a particular state.

Our plan was to work closely with local authors native to the state we were covering. This presented a bit of a problem, though, as we didn't always know just the right person to tell a particular state's stories. That was the exact dilemma we faced in the case of Colorado. Fortunately, Weird people just seem to gravitate toward us. And that is how we first became acquainted with author Charmaine Ortega Getz. One day a while back, we received the following message from a strange

Coloradoan that read, "I am a fan of all things weird and have been enjoying the Weird books . . . with one exception: Weird Colorado. There is no *Weird Colorado*! And why ever not, pray tell? I can assure you, there is more weird here than has been dreamt of by *Weird U.S.* So, how does one go about applying for the job of writing a *Weird Colorado* book? Can I, can I, can I, huh?"

After checking into Charmaine's writing credentials, it was clear to us that she not only possessed a great talent for her craft and was a wonderfully gifted storyteller, but that she also had what we refer to as the "Weird Eye." The Weird Eye is needed to seek out and find the sort of stories we were looking for. It requires one to see the world in a different way, with a renewed sense of wonder and curiosity. And once you have it,

there is no going back—you never see things the same way again. All of a sudden you begin to reexamine your own environs, noticing your everyday surroundings as if for the first time. And you begin to ask yourself questions like, "What the heck is *that* thing all about, anyway?" and, "Doesn't anybody else think that's kind of *weird*?"

So come with us now and let Charmaine take you on a tour of *her* Centennial State —and see just why the state really lives up to its other nickname—"Colorful Colorado." With all its unique wonders, mysterious places, unusual characters, and unexpected sites, it's a place we like to call Weird Colorado.

—*Mark Sceurman and Mark Moran*

For weirdness to flourish, it has to have the right compost made up of dramatic history, amazing environments, and truly unique, off-the-grid characters. Colorado is blessed with all three.

I've lived in Colorado for more than a decade, since following the love of my life here from California in the late 1990s. But even as a journalist who has long been fascinated with truth more colorful than fiction—and married to a lifelong Colorado native—I didn't realize just how blessed this state is until I agreed to write this book.

Let's step back a moment. When *Weird N.J.* came out, followed by *Weird U.S.*, I was hooked immediately. Imagine my disappointment when the Weird books started rolling into the bookstores, and there wasn't one on Colorado.

The best I could find was a single story in *Weird U.S.* (Bishop's Castle, the one-man architectural wonder deep in the San Isabel National Forest). In between writing assignments about city zoning, high-altitude gardening, camp-out cookery, and the history of men's secret fraternal societies, I pondered this inequity.

At last, I sent an e-mail to Mark Moran and Mark Sceurman, the earthly gods of Weirdness. It said, "Gentlemen, you don't know from weird in Colorado." I gave the Marks a summary of some of the stories I collected in the few years I had lived in the Mile-High State to date.

There was Frozen Dead Guy Days in tiny Nederland, of course, a celebration I had attended since its inaugural event. Back then, the festival was so small that the snowboarders from Boulder headed farther up the mountain didn't bother to get off at Ned's bus stop. Now it's an event that draws hundreds of people seeking to get their freak on every March.

Then there is the student cafeteria at Colorado's flagship university named for Alfred Packer, the nineteenth-century mountain guide who turned his party of fortune hunters into survival grub.

And who could forget the annual commemoration in Fruita of Mike, the rooster that lost its head but not its will to live?

Mark Moran's e-mail response read something like, "Well, OK, then, send us those stories." So I did. Three of my stories appeared in the second edition of *Weird U.S.* and sometime in 2007, I got an invitation from the Marks to write *Weird Colorado*.

"You think there's enough weird in Colorado for a whole book?" my husband Steve, the lifelong Coloradoan, asked.

After a year of criss-crossing the state in my purple Subaru, interviewing a few hundred people, searching through old bookstores, libraries, and the Internet, I can confidently say, "You betcha, my sweet baboo."

Colorado may not be one of those states that immediately springs to mind as a haven of the strange and bizarre. It's a vacation destination for those who love the glorious outdoors, snow sports, rock climbing, and the many microbreweries, just to name a few well-known features. For folks who don't look more closely, the nearest things to "weird" in Colorado are the two liberal cities—Boulder and Durango—in a state that historically was a lot redder until 2008.

True fans of weird know it's not just about the bizarre and strange, but about the unusual in *all* its fascinating, beautiful, repellent, hilarious aspects.

So searching in Colorado for weird is not hard. In fact, there is a slew of books that has covered much of the state's more colorful people, places,

and things, many of which have inspired me and are mentioned in the Acknowledgments.

I also had the help and encouragement of many generous, good-humored folks who sometimes weren't sure of what I was doing but were willing to trust that it wasn't mean-spirited. Weirdness is often found in a local legend, a neighborhood story, a place well off the beaten path—unwritten about and often half forgotten.

My challenge for *Weird Colorado* was to find the fresh angle for well-known stories too good to ignore, as well as to unearth the tales that hadn't had their due yet. As a journalist, I wanted to provide as much of the real deal, the true story, as possible.

My hope is that I've written a book that will disappoint no one, particularly anyone who had a hand in helping me shape it. And that it will provide as much joy in reading as I had with writing it.

Thanks, Marks, for helping me to get better acquainted with Colorado!

—*Charmaine Ortega Getz*

outlandish, the bigger than life, even the paranormal. Unlike a tall tale or fairy tale, the most unusual happening could come off as believable even if not believed.

That's because a legend doesn't need a moral, a structure, or even a neat ending. It needs truth: a historical basis, some real-life characters, confirmable details, an actual physical setting. Weave these around the otherwise unbelievable element until you have something people would prefer to believe even when they know better . . . that's when you have a legend.

Legends were made in Colorado.

Legend of the Blue Mist

They've been told around campfires in Estes Park for decades—tales about Miner Bill, the crazed old prospector who raved about a "Blue Mist" that would descend sometimes on cloudy, overcast evenings. When the mysterious mist retreated, it always left fresh animal remains and huge three-toed claw marks on tree trunks and soil.

When Miner Bill failed to be seen in town for an unusually long time, folks grew concerned. Someone finally made the difficult slog to the mountain where Miner Bill's isolated cabin stood and came back with a grim report. The bones and sinews of Miner Bill and his dog were surrounded by tracks of a peculiar three-toed mark. . . .

Estes Park is a beautiful, small mountain town; one of the town's streets is called Blue Mist Lane, and the Lula W. Dorsey Museum keeps a number of artifacts that supposedly belonged to the legendary prospector.

Shortly before World War II, a young wrangler named Bill Robinson started work at various livery stables and ranches. He often led horse rides and was a master storyteller who held forth at campfires to an audience of breathless visitors. Robinson had known Miner Bill, born William Clyde Currence

in Virginia around 1868. Currence left his family's Nebraska homestead in 1883 and wound up a prospector on Ute Mountain, Colorado. In 1904, several acquaintances took him to the Montezuma County jail because he was berserk and incoherent. After a sanity hearing, Bill went to what was then called the Colorado State Insane Asylum in Pueblo but was released a year later.

He turned up in Estes Park in 1908. He raved about astrology and "divine things," but he was rational enough to stake his mining claims with a partner and build a couple of cabins. However, the mining claims were fairly worthless, and anyway, the men were digging up land that belonged to the government. Eventually his partner gave up and left, but Bill stuck it out until 1930 when he finally moved to town, a disheveled, raving old coot.

Miner Bill died of arteriosclerosis in 1951. With no relatives to claim the body, his corpse was handed to the Colorado State Anatomical Board for medical study. His remains were cremated, and the ashes scattered in Denver.

His old cabins still stand—on protected Rocky Mountain National Park land, by the way. There's a rocky outcropping on Mount Chapin near Fall River Road called Miner Bill's Spire.

What about the Blue Mist and the mysterious deaths? Well, Bill Robinson, the master storyteller, who died in 2003 at age 75, made up that part.

The Blue Mist: An Estes Park Legend, published by the YMCA, has a foreword and biography of Miner Bill written by Jack Melton, director of the museum. Melton is an ardent student of American folklore.

Melton doesn't seem to think there's any merit to Robinson's tale, but we're not so sure. "There were so many other details in that story that were true," Melton concedes.

Regardless, camp counselors and other summer workers get together to swap more tales of the Blue Mist. Anytime a hiker disappears—which is not

It always left fresh animal remains.

uncommon, considering the area's rugged slopes—it is said that the Blue Mist was seen just before or after.

Out of the Blue Mist Legend

In the summer of 1984, my friend Randy and I worked at the YMCA of the Rockies near Estes Park, Colorado. We were hired as seasonal help, and the job offered little: long hours of menial labor and low pay. Room and board was included and, for a mountain climber like me, it was the summer of heaven, nestled as we were against Rocky Mountain National Park and its spectacular scenery.

Randy and I intended to be the first in our group of climbing friends to reach the top of Sprague Mountain and Stones Peak. It's a twenty-one-mile journey, with most of it above the tree line, and dangerous on many counts. So to play it safe, you need to start hiking by no later than one A.M. to get back before the light show begins.

About five miles into the climb, we stopped for a snack and some water, dropping our thirty-pound packs and turning off our flashlights to conserve batteries. We were surrounded by inky blackness, as there was no moon. The stars hung above us in brilliant banners.

As I was stuffing my water bottle back into my pack, something caught my attention. Down in the valley below us was a glowing blue haze. Before I could mention it to Randy, he grabbed my arm and pointed toward it. We had the same thought: It was the Blue Mist!

We had heard about Miner Bill, the prospector who told stories of a floating blue mist that drove his dogs wild. Eventually, those misty visits drove him mad. More recent stories told the disappearance of hikers soon after the sighting of a glowing blue cloud.

Yeah, we knew the Blue Mist was just a legend. Yet, there in the valley below us a luminescent blue haze floated above the trees. It had the appearance of a nebula, with a brighter, glowing center surrounded by a more diffuse disk. It resembled a monstrous blue eye, staring up at us. We agreed that it had to be the lights down at the Bear Lake parking lot.

Quickly shouldering our packs, we headed out and didn't look back. However, the luminescent blue specter was etched forever into my brain.

You see, when Randy and I stood there alone in the blackness and mutually agreed that the blue haze was from the lights at the Bear Lake parking lot, neither of us dared speak of what we knew to be true.

There are no lights at the Bear Lake parking lot. —*Steve Sorensen*

Warning: *It's a highly challenging hike up this zigzag trail, day or night, even for the experienced climber. Sudden storms can trigger dense fog and rockslides. Bears are common and cell phones probably won't work.*

Face on the Barroom Floor

A mysterious painting on the floor of the Teller House Restaurant in Central City has baffled generations. Many believe that it inspired a famous poem. Others have heard that it was drawn by a vindictive man, upset that his girlfriend was cheating on him so that all who visited would step right on her.

Just what is the story with this mysterious visage?

Central City, thirty-five miles west of Denver, is famous for its gambling casinos and well-preserved nineteenth-century mining-era buildings, including a small jewel of an opera house that is still in business today.

Teller House is the best-known building in Central City, situated literally next to the opera house. At the time it was built in 1872, it was said to be the finest hotel west of the Mississippi River. Painted on the heavily varnished wooden floor of its splendid old bar is the face of a beautiful woman with a sidelong glance.

There are several stories about the origin of the face in books and on the Internet. Most of them are wrong because the picture has been confused with an older poem that inspired it—"The Face on the Barroom Floor," written by Hugh Antoine d'Arcy in 1887.

Central City was one of the most successful mining towns in Colorado. When the mines gave out, though, so did much of the local economy, and the place was nearly a ghost town by the 1920s.

A group of citizens came together to work for the preservation of the town. The Central City Opera House Association hired a Denver artist named Herndon Davis in 1936 to create a series of paintings. (Davis was an illustrator for the *Denver Post* and the *Rocky Mountain News* and moonlighted as a mural artist.)

The project director, Ann Evans, was a granddaughter of the early Colorado territorial governor John Evans and a bona fide grande dame in Denver society. She disliked Davis's less-than-romantic portraits of gunslingers, miners, and whores, and they quarreled about them.

As a result, Davis either quit or was fired; no one really knows for sure. What we do know came from Davis himself, in a 1954 *Denver Post* interview preserved in the historical archives of the Denver Press Club (reprinted from its Web site with the organization's permission):

The Central City Opera House Association hired me to do a series of paintings and sketches of the famous mining town, which they were then rejuvenating as an opera center and tourist attraction.

I stayed at the Teller House while working up there, and the whim struck me to paint a face on the floor of the old Teller House barroom. In its mining boom heyday, it was just such a floor as the ragged artist used in d'Arcy's famous old poem. But, the hotel manager and the bartender would have none of such tomfoolery. They refused me permission to paint the face.

Still the idea haunted me, and in my last night in Central City, I persuaded the bellboy, Jimmy Libby, to give me a hand. After midnight, when the coast was clear, we slipped down there. Jimmy held a candle for me, and I painted as fast as I could. Yet it was 3 A.M. when I finished.

As the story goes, Jimmy scraped off the varnish with a brick beforehand while Davis stoked up with a few drinks. Afterward, Davis fled town.

As it happened, the management at Teller House loved the mysterious little unsigned painting and kept it. To explain its presence, employees told tourists that it was the actual painting in the old poem, or that it, at least, inspired the poem.

Another story given out was that a drunken miner painted the face of his unfaithful girlfriend where people would have to walk all over her. Whatever, the story of the mysterious face with its sidelong glance brought droves of tourists to the bar.

Davis worked outside of Colorado for some time and heard about the now-famous Teller House attraction when he returned to Denver in 1946. He stomped back to Central City and painted his signature on the portrait but claimed that the bar's management removed it to keep the mystique.

The model for the Face was Davis's wife, an artist named Edna Juanita "Nita" Cotter. She wasn't thrilled about the location of her portrait, which is why it's believed Davis always said it was "just a face," but he refused to reproduce it. His wife begged their friends to stay silent about it until her death in 1975.

Davis was working on a mural for the Smithsonian Institution in Washington, DC, when he suffered a fatal heart attack in 1962. He is buried in Fort Logan National Cemetery in Denver.

The Face is now protected with a frame, but it's still on the barroom floor.

Emma Crawford

Pretty, young Emma Crawford was a "lunger," one of the unfortunate and desperate hordes who came to Colorado seeking a cure from tuberculosis, sometimes called consumption or the white death.

Manitou Springs was famous for its mineral water that was supposed to have healing properties. Emma arrived with her mother in the 1880s, and they lived in a house from which Emma could see Red Mountain to the south.

Emma was engaged to a civil engineer named Hildebrand, or Hiltbrand, who was employed on the construction of the nearby Pikes Peak Cog Railway. They were to marry once Emma had recovered.

The Crawfords were spiritualists who believed they each had an Indian guide in the spirit world. Emma one day thought she saw her guide summoning her to Red Mountain. According to the story, Emma at some point managed to climb to the peak and tied her scarf to a tree to prove it. Her health apparently went into a sudden decline soon after because on December 4, 1891, a few days before her scheduled wedding, Emma died.

Her fiancé knew Emma wanted to be buried at the summit of Red Mountain and although he failed to obtain a deed for the site, he recruited eleven men to help him put her casket there anyway. There was no road to the summit, so it took them all day, in two shifts. It's said that so many spiritualists later trekked to Emma's grave that a path was worn into the mountain.

Local legend says that a flood and resulting landslide one day unearthed Emma's coffin and sent it all the way back down Red Mountain and into town. It's a fun image but not quite what happened.

When a railroad attempted to build on the site in 1912, Emma's grave was moved to the south side of Red Mountain. Unfortunately, this was a gravel slope, and years of heavy

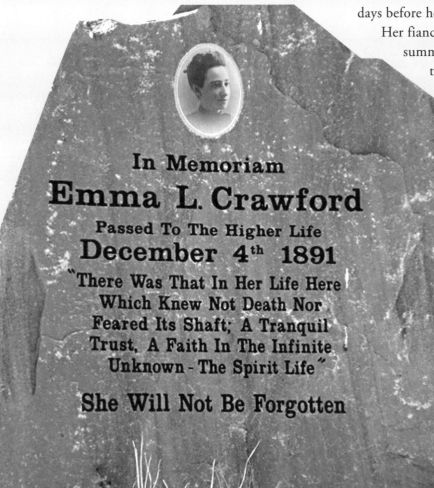

In Memoriam
Emma L. Crawford
Passed To The Higher Life
December 4th 1891
"There Was That In Her Life Here Which Knew Not Death Nor Feared Its Shaft; A Tranquil Trust, A Faith In The Infinite Unknown - The Spirit Life"

She Will Not Be Forgotten

truly final resting place, the city had been honoring her memory (since 1994) with an annual ghost walk, hearse parade, and other events. However, the real highlight

A few days before her scheduled wedding, Emma died.

is the Emma Crawford Coffin Races on the main drag, Manitou Avenue. Teams of costumed folks guide highly creative coffins on wheels with an "Emma" in each one.

rains pounded away at the soil until Emma's coffin was unearthed in August 1929. A couple of boys found her skull, and her bones were soon gathered and deposited in the city hall at Manitou Springs. For two years, officials tried to find Emma's next of kin.

Eventually, her remains were moved to an unmarked grave in Manitou Springs's Crystal Valley Cemetery. A gravestone was finally installed in 2004, adorned with Emma's picture, a poem, and the promise SHE WILL NOT BE FORGOTTEN.

Even before Emma reached her

Manitou Springs Spa

Known for its healing mineral springs, Manitou Springs is a little mountain resort at the foot of Pikes Peak. You can freely help yourself at a variety of fountains that spew, sputter, gurgle, and dribble water with a different taste at each site.

For many years, the biggest and best spring in town was part of a formerly elegant old spa. However, the three-story, thirty-four-thousand-square-foot building smack in the middle of the town's historic center had been neglected and gradually declined.

"When I was a kid," says Chuck Murphy of Colorado Springs, "it was still a pretty neat place. I remember my father taking me so we could use the steam baths and sauna. In the lobby, there was always a lady in a starched white uniform who would hand out little Dixie cups of the water. It was so good, you bought the bottles of spring water to take home."

The building was a state-of-the-art wonder in 1921—a mix of residences, shops, restaurants, and the spa. It later became antiquated and in dire need of repair and updating. Successive owners were unable or unwilling to deal with the cost of a money pit, let alone the red tape involved in the restoration of what was officially a historic landmark.

Several legends grew. One stated a Native American shaman cursed the site: "No white man's enterprise will ever thrive there!" the curse supposedly decreed. A second story told of a cursed owner who decided to enclose the Soda Spring in 1918 and charge for the water. After that, any time misfortune occurred at the building, the curse was blamed. Finally, another story surrounded a more recent owner, who allegedly reneged on a deal with a local shaman to restore the building in return for the lifting of the curse.

Soon people were talking about strange noises and lights late at night, glimpses of people walking about

The New Bath House and Mineral Springs, Manitou, Colorado.

inside, and other weird happenings.

"The *real* story was that there was a succession of owners with a dream and a scheme, but they always ran out of money," says Chuck Murphy. "The last owner couldn't keep it up by himself and couldn't sell it."

In 1999, the old bathhouse was finally condemned. At that point, Murphy became involved. His company, Murphy Constructors, had done successful restorations of other historic buildings in town, so he recruited a couple of big investors and pitched a deal to the town that it couldn't refuse.

By the time renovations began in 2005, vandals and squatters had left their marks. After salvaging anything left of value, Murphy tore the building down to its concrete and steel skeleton. The spring was preserved, and the calcium deposits were carefully stripped from the Italian marble floor. However, the project was mired in bureaucratic red tape that slowed the restoration project during the next two years.

"I have a friend who has lived in Manitou Springs for thirty years," says Maureen Murphy, Chuck's daughter, who works for Murphy Constructors. "She told me about a woman who let herself into the site at midnight, went up to the top story, and performed a blessing ritual. She told my friend that if there was a curse, it would remove itself in the form of big black birds. They saw two big black birds fly out of there."

Chuck Murphy is just glad that his "passion project" was finally finished in 2007. No mysterious accidents. No paranormal episodes. No deaths. In fact, it's once again a popular gathering place and maybe—just maybe—the shaman's curse has finally ended.

Manitou Springs's Annual Great Fruitcake Toss

The Annual Great Fruitcake Toss is Manitou Springs's answer to cabin fever and too many "Christmas bricks." Every January since 1996, people assemble at Memorial Park to have a go at flinging the despised holiday food in creative ways.

The event began as the brainchild of the Chamber of Commerce's executive director, Michele Carvell, who remembered her childhood aversion to her great-aunt Elsie's holiday gift as well as the lack of enthusiasm among her friends for the fruitcakes in their lives.

At the time, the Chamber was looking for a seasonal event that could be put on with minimal cash. Carvell brought up the perennial fruitcake dilemma and suggested doing something more fun than simply regifting them.

At first, it was simple—a strong arm and a fruitcake. The thrower who achieved the most distance won. The satisfying thrill of soaring cake soon gave way to the ancient human need to keep making things more interesting and, inevitability, the competitive spirit.

Devices were entered into a separate category so as not to compete with pure human power—slingshots, of course, and golf clubs, even an archery bow (fruitcake impaled on an arrow). Then somebody trundled in a crowd-pleasing working reproduction of a trebuchet, or medieval seige catapult.

Soon, people started messing with the fruitcakes themselves. The event organizers had to create rules: nothing more than the traditional baking ingredients, no foreign objects to add heft, weight restrictions for cakes according to type of launch, no foil, and no duct tape.

Teams formed and competition was stoked. In 2002, a group of engineers from the Boeing Company lost to a team of Girl Scouts. The engineers came up with the Omega 380, a launcher fueled by compressed air pumped by an exercise bicycle. The artillery-like device fired fruitcakes so far that a Global Positioning System (GPS) device had to be used to track them.

"When Team Boeing brought in a pneumatic cannon and launched missiles more than 1,400 feet, well, that was amazing, but the whole distance thing started to feel pointless, you know?" says Floyd O'Neil, the Chamber's director of special events.

Not only did it seem ludicrous to have to use a GPS to track flying fruitcakes, but the darn things were hitting cars, homes, and businesses and threatening to bonk innocent townspeople on the streets.

"Got one on the roof of the Moroccan restaurant, hit some into the neighborhood behind it," says O'Neil. "Didn't exactly seem neighborly. So we moved the event to the track at the Manitou Springs High School. More room, less risk of hitting stuff."

However, the audience had to be kept well back away from the launchers' area to prevent spoiling the school's track field. So, the event was moved back to the smaller Memorial Park, the focus was changed, rules were tweaked, and new events were added.

There are now eight categories of competition, and only three include distance as a factor. Teams aim their fruitcakes at targets (old television sets and computer monitors are popular) placed at different distances. People can also attempt to catch the fruity missiles with baseball gloves, buckets, fishing nets, and the like. Kids and adults have separate categories.

The winner in more recent years is awarded a modest trophy and a T-shirt. The only entry fee is a donation of a nonperishable or canned edible for the local food bank—as long as it isn't a fruitcake.

Angel of Shavano

Mount Shavano is named for a Ute tribal leader but is best known for an image on its east slope.

The Angel is a trio of intersecting snow-filled gullies that looks vaguely like a human figure with arms upraised. It only appears in the spring and just for a few weeks to a month.

Various books about Colorado and its place names say there are several Indian legends about the image but usually don't give many details. One local story is that the Angel appeared after Shavano prayed for his dying friend, the scout George Beckwith.

Another is that an Indian princess sacrificed herself so that the gods would send much-needed rain. Every year, she comes back to weep rain for her people in the valley below.

There's also a non-Indian version of that one. This tale stuck a frivolous young goddess on Mount Shavano until she learned to shed tears for others. She became so good at it she's allowed to return year after year.

Something like this last version was written in the 1920s and circulated widely with photos of the Angel. It still couldn't compete with the Mountain of the Holy Cross for pilgrimage power, but the area has come into its own for its outdoor recreation and the funky charm of its small towns.

For many, sighting the Angel after a Colorado winter is miracle enough.

The Vampire Grave

Take a hand-etched grave marker with the word *Translvania* on it, put it in an old cemetery, and *voila*, you have a vampire story that won't die.

"We have no idea who the guy is," says Dick Schillawski, past president of the Lafayette Historical Society. "He died in 1918, and he's buried in the old section for indigents in the Lafayette Municipal Cemetery. That's all we know."

In stories that repeatedly make the rounds of Internet paranormal sites, the gravestone is written in a foreign language and states that one Fodor (Theodore) Glava, born in Transylvania and died in 1918, is buried there. Local legend says there's a tree growing out of the grave (maybe that's the stake in his heart?) and a couple of frazzled rosebushes that are really the vampire's nails continuing to grow. (The rosebushes were cut down a few years ago.) The stories keep coming—about disembodied

voices and strange lights around the grave, lone visitors beaten up by an unseen assailant, and apparitions that hover around the tombstone.

It's not an isolated location, and there are no barriers to access, making it easy for ghost hunters with flashlights and cameras to visit the cemetery at night (when it's supposed to be closed), hoping to track paranormal activity. The cemetery is at a busy intersection, across the street from a fire station, and next to the local recreation center.

The *Lafayette News* occasionally reports items that show up on the grave at Halloween: a voodoo doll and stickpins, a pile of salt, a glow-in-the-dark rosary, and more.

If there is some occultic reason for these offerings, they're quite unnecessary. The American Association of Paranormal Investigators (AAPI), based in Aurora, Colorado, discovered the true story of the grave by digging

through old files. The findings are posted on the AAPI Web site, and we were given permission to report them here.

Interestingly, not just one person is buried in the Vampire Grave, but two—to save space, no doubt. The dead can't complain, and both men were immigrants, their families still in Europe, employed by the nearby Simpson Mine.

Not just one person is buried in the Vampire Grave.

Both men died on different days in December 1918. According to obituaries in the now-defunct *Lafayette Leader* newspaper, Theodore Glava, forty-three, was from Austria-Hungary, and died after a relapse of influenza. John Trandifir, twenty-seven, was from born in Transylvania (now called Romania), and officially died of pneumonia—or, more likely, the Spanish Flu, as it was called in the first pandemic of 1918. There is no mention of a funeral service for Glava. Trandifir was a member of the Greek Orthodox Church and received a formal send-off with a priest and music.

The double grave's marker is clearly homemade. Besides the misspellings, the letters appear to have been made in wet cement with a stick. The letters have blurred over time, the information offered is jumbled, and it's easy to see how visitors could be confused. Many of the cemetery's old graves look untended and add to the spooky allure of the place.

On the Roadside America Web site, a paranormal investigator named Drea Penndragon reported her group's experience with a tape recorder at the Vampire Grave in which they allegedly picked up a voice asking clearly, "Do you want to see my stake?"

Visiting the Vampire

Have you seen the Vampire Grave in the Lafayette graveyard?

My friends and I have made trips to see a crudely etched gravestone at that cemetery—because its most famous resident, Fodor Glava, was from Transylvania. And, growing in the middle of his plot is a tree. It clearly grows above the spot where Glava's heart should be positioned. We have always heard that the tree grew from a stake that was planted in Glava's heart—because he was, and is, a vampire.

Also written on the Vampire Grave is the word *Trandofir*, Romanian for "rose." There used to be rose bushes at the grave—they got so thick that the town cut them down a few years back, though. We have always understood it that the roses that grow are actually Mr. Glava's fingernails, sprouting forth from his resting place—he is trying to claw his way out!

Some people have seen a mysterious ghostly figure at the Vampire Grave. We never have—but each and every time we go there, you can feel that there's a stillness in the air, and a dark sense about this place. The Vampire Grave is easily one of the best places in this entire area to go when you want a good scare—just be wary of Mr. Glava rising from his grave to meet you when you visit! —*Theresa Collins*

Fortune-telling in Crystola

Towns in old Colorado always sprang up wherever a new railroad line was built, which is how the north slope of Pikes Peak near Ute Pass turned into a ranching community and summer vacation area called Trout Park in 1870.

Among the settlers who moved into this beautiful area was a former Illinois legislator named Henry Clay Childs. Childs and his wife, Catherine, were dedicated spiritualists, and it was on the advice of a spiritualist that they moved to Colorado. They entertained their neighbors with séances and consultations with a crystal ball and frequently had mediums and other spiritualists as guests.

Childs was interested in finding gold on his property and studied metallurgy and minerals in his laboratory. One of his guests, who claimed to be able to find gold through his psychic powers, persuaded Childs and other believers to organize the Brotherhood Gold Mining and Milling Company in 1897. The company brochure promised easy gold:

> In some cases, the prospector is saved the trouble of locating a mine by an accommodating wizard, who, instead of locating the future bonanza for himself, will locate it for anybody who will put up a sufficiency of cash in advance.

It was also publicized in local newspapers that the method resulted in a large number of rich deposits found in the area. If so, it was a suspiciously short-lived trend but not before it had attracted quite a lot of investment. By 1899, the company was renamed the Crystola Brotherhood Town, Mines and Milling Company, and Trout Park came to be known as Crystola. The company built a gold-processing plant and a storehouse for the gold it confidently predicted would pour in.

What did pour in were fortune seekers, including lots more spiritualists. The little town grew, but the promise of mining wealth never materialized. As regional historian Jan Pettit wrote in *Ute Pass: A Quick History*: "More money was invested here with no return than anywhere else in the region."

Childs never found gold himself, and when his wife died, he became reclusive. Rumor says that when he died and was cremated in 1910, his crystal ball was buried with his ashes. The Ute Pass Historical Society says there's a local story that someone dug up the spot, but the crystal ball was not found.

Childs left his estate for the founding of a spiritualism school in Crystola. Friends did their best to fund it with attempts to attract "progressive thinkers and earnest students," according to one piece of advertising, but the school never took off.

Crystola was finally, literally, nearly wiped off the map when a dam broke during a storm in August 1929, and water swept away nearly all the summer cabins at one end of the area. Most of the commercial buildings that didn't burn down were dismantled and reused elsewhere. What remained became an off-the-beaten-path place of entertainment with a popular roadhouse and brothels.

Today, you can zip past the sign for Crystola if you're driving on Highway 24 between Manitou Springs and Florissant. Other hamlets in the area have done better, and Crystola is now considered part of the village of Woodland Park. However, Crystola is still worth a stop, if only to check out its scenic beauty, ponder its unique history, and enjoy the legendary roadhouse.

Crystola was finally, literally, nearly wiped off the map.

Is That a Dead Bear in Your Freezer, Sir? Tales of the Crystola Roadhouse

It was originally a hotel built on the site of Crystola's former grocery store and called the Crystola Inn for many years. It was rebuilt in 1945 and sold to a returning World War II veteran named Gabe Brock about a year or two later. In its heyday of the 1950s, it featured a dance hall and a stage for live entertainment, some of them well-known acts such as the Mills Brothers. It also offered completely illicit gambling in the basement.

Former pro hockey player Darryl Maggs bought the place in 2006, restored much of it, added to it, and collects local history and stories, many from customers "back in the day."

"They had a full gambling setup down there," Maggs says. "They were friends with other gambling establishments in Woodland Park and whenever they got a tip that the district attorney was coming to raid the place, Gabe would bring out old gambling wheels and things and hide his good stuff. He'd bring out it all again when the raid took away the junk."

The menu featured a frequent "Poacher's Special," and it was no joke. Gabe Brock was caught with a dead bear out of hunting season in his freezer once. Being a man of foresight, he had used his connections to score a blank game tag ahead of time.

When the district attorney popped in with a game warden to inspect his freezer contents, Gabe had a predated tag on the animal that indicated it had been lawfully shot in season.

Gabe's son, Steve, ran the Crystola Inn until the 1980s. It then passed through several owners and was in huge need of an overhaul when Maggs bought it. He spent a month sleeping on site while he was doing the work. These days, there aren't any high-stakes games to bring in customers. Maggs concentrates on offering the kind of food and drink that earn rave reviews in area newspapers and continues the tradition of offering live entertainment.

It's not what the fortune-hunting spiritualists would have imagined, but it does prove there's at least one hidden gem left in what remains of the old town.

The Solid Muldoon

Southwest of Pueblo, in the foothills of the Wet Mountains, is a valley that was once a hideout for a bandit named Juan Mace. The settlement named for him decided to go for a more sophisticated name when the U.S. centennial rolled around in 1876. It picked Beulah, a nice biblical name that was certainly better than Mace's Hole.

In 1877, on a hill about eight miles east of Beulah, W. A. Conant said he was looking for fossils when he came across what looked like a petrified human form sticking partially out of the ground. As he and his son dug it up, the head broke off, revealing what appeared to be vertebrae. They took the skeleton into Pueblo where it generated some interest as well as skepticism about its supposed origin as a prehistoric human, more than seven feet tall with a vestigial tail and ape-like feet.

The *Pueblo Chieftain*, the local newspaper, expressed open disbelief and dubbed it "The Solid Muldoon" after a popular song about an Irish immigrant wrestler named William "Solid" Muldoon—"a solid man!"—written by the entertainer and songwriter Edward Harrigan.

Public attention was stoked when the legendary showman P. T. Barnum contacted Conant and offered $20,000 for "the solid man." Conant refused and started exhibiting his petrified giant for a fee. Crowds flocked.

Conant invited scientific authorities to examine the figure. Some of them pronounced the figure to be human. Some suggested that it was the Darwinian "missing link" in the evolutionary scale between ape and human.

Others, such as a Yale professor, declared the Solid Muldoon to be an outright sham but that just brought more crowds to judge for themselves. The Solid Muldoon was exhibited around the country. Six months later, it was starring at P. T. Barnum's American Museum of oddities in New York City.

There is one account that a co-conspirator named E. J. Cox, who wasn't paid for his part, spilled the beans. The hoax was soon out of the bag, and one of the names that tumbled out with them was connected with a previous, similar hoax—still one of the most famous of all time—the Cardiff Man.

George Hull was an atheist who argued with a minister over Genesis—particularly over the reference of giants once existing—and concocted an elaborate head game to play with fundamentalists. Hull commissioned the creation of a ten-foot-tall gypsum statue, had it treated to make it look aged, arranged for it to be buried for about a year, and later dug it up before witnesses in Cardiff, New York, in 1869.

"Humbug!" yelled scientists. However, the public flocked to see the Cardiff Man at twenty-five cents a peek. What gratified Hull even more was that a few fundamentalists

defended the possibility of it being a "petrified giant" on biblical grounds. Barnum helped Hull promote the Cardiff Man until his bid to buy it was rejected. Then he created his own "giant" and promoted it as the real Cardiff find. Hull sued him for defaming his giant as the fake. The hoax unraveled in court in 1870; the judge ruled Barnum could not be sued for calling a fake a fake.

Hull must have itched for a second chance at fame and money. He studied chemistry and created a special cement to cast a new giant. To fool scientists, he put in real human bones from a medical source. He shipped his six-hundred-pound creation to Colorado Springs. W. A. Conant, a friend who had worked for Barnum, helped Hull transport and bury the statue near Beulah, and then staged his "discovery."

Some say Barnum financed whole setup. It's not much of a stretch to guess that the earlier court battle with Hull was staged for the publicity.

It's not certain what happened to the Solid Muldoon when the hoax went bust. The most common tale is that Denver's premier con man, Jefferson "Soapy" Smith, bought and exhibited the statue for some time before it disappeared

There were at least a couple of other things called the Solid Muldoon in Colorado: a newspaper in Ouray and a mine. No one is sure if they're named for the wrestler, the 1874 Harrigan song, or the hoax statue.

In 1977, the Colorado State Fair commissioned a Pueblo art student named Joel Carpenter to recreate the Solid Muldoon for the centennial fair. Carpenter worked from old photographs and period descriptions to reconstruct the six-hundred-pound statue from a wire beam, stucco wire, and plaster.

Moving the new Solid Muldoon was so challenging that it broke before it could star at the fair. It went on a short regional tour and then was put on display in a Pueblo museum. Eventually, in 1984, the Beulah Historical Society volunteered to give the statue a wake and proper burial on the hill where the discovery of the original Muldoon was staged.

The replica is buried under a marker. The site is now called Muldoon Hill. It's sometimes referred to as the Muldoon Cemetery.

P. T. Barnum's 'Hood

The famous promoter and circus showman Phineas T. Barnum bought 760 acres for development just outside Denver city limits in 1871. It was annexed to the city in 1896. It currently stretches between West Sixth Avenue to West Alameda Avenue, and Federal Boulevard to Sheridan Boulevard.

For decades, there were legends that Barnum had actually lived in that neighborhood, had planned to establish an off-season headquarters for his circus, had done so at one time with elephants and other performance beasts stabled in local barns and whatnot, and so on.

None of this happened. And, no, it was not another of Barnum's famous hoaxes, although a reputed hoaxer claims to be a direct descent of Barnum and living in "Barnum's house," according to a weekly Denver newspaper.

Barnum first became famous for his American Museum in New York City, which exhibited such entertaining frauds as George Washington's wet nurse and the Feejee Mermaid. He started his circus business in his sixties with a show called P. T. Barnum's Grand Traveling Museum, Menagerie, Caravan & Hippodrome. It is known today as Ringling Bros. and Barnum & Bailey's Circus.

Besides show business, Barnum was into land speculation, wheeling and dealing cross-country as he gave paid lectures on how to become rich and abstain from alcohol.

He was a friend of the famous newspaperman and temperance activist Horace Greeley, who was the inspiration for the founding of the town of Greeley (first called Union Colony) in northern Colorado. Barnum had family in Colorado, so he had several reasons to visit frequently.

Even Barnum was not immune to a slick con, and he fell for a scheme in which he bought reportedly prime real estate near Denver. It turned out to be a largely undeveloped

mud tract. Once he had seen it—and had a good taste of Colorado climate—Barnum realized it would be no place for wintering his traveling circus as he first planned.

He sold some of the land and created Barnum Town from the remainder. He also bought a hotel called Villa Park House in Barnum Town at Tenth Street and Hazel Court. Eventually, he sold the land to his daughter, Helen, for a dollar.

Helen had a house on Lincoln Street before she and her second husband, William Buchtel, moved into the Villa Park Hotel. They lived there for four years while William was mayor of Barnum Town. Barnum himself spent only four separate weeks visiting Colorado. His circus partner, James Bailey, brought the show to the state for the first time in 1880.

Much of this information came from two women with a deep interest in Barnum's ties to Colorado. Cathe Mitchell was hired by the Denver Parks and Recreation Department in 1998 to research whether Barnum Park would be historically accurate if renovated to include a circus theme. The Colorado historian and author Ida Uchill wrote a book published in 2001 called *Howdy, Sucker! What P. T. Barnum Did in Colorado*.

What they found convinced them that the claims of a charming old man living in the Barnum Neighborhood were as fake as the fabulous hoaxer himself, according to a March 1, 2001, article in the Denver *Westword*.

Then seventy-nine-year-old Bart Barnum claimed he was the great-great grandson of P.T. He lived in a house on King Street in Barnum Neighborhood that he said his famous ancestor lived in for ten years. He, himself, he said, was born and grew up in it.

Barnum House, he said, was originally a carriage house built in 1878 that P.T. converted and moved into when his mansion burned down. The house had been situated two blocks north and was moved to its present location in 1956. The present owner said he moved back into the house about thirty years previously and that he had inherited it from his father, who insisted Bart always live in it and never sell it.

The only problem with Bart Barnum and his house, Cathe Mitchell and Ida Uchill said, was everything.

P. T. Barnum had no sons and all his living descendants, in Colorado and elsewhere, can prove their lineage. Neither of "Bart Barnum's" parents is listed on P. T. Barnum's family trees, according to these investigators.

Uchill found that "Barnum House" was originally a barn purchased by James Failing in 1921 and converted into a house. A 1956 *Denver Post* story noted that it was moved from what was called the old "Barnum estate" to its present location.

And "Bart Barnum," in the course of

Westword's interview, finally admitted that he was Robert Failing, son of the man who bought, converted, and moved the house he lived in. He knew he was somehow related to old P.T., probably through his mother. He was old Barnum's great-great-grandson, he insisted, and simply preferred to use the Barnum name rather than his own more "negative" surname of Failing.

Whether the family story is one he heard from his parents or invented himself is not known. However, Barnum/Failing appeared by all accounts to be a completely sane, humorous, and intelligent individual, and he stood by his claims at the time the *Westword* story was published.

Many people appeared to have been persuaded by Bart Barnum's story. The handsome, two-story house was once listed by the state as a tourist attraction. Its owner is still occasionally asked to give tours or lectures on the history of the house and P.T. Barnum.

Perhaps so long as one knows one is being taken for a ride, what actually matters is that it's an entertaining one. The old master himself, Phineas T., can't argue with that.

Mountain of the Holy Cross

Foreign travelers in Colorado started hearing about it early, probably as soon as the Christian cross became familiar to the Native Americans.

The sacred image could be seen at certain times and places on an inaccessible mountain peak, the travelers were told. It came and went with the snows, and sometimes as one approached the peak it would disappear before one's eyes.

The tale sparked an intense desire among non-Indians to locate this mystery cross. Samuel Bowles did it in 1869. He was the first to describe it in print in his book about Colorado, *The Switzerland of America.*

Bowles was a newspaperman from Springfield, Massachusetts, who was on Grays Peak, forty miles away, when he saw the image. His description—"It is as if God has set His seal, His sign, His promise there, a beacon upon the very center and height upon the Continent to all its people and all its generations"—helped fan the concept of Manifest Destiny, the idea that the United States had a divinely approved mission to expand and conquer the land.

Such signs seen in natural wonders gave comfort to people for whom wilderness was scary and potentially dangerous, and seemed to justify appropriation from the pagans who had long lived there. The same year Bowles published his book, the Ute tribes were pressured by the United States to give up the area.

Five years later, the U.S. Geological Survey sent a team headed by Ferdinand Hayden. Part of Hayden's mission was to find this elusive mountain, which he did when the team reached the summit of Notch Mountain in the summer of 1873.

Along for just this opportunity was photographer William Henry Jackson. He lugged hundreds of pounds of equipment up Notch Mountain without pack animals and spent the night in the frigid open air so he'd be awakened by first light. He was rewarded by an unobstructed view of the image and took the first photograph of the legend.

Hayden's second expedition the next year included artist Thomas Moran. He later created a seven-by-five-foot oil portrait of the scene. Moran enhanced the Cross image considerably and softened the stark peak by wreathing it in clouds and adding beautiful wilderness in the foreground.

The photo and the painting were exhibited at the Centennial Exposition in Philadelphia in 1876. The images fascinated people who saw in them a divine hand that practically beckoned people to the West. Jackson won several awards for his photograph, which has become an iconic image of the early West (it's now in the Smithsonian Institution). Moran's painting was bought in 1880 by Dr. William Bell, a member of the Denver and Rio Grande Railroad consortium and is now in the Autry National Center in Los Angeles, but for years it was a major advertising image used by the railroad to lure people to Colorado. Moran was also hired to create wood engravings for its publications.

One mining town in the Holy Cross Wilderness Area named itself for the image in the 1880s although the image couldn't be seen from there. (See the Abandoned Colorado chapter.)

Drawing people to Colorado wasn't that much of a problem. But for years you had to be pretty determined to travel to the place fifteen miles south of Vail where you could actually see the Holy Cross image.

The peak itself is one of Colorado's Fourteeners, mountains at least fourteen thousand feet tall. The best place to see the Cross is from one of the nearby peaks, but they're not exactly dwarves either. It's rugged country, and people accustomed to living nearer sea level find a trek in this

altitude quite difficult.

What really keeps the image elusive is that it can only be seen during June or July, when the snow has melted enough so that the two intersecting crevasses are revealed, but the snow in them remains.

By the 1920s, improved Colorado roads and a desire to spur tourism had improved access to the point at which more people felt it was possible to make the trip, even if some of it included a donkey ride. For the faithful, the challenges of reaching the right spot at the right time made the journey a true pilgrimage.

Rumors grew that some sick pilgrims were miraculously cured after a visit to the Cross. By the 1930s, the Denver newspapers were commenting on the steady stream of desperate folks bound for the Mountain of the Holy Cross.

The Notch Mountain site was designated a national monument in 1929, but the Great Depression and World War II limited travel for a lot of people and the Cross showed signs of erosion. The designation was revoked in 1950.

Today, there are other reasons to visit the popular wilderness area—terrific outdoor recreation and fishing, interesting small towns, and a few old ghost ones for exploring. The Mountain of the Holy Cross is more known for its hiking trails, wildlife, and fantastic views than for its history as a symbol.

The Holy Cross image is still visible today, although one arm is less clearly marked than it used to be, probably due to natural shifts in the rock formations. Access is easier than it ever used to be, so long as you go in June to July. Then again, snow can linger in the Sawatch Range into mid-summer, and summer storms are a near-daily occurrence.

The Holy Cross Ranger District says the best place for viewing the image is still from the summit of Notch Mountain, which requires a hike on foot. An easier way see it is by taking the west side of Shrine Pass Road, a dirt road off I-70 below Vail Pass, as it slopes toward Red Cliff. There's also a gondola ride you can take on Vail Mountain that can put you within sight of the peak when conditions are right.

Check with the rangers before thinking of heading out. You can find out which roads and trails are safe to take and what the weather conditions are—and if the Cross has been seen lately.

Mount of the Holy Cross, Colorado

Denver and Rio Grande Western Railroad
Scenic Line of the World
Royal Gorge Route

Old Man Mountain

It's forbidden, mostly.

Sometimes known as Man Mountain, or Old Man's Mountain or Sitting Man, the literal translation from the Arapahoe language is Man-Where-Sit-He. It's situated on the Fall River in the town of Estes Park, and the summit is owned by the state and managed by the University of Northern Colorado.

It doesn't look like much. At around 8,600 feet, the granite peak is dwarfed by Colorado's more spectacular mountaintops.

From the area of the venerable Elkhorn Lodge and Guest Ranch, located along an ancient Indian trail, you might be able to spot two rock formations in the shape of human faces—one facing north, the other south.

That's the first clue that's there's something special about this place. Man Mountain is Colorado's oldest documented religious site. It's been a center of vision-quest activity, where Native Americans since ancient times have gone to commune with the spirit world.

This was first confirmed about 1900, when Arapaho elders were interviewed by interested Estes Park residents about the large number of artifacts found on the site and the little piles of rocks geologically foreign to the area.

Native Americans from many nations had long visited Man Mountain, and the tradition was to bring special rocks from their homelands or something valuable to leave there. Families or tribal groups would make stacks of the rocks they brought. Other rocks might have been used in temporary sweat lodges built in the vision-quest tradition.

In the 1930s, well-meaning Estes Park residents gathered all the artifacts they could to save them from theft or destruction and placed them in various Colorado universities and museums. Some small piles of foreign rocks, however, can still be seen in out-of-the-way locations on Man Mountain.

In 1976, the University of Colorado studied Man Mountain and concluded that some of the artifacts left were as much as ten thousand years old. Other authorities were able to establish the origin of the foreign rocks (from places such as Wyoming rock quarries) and the purpose behind the stacks left behind by Indian pilgrims.

The state of Colorado forbids access to Man Mountain without permission, and NO TRESPASSING signs are posted. However, according to the Elkhorn Lodge, which has been in continuous operation at the same location for 134 years, it has permanent access to the trails that lead through the property and onto Man Mountain.

Lodge guests are allowed on the trails but must show knowledge of the area's special status and an appropriate respect for Native American religious traditions.

Penitente Canyon

The Penitente Canyon Special Recreation Management Area is secluded and definitely off the beaten path, which is how it originally came to be named for one of the Southwest's most mysterious and legendary religious groups—Los Hermanos Penitente, the Repentant Brothers. This is supposed to have been one of the secret places where they met and literally reenacted Jesus' crucifixion on Good Fridays.

Under Spanish law in New Mexico and southern Colorado, Native Americans could be enslaved for ten or twenty years or as long as their masters lived. Once freed, however, these *genizaros* were regarded as being on the lowest rung of the social ladder. Considered ethnic outsiders by both Pueblo Indian and Spanish communities, this group spoke its own dialect of Spanish, married only within its own community and, gradually, in the early nineteenth century, came to celebrate a blend of Catholic ritual and Native American beliefs in a unique system without priests.

Instead of churches, the men and women met in *moradas*, or special meeting houses. They still do, according to some local legends.

In northern New Mexico and southern Colorado, membership is passed through families, and outsiders are forbidden. Members believe in performing acts of charity in their communities.

Although there is a female counterpart to Los Hermanos, men lead and meet secretly to perform some of their sacred rites that in the old days included self-flagellation as penance for their sins. The most famous thing known about the Penitentes was their secret reenactments of Jesus' crucifixion on Good Friday. In many cases that was literal, even to a man being nailed to a heavy cross. For the man picked because of his virtue and piety, it was an honor.

The Catholic Church tried to suppress the ritual practices and bring the Penitentes back into the mainstream fold, but it only drove the group underground.

While the Penitentes usually bar nonmembers from attending their rituals, word and a few rare photographs got out in the early 1900s. Sensationalized reporting portrayed the men as religious nuts, and the Penitentes took their practices even deeper into the shadows.

Perhaps figuring the membership had dwindled to old folks and that the more sensational practices had been discarded, the Catholic Church lifted its ban on participating in Los Hermanos in the 1940s.

The Penitentes today are private and prefer to keep their special practices out of the public eye. In many Hispanic communities in the Southwest, however, they continue to have an honored presence.

They literally reenacted Jesus' crucifixion.

Penitente Canyon is still secluded and not advertised much, but it's so pretty that it's become a popular spot for rock climbing, hiking, camping, and picnicking.

On a day when people and dogs are wandering around and children are playing tag in the tall grass and wildflowers, it's hard to imagine secret religious rituals could continue to be held here. Whether they do or not, there still remains a reminder of its mystical past.

High up on one of the many rock faces' smoother surfaces, there's an image of the Virgin Mary in fading blue paint. One story about it is that a Hispanic soldier, returned from World War II, painted it in the 1950s in gratitude for his life.

He would have had to be suspended over a cliff on a rope to do it.

To find Penitente Canyon: Travel north out of Monte Vista on Highway 285 for eighteen miles to County Road G. Make a left and continue west to the intersection just past the La Garita ("the lookout") store. Go south along a dirt road. Signs will lead to the canyon.

Ancient Mysteries and Natural Wonders

Ancient Colorado is not just preserved in museums or in well-known places such as the Mesa Verde cliff dwellings. The evidence of ancient peoples, extinct species, and vanished landscapes is hidden in plain sight to most of us because we don't how to recognize it, or it's off the beaten path without the ballyhoo of the big tourist attractions, or it was diminished before we ever had a chance to enjoy it.

The people who found these places before us may have stopped to admire, but too often, they stopped to loot, damage, and even destroy. We're lucky to have what's left. If nothing else, we have some great stories.

Fortunately, we also have a lot of the lost world in places you might never expect, such as the golf course with a stretch of dinosaur tracks a ball's throw from the twelfth green. We have forest trails with hundreds of old pine trees deliberately bent over by human hands, and a cave with ancient markings that are highlighted with a beam of light on the equinox.

To paraphrase what one tracker of ancient evidence says in this chapter, once you know what you're looking for, you can see it everywhere.

Tracks of Time

When it comes to fossils, bones generally receive most of the attention. It's hard, after all, to beat the sight of a reassembled *T. rex*, Stegosaurus, or other impressive beastie.

The preserved tracks of vanished species, including ancient humans, have attracted more scientific respect recently. Probably more than anyone we have to thank Dr. Martin Lockley, professor of geology at the University of Colorado Denver and curator/director of the school's Fossil Footprint Collection, for raising this neglected science into new light.

Lockley has been studying fossil footprints and other tracks left by ancient species, including humans, for more than twenty-eight years. He says there's a lot we can tell from these impressions.

"They're not the only thing that can tell us about the behavior of these extinct species," he says. "But they're the only direct evidence. For example, they can tell us about migration patterns, whether their makers traveled in groups and how, their daily activities, and lots more."

He started the Dinosaur Trackers Research Group about twenty years ago. Graduate students, faculty, and colleagues who formed the group have journeyed across the United States, Europe, east and central Asia, and Africa in pursuit of documenting and sometimes collecting fossil footprints.

Part of what the Trackers do is make molds of the prints for later replication. A commercial company makes the copies, mostly for academic and scientific study. The Trackers' collection is one of the largest and most varied in the world, with more than a thousand specimens. It's currently kept in storage on campus and is brought out occasionally for exhibits.

However, you don't have to visit a museum or wait for an exhibit to come to your area to see ancient tracks. Lockley says they're all around us.

To learn more, you can look up some of the books Lockley has written, such as *The Eternal Trail: A Tracker*

Looks at Evolution or *Tracking Dinosaurs: A New Look at an Ancient World*. You can also visit some of the many places in Colorado where the fossil traces of birds, beasts, plants, and insects are visible, right where they were made. The sites are open all year—access may depend on weather permitting—and there's no charge in most cases.

Dinosaur Ridge

Easily one of Colorado's most unique museums. It's run by The Friends of Dinosaur Ridge, a nonprofit group with a visitor center located between Morrison and Golden, close to where Highway C470 (Cretaceous 470) and North Rooney Road meet (16831 W. Alameda Parkway).

Look for the giant Stegosaurus (the official Colorado state fossil) statues outside decked out in colorful designs unknown to zoology. The visitor center is at the bottom of Dinosaur Ridge, the hogback formation where Arthur Lakes and H. C. Beckwith first came across the humongous dinosaur bits that brought the Bone Wars to Colorado and the West.

In the 1930s, construction of a new road to be called Alameda Parkway uncovered a slew of fossil finds on the east side of Dinosaur Ridge. Over the decades, people helped themselves to a lot of the more accessible fossils. Concerned folks lobbied the U.S. National Park Service to designate the Morrison Fossil Area as a U.S. National Natural Landmark in 1973. In 1989, the Friends of Dinosaur Ridge was formed to protect the site and teach visitors about its unique history.

The Alameda Parkway is now closed to everything but foot traffic, emergency vehicles, and bicycles. You can hike through the area, or you can hop on a shuttle—dubbed the Vanosaurus—at the visitor center for a guided tour.

Either way, Dinosaur Ridge is accessible all year, from dawn to dusk, the visitor center is open seven days a week, and the shuttle ride requires only a small fee. However, if

you really want to know where the good stuff is and what you're looking at, the guided tour is highly recommended.

For instance, most people wouldn't otherwise know that the curious ridges on the slopes of Dinosaur Ridge are the marks left by the vast, shallow inland sea that once stretched from the Gulf of Mexico to Canada. Over considerable time, the sea receded and the geologic forces pushed the hardened sandy shores upward so that now viewers can see tide tracks higher than their heads. A guide can point out squiggly lines made by worms on what was the sea floor and places where the soil bulges in petrified humps—that's where a dinosaur pushed against the mud.

There are imprints of extinct ferns and insects, and bits of mangrove trees—more common to swampy areas—that have turned to carbon. In some places, what look like bulging discolorations in the rocks are really bones. The showiest and most identifiable "exhibits" in this outdoor museum are the animal tracks. Sometimes, they're just big impressions of some mystery beast. At others, they are evidence of more identifiable critters, such as a plant-eating mama Iguanodon and her baby.

Fossil Trace Golf Club

The golf course just outside the city of Golden off Sixth Avenue (U.S. Highway 6) is named for the evidence of an ancient tropical world discovered in old clay quarries once used for producing bricks.

The clubhouse has an exhibit inside that shows some of the trace fossils—a path leads to the old quarries where you can see those still on the walls. Interpretative signs are posted to help you discern what some of the fossils are. Within yards of a golf ball's flight, you can see Triceratops footprints, birdlike tracks, the clear impressions of palm fronds, and more. Non-golfers can view these tracks and impressions by taking a path from the entrance at the corners of Sixth Avenue and Nineteenth Street.

Purgatoire River Valley

The biggest site of dinosaur tracks in North America is in the Comanche National Grassland, south of La Junta, Colorado.

Once upon an extremely distant past, the river here was an enormous freshwater lake with a big muddy shore. That made the perfect canvas for layers of tracks made by ancient creatures. Fortunately for us, the mucky paths dried with more than a thousand tracks intact, were buried under sediment, and turned into stone.

The area is rugged and can be hard to explore, so the tracks weren't given serious scientific attention until the 1980s. The valley is thirty miles from the nearest town of La Junta; some of those miles are unpaved. You can park at a trailhead and hike or bicycle (if you brought one) to the dinosaur track site, a bit more than five miles farther.

You can make a reservation with the U.S. Forest Service in La Junta to drive your four-wheel vehicle on a specific route on Saturdays in May, June, September, and October. The cost is $15 for each adult and half that for kids. The tracks extend for about a quarter of a mile, mostly on the other side of the Purgatory River from the parking lot. So, if you want to see them, you'll have to wade through water that is usually very shallow but also very fast and very cold.

The animals that crushed soil, plants, clams, crustaceans, snails, and fish in their ponderous progress were two kinds of dinosaur species: the meat-eating Allosaurus follow those of plant-eating Brontosaurus.

Parallel tracks of the same kinds of dinosaurs suggest sociability. The tracks may have been frozen in time, but their time is finally starting to run out. "Set in stone" doesn't mean much when that stone is crumbling, the erosion hastened by rain and river overflow.

A Town Called Dinosaur

Northwest Colorado used to be outlaw country. Sparsely settled and starkly beautiful, it was where Butch Cassidy and the Wild Bunch hid from the law. The plains here didn't have the gold or minerals to attract the fortune-hunting hordes that tore up mountainsides and muddied creeks elsewhere in Colorado, which was good for the farmers and cattle ranchers, the mainstay of the local economy for decades until oil drilling arrived in more recent years.

Recreational tourism, largely generated by the Green and Yampa Rivers that flow through spectacular canyons, is also a part of the local economy.

In 1909, rich fossil beds were discovered in an eighty-acre area in Utah near the border with Colorado. President Woodrow Wilson declared this area Dinosaur National Monument in 1915. Its boundaries were expanded into

Colorado in 1938, which made its current size more than two hundred thousand acres.

Tiny Artesia, just west of Dinosaur Monument headquarters in Moffat County, three miles east of the Utah border, must have watched thoughtfully as the stream of visitors whizzed by on U.S. Highway 40. When your town is only eight-tenths of a square mile and has a population of 319 (as of the 2000 U.S. Census), you have to be creative about siphoning off some of that lucrative traffic through your Main Street. In 1965, the town council made a bold move to name itself for the best-known attraction in those parts.

"Oh, goodness, yes, I remember that," says Elva Murry, a lifelong area resident, community college teacher, and artist. "My husband, Elmer, was on the council. He was all for it. Change *Artesia* to *Dinosaur*, and all the street names to dinosaur names. The town was quite divided. I was not on the side that wanted the change, I have to say."

But in the end, ambition won out.

"It did seem to bring us a little more attention," says Murry, "although it didn't change us very much. And in the end, we didn't change *all* the street names. We got to keep the one we live on, and it's something I can spell."

Which means Murry doesn't live on Brontosaurus Boulevard, Stegosaurus Freeway, Triceratops Terrace, Brachiosaurus Bypass, or Diplodocus Drive.

Dinosaur has motels, a cafe, and other amenities you're not likely to find in the long stretch of country between Rangely and Dinosaur National Monument. Don't miss the little city park and its statues of dinosaurs.

Dinosaur Diamond Prehistoric Highway

If you can't get enough of dinosaurs and scenic beauty, then Colorado has a road trip for you. This roughly diamond-shaped journey runs through two states, two national parks, and a couple of national monuments. That's a whole lotta of forested mountain road, colorful rock formations, canyons, rivers, cliffs, and Native American rock art.

All along the way are quarries and small museums in which you can learn about ancient cultures and watch fossils being unearthed and prepared for museum display. There are plenty of reconstructed skeletons and dinosaur re-creations in the toothy pseudo flesh.

Most of the 512-mile Dinosaur Diamond Prehistoric Highway (Dinosaur Diamond) is within eastern Utah. But a pretty good segment of the total loop is in western Colorado, where it's officially known as Dinosaur Diamond Scenic and Historic Byway.

At the south end, it curves near or through Fruita and Grand Junction before it heads north to Rangely and tiny Dinosaur, outside the entrance to Dinosaur National Monument. (Dinosaur National Monument area pictured below.)

The One and Only Mesa Verde

They're iconic images of the ancient world—rows of stark stone structures in long niches under cliff overhangs. No matter how familiar you are with the photographs, you're bowled over when you see them for yourself. The ruins of Mesa Verde have been a crown jewel among ethnic cultural treasures for decades (the park is a UNESCO World Heritage Centre), and the park's story is yet another example of how an irreplaceable Colorado landmark was looted and almost destroyed.

We don't know much about the particular ancient Native American folks who lived in this region of the Four Corners (where the southwest corner of Colorado abuts the corners of New Mexico, Arizona, and Utah). We do know now that the once-common term to describe them in scientific circles, *Anasazi*, was a mistake (it's a Navajo term that means "ancient ones" or "ancient enemy"). We know—or believe we know—that they didn't become extinct but moved away—their descendants are found among Native American nations of today, including the Hopi in Arizona and the Pueblo nations of New Mexico. The ancient Pueblo people settled in the area about 600 CE and lived there for more than seven hundred years. Sometime in 1300 CE, they moved out.

The famous cliff structures aren't the only ancient Native American ruins in the area, but they're the best-preserved blocks of dwellings at least partly due to their sheltered locations. After the area was deserted, other Native Americans tended to avoid the ruins. The Spanish priest and explorer Father Silvestre Velez de Escalante mentioned the cliff dwellings in his journal in 1776. The term *mesa verde*

means "green table" in Spanish. In 1846 and 1848, a couple of American expeditions also recorded seeing ancient ruins in the area. However, the cliff dwellings remained otherwise unknown to the larger world until December 1888. That's when ranchers in pursuit of stray cattle happened to see the cliff dwellings in Mancos Canyon.

If you want detailed scientific and ancient cultural history about the place, read *The Mesa Verde World: Explorations in Ancestral Pueblo Archaeology*, edited by David Grant Noble. However, if you want to know the whole down-and-dirty story of how the ruins were found, explored, exploited, and then finally appreciated and preserved, you shouldn't miss *Women to the Rescue: Creating Mesa Verde National Park* by Duane Smith.

As soon as the ancient ruins were publicized, souvenir hunters, treasure seekers, and scholars descended upon them and began the removal of just about everything portable. People sometimes threw dynamite into the buildings to rid them of rattlesnakes and unearth more goodies. Artifacts wound up in private collections and museums all over America but without the vital information of their original context.

In 1882, a Colorado Springs correspondent for the *Daily Graphic* in New York went to view the "buried cities."

What Virginia McClurg saw started her on a campaign to save the ruins. She and other like-minded people pushed to make the area a national park, which President Theodore Roosevelt finally did in 1906, as well as signing the landmark American Antiquities Act.

Today, Mesa Verde National Park—the first national park meant "to preserve the works of man"—is open daily and year round. Archaeology and other research are ongoing, and recent large wildfires have uncovered even more evidence of the ancient human occupants: old farming structures, towers and pit houses, petroglyphs, and so on. The usual signs of national-park tourism are carefully incorporated so as not to be intrusive, allowing visitors to imagine life on the Colorado Plateau as it might have been more than a thousand years ago.

Tours must be arranged through the park service, and rangers conduct them to keep people from roaming around the ruins on their own.

Florissant Fossil Beds National Monument

Wandering around this six-thousand-acre park full of geologic wonders and fossil displays, well supervised by a staff of rangers, you might find it hard to believe it was once the center of rampant looting and greed for more than a hundred years. We're lucky to have what remains.

Millions of years ago, volcanic eruptions buried a valley deep in fine-grained sediment about thirty-five miles away from today's Colorado Springs. The sediment hardened into shale. Trunks of blasted redwood trees became a petrified forest, and that forest had a petrified population of plants, insects, and animals whose details were forever imprinted on the shale.

Native Americans referred to this place as the Valley of Shadows. European trappers and settlers who came through were impressed, and they helped themselves to fossil souvenirs. By the 1870s, the petrified forests were established tourist attractions. Scientists took away cartloads of fossils, sending many to museums and universities. Their reports and published articles about the amazing finds of delicately preserved extinct species brought wagonloads of sightseers—all of whom wanted to take a few souvenirs home with them, too.

Eventually, almost every easily recognized and removable fossil imprint on the valley floor was gone. People even tore out as many petrified redwood tree stumps as they could, although the effort took steam-driven saws and dynamite. Local trains ran "specials" to

ENTRANCE GATE AND LODGE OF THE COLORADO PETRIFIED FOREST

bring more souvenir hunters during the tourist season.

By 1883, a few locals realized that the great tourist attraction was being whittled away and formed the now-defunct Colorado Museum Association. However, some of its members sought merely to keep the fossils at home for easier exploitation, rather than to preserve them for future generations. The tourists who came to the land owned by these members could take away just about anything they wished, particularly if they paid the landowner a fee.

There was something of a feud between two of those landowners competing for the tourist trade—the Colorado Petrified Forest Ranch owned by Palmer Singer and the Pike Petrified Forest owned by H. D. Miller. In 1950, Miller's zealous manager, John Baker, allegedly was caught spreading nails on the road leading to the Singer business and was shot in the leg by a Singer employee. Baker reportedly harassed the Singer enterprise until his employer's operation expired in 1961.

In 1969, at the urging of the *Denver Times* newspaper fifty-four years earlier, the federal government approved the creation of a national monument. Today Florissant Fossil Beds National Monument is managed by the U.S. National Park Service, and the wonder is that there is still so much left to see. Paleontologists are still uncovering the solid shadows of thousands of extinct plant, animal, and insect species.

It is now illegal to remove anything from the grounds.

For most of this information, we can thank Florissant resident Celinda Reynolds Kaelin, author of Pikes Peak Backcountry: The Historic Saga of the Peak's West Slope.

Pikes Peak and Its People

There is probably more myth attached to "America's Mountain" than to any other natural landmark in Colorado. It's the second-most-visited peak in the world—after Japan's Fuji. All because of its colorful mixture of history, legend, and outright lies.

Even the spelling of its name has caused controversy for years. Originally, it was called Pike's Peak (note the apostrophe) after the man who discovered it, but no one was sure if the apostrophe was needed or not. In 1891, the mountain officially became Pikes Peak (sans apostrophe) because the U.S. Board on Geographic Names didn't like apostrophes. The Colorado State General Assembly sealed the deal in 1978 by actually outlawing the use of an apostrophe for Pikes Peak. (In this book, we'll "follow the law" and stick with Pikes Peak.)

As for the mountain itself, it never was a volcano. True, the stuff of which it's made, granite, was once molten rock that came from as deep as twenty miles beneath Earth's surface. However, a process called uplifting shuffled the rocks skyward until they formed a mountain.

The volcano legend will be explained later.

A few thousand years of weather erosion carried away the soil and exposed the granite, and then about a million years more of glacier movement carved the peak's current shape. The period of that particular ice age ended about eleven thousand years ago.

At 14,110 feet, Pikes Peak ranks thirty-first out of Colorado's fifty-four Fourteener mountains—one that exceeds 14,000 feet. It's certainly not the tallest peak in the United States, let alone in the Mile High State, so how did it come to be known as *the* high point of Colorado?

As is true with all real estate, Pikes Peak's success has to do with its location. It's situated where it can be seen on a clear day from as far north as Denver, more than sixty miles away, and from far to the east over the Great Plains. The

peak, composed of a pinkish stone called Pikes Peak granite, has served as a beacon to humans for millennia.

Earliest Visitors

The first people known to have given this particular Four-teener a name were the Native Americans known as the Tabeguache (also called Uncompahgre) band of the Ute tribe. The Utes are the oldest continuous residents of Colorado. Their actual name for themselves is pronounced *Noochee*, "the people." *Ute* came from a word the early Spaniards called them and is how the state of Utah was named.

In the traditional Ute religion, when Sunawiv the Creator formed the new Earth, the god's daughter looked down from their home in the sky and saw a mountain so pretty she just had to go down and see more of it. While she was there, she was seduced by a handsome young man, who was actually a bear in disguise. The bear-man was punished by being made to walk on all fours forever after. The Utes are the result of this unusual tryst.

Their ancestors called the pretty mountain *Tava*, the Ute word for "sun." The surrounding range was called the Shining Mountains. Members of the Ute Ceremonial Circle would make an annual trek to nearby Crystal Peak for special stones, then travel over a ridge trail to Tava. One person would then be selected to take the special stones to the summit for a four-day vision quest.

You can still see Prayer Trees along this trail known as Cedar Mountain Road today. Prayer Trees are young pines bent over and tied down with leather thongs to form altars.

"The Tabeguache say that when the wind blows through the branches, it blows breath into the prayers said there," says Celinda Reynolds Kaelin, history writer and president of the Pikes Peak Historical Society. "Many of these trees are ponderosa pines, which live to be hundreds of years old, so there are many, many of these Prayer Trees, which you can see were formed a very long time ago."

The mineral springs at the foot of Tava were also considered sacred, and white explorers reported finding gifts of beads, deerskins, and other goods placed into the waters or the surrounding trees (see Local Legends for the story about the alleged curse of Manitou Springs).

Pike Picked a Peak

The first white men to see the mountain were Spanish explorers. The first Americans were members of Lt. Col. Zebulon Pike's expedition in the early 1800s. Pike's journey is one of those unresolved controversies history buffs love to chew over. His official mission was to explore, map, and record the southwestern borders of the Louisiana Purchase. Unofficially, it also was to snoop out the strengths and weaknesses of Spanish-controlled territory.

If captured by Spaniards on their turf, Pike was to claim he'd become lost. Some historians think Pike really was lost when the Spaniards caught up to him near present-day Alamosa on February 16, 1807. At any rate, Pike's capture and subsequent journey to Chihuahua, Mexico, gave him exactly what he wanted. By the time the Spaniards decided he was harmless enough to ship back to U.S. territory in Louisiana, Pike had picked up quite a lot of useful military information.

Pike's expeditions have been called the poor man's version of the Lewis and Clark journeys. He wasn't much of an explorer, and some of his military decisions were ludicrous (for instance, he decided to press on in winter with neither provisions nor clothing for harsh conditions). Despite all that, Pike managed to hold onto his career and died in battle in 1813 with the rank of brigadier general.

However, the conspicuous Colorado peak is what kept Pike's name out of complete obscurity for a long time. There is a Colorado myth that the word *piker*, meaning "an overly cautious gambler," arose from Pike's boast that he had ascended the mountain that he named for himself, when he had actually climbed a neighboring slope.

Pike was known to have been pompous, but he wasn't a blowhard. He was intrigued enough by what he originally called the Blue Mountain or the Grand Peak that he took three other men along in an attempt to climb it on November 15, 1806. The group was ill equipped for below-zero temperatures and deep snow. The men spent days on a miserable ascent to the top of a mountain, only to realize the peak they sought was still about fifteen miles away. They gave up and went back to their base camp. Pike marked the elusive summit as the "highest peak" on his area map.

We now know the mountain they climbed as Mount Rosa, 11,499 feet high. Pike and his group might not

General Pike?

have climbed a Colorado Fourteener, but they were the first known men of European descent to make an alpine mountain climb in North America.

In 1820, Edwin James, a young naturalist with the expedition of Maj. Steven Long, became the first known white man to climb "Pike's highest peak." Attempts to name the mountain went back and forth between James Peak and Pikes Peak for some time.

Bust or Busted

Daniel C. Oakes was an Iowa homesteader who participated in the great California Gold Rush of 1849. He led a bunch of prospectors to the Colorado Rocky Mountains nine years later. After he failed to turn up anything worthwhile, Oakes returned to Iowa and wrote a guidebook that considerably overstated his knowledge of Colorado gold panning. The guidebook was widely published in the East. Along with newspapers' published letters of exaggerated gold discoveries, Oakes's guidebook set off a stampede in 1859 of fortune seekers who adopted the slogan "Pikes Peak or Bust."

Towns along the popular routes to Colorado through Iowa, Missouri, Nebraska, and Kansas did all they could to milk the "Peaker" migration. They stuck PIKES PEAK signs on hotels, eateries, general stores, express wagon lines, and riverboats. And they charged sky-high prices for everything until many a would-be prospector found himself broke before ever reaching Colorado.

As many as 150,000 Peakers started out for the fabled goldfields, but about a third met misfortune and turned back before reaching them. Others who made it to Colorado stayed only long enough to see that the pickin's were no way as easy as advertised.

"Busted, by thunder!" went the new slogan. A huge eastward migration ran slap up against fresh hordes of hopefuls on their way to Colorado. Many of the newcomers who heard that it was "all a humbug," turned around and headed home. Many of those "busted" felt they had been badly misled. There were threats against those who had written the glowing reports in books and the eastern newspapers. One man became a particular target.

A sawmill hitched to his wagon, Daniel Oakes was on his way to Colorado in 1860 for new business opportunities (and an eventual future as a Colorado elder statesman) when he met the waves of stampeders on their return. Oakes was shocked to find himself buried in effigy in numerous graves along the way. The epitaph on the makeshift grave marker usually went something like this:

> *Here lies the body of D. C. Oakes*
> *Who started the damned Pikes Peak hoax*

Tall Stories

People did make their fortunes in Colorado (see "Leadville and the Fabulous Ice Palace" under Fabled People and Places), but no gold was ever found on Pikes Peak or even within a sixty-mile radius. In 1871, the U.S. Army Signal Corps stuck a weather station atop Pikes Peak where it rotated unfortunate

enlisted men, one at a time, until 1889. The only duties were to maintain the station and record wind velocity, temperatures, precipitation, and so on. The results would be sent by telegraph to headquarters.

Even when the men were allowed to bring family, the duty couldn't have been a choice one. From 1876 to 1881, Sgt. John O'Keefe obliged reporters with tales of his experiences that passed on to publications back East. O'Keefe's most widely reprinted report was about the massive rat invasion he and his wife, Nora, fought off one night. The rats that populated the mountain crevices, he wrote, had developed a taste for raw meat "rivaling that of the Siberian wolf." After a big meat delivery, rats poured into the station, ate the beef in nothing flat, and then turned on the O'Keefes. Mrs. O'Keefe seized a length of

electrical coil attached to a large battery, flipped the switch, and electrocuted every rat in contact. The other rats fled.

The army's attitude was indulgent until it discovered that some of O'Keefe's weather reports were also fiction. Turned out, he'd write his reports days in advance so he could go off and enjoy a good pub crawl. The army put a stop to that, as well as the stream of tall tales.

When O'Keefe returned to civilian life in Denver as a telegraph operator, his fans threw a banquet for him with many a suitably florid toast.

A Soft Ride

By the 1880s, settlers of mainly European descent had booted the Utes out of the coveted region and onto reservations. The Tabeguache band in the Pikes Peak area was sent to Utah. The image of America's Mountain was reproduced endlessly (often inaccurately) across the nation on everything from coins to soap ads to amusement park rides. The toymaker Parker Brothers created a board game called Pikes Peak or Bust in 1895.

Pikes Peak was a major tourist attraction, although tourists had to be plenty fit to make the trip. Visitors made the two-day trek to the summit by foot or on a donkey. The easiest way was a wagon ride up to Half Way House and the rest by mule.

One man's sore butt may

have changed access to the peak forever. It belonged to a prosperous inventor with a thing for comfort—Zalmon G. Simmons, founder of the Simmons Mattress Company. Simmons went up Pikes Peak in the late 1880s to check on another one of his inventions, the insulator for the telegraph wires at the weather station. He took the donkey ride both ways.

On his return, he made a beeline for the mineral baths at Manitou Springs. The owner of his hotel (rumored to have been the now-venerable Cliff House) waited until Simmons had a good soak before he casually mentioned that the locals had been talking about putting a railroad to the top of Pikes Peak for some time. Simmons certainly saw the benefit of that. He set out to raise the funds, and by 1891, the Manitou & Pikes Peak Cog Railway was open for business.

Half Way House and the donkeys are gone today. You can ride in a modern cog rail car up the steep side of Pikes Peak at a slow speed designed to acclimate you to the reduction of oxygen. This trip is designed for only short stays at the summit, because most people will quickly feel the unusual effects (dizziness, nausea, swelling of the limbs, even swelling in the brain) of being so high above sea level. If your brakes are good, you can drive the spectacular nineteen-mile toll road built in 1915. Even better, visit in July for the annual Race to the Clouds, held every year since 1916. You can watch cars and motorcycles race against the clock on narrow, mostly gravel, two-lane switchbacks with plenty of blind curves.

Pikes Peak has come a long way since it was the paradise of the Tabeguache Utes. But the ancient story has not been forgotten. In 1999, members of the northern Ute Reservation in Utah began making regular visits again to the remains of the old sun-dance grounds on the side of the mountain they call Tava.

The Pikes Peak Historical Society has an endowment fund set up just to sponsor this weeklong visit every year.

Paint Mines Interpretive Park

This is one of those gems of Colorado that even many longtime Coloradans haven't heard of—a jaw-dropping, where's-my-camera, natural wonder of a place that stands out even in a state full of 'em. The 730-acre park maintained by El Paso County is southeast of Calhan and northeast of Colorado Springs.

The beautiful wetlands, native-grass prairie, diverse wildlife, and seasonal wildflowers aren't what make this park stand out. The abundance of cliffs, spires, hoodoos, and labyrinth-like gullies that would be striking enough anywhere aren't the main eye-catchers either. It's the colors—layers and multiple shades of purple, red, orange, yellow, and gray clays left more than 55 million years ago. State archaeologists have estimated Native Americans have flocked here to entrap game and dig the clay to make paints as many as nine thousand years ago. They used the bits of petrified wood from the tropical trees that once flourished here for darts and arrow points. Settlers used the clay for bricks.

The park is accessible year round, weather permitting. Locals say the best time to view the colors is just before sunset.

Rock Art

Petroglyphs are images scarred into rock by chipping or pecking with a sharp object, while pictographs are painted images made with crushed minerals or vegetation mixed with something like grease or blood. These types of art can be found in many places around Colorado, and their age can range from thousands of years ago to much more recent. Some of this art has deep cultural and religious significance.

Picture Canyon and the Mysterious Crack Cave

Comanche National Grassland is, as the name suggests, rolling prairie and remains relatively unchanged since the late 1880s. After the dust bowls of the 1930s drove ranchers and farmers away, the U.S. Forest Service bought many of the marginal farms that now make up the majority of the Grassland.

You can still see the remnants of farm buildings, fences, and cemeteries built with local rock. Here in southeastern Colorado, just a howdy away from Oklahoma, the rolling prairie laps against the rims of sandstone canyons embellished with rock art.

In particular, Picture Canyon's walls have served as an outdoor gallery for centuries. Native American images include women, warriors, bison, and horses and are worth a visit at any time, but if you're willing to rise before dawn on the spring and fall equinoxes, you can gain entrance to a cave in the canyon that is inaccessible the rest of the year.

Crack Cave is named from the very narrow passage that runs about fifteen feet from its entrance inward. When the sun rises over the east canyon wall on the equinox, light shines through the cave entrance and falls onto an inscribed stone lump on the north interior wall. The spot is highlighted for only ten to twelve minutes before the light disappears. Some scholars of ancient languages say the lines are a form of writing similar to a Celtic language called Ogam, also spelled as *Ogham*.

No one knows for sure where Ogam originated, but it's associated with ancient Celtic communities in the United Kingdom and is believed to have flourished in the fifth and sixth centuries. Inscriptions have been found on monuments or as labels or messages on objects. Other theories are pretty wide ranging. Ogam may predate Christianity, or perhaps early Irish Christians invented it.

It could have been meant as a secret code or as an alphabet with a special purpose.

If the markings inside Crack Cave are Ogam, then it's evidence there were Europeans in Colorado long before the Spaniards arrived in the sixteenth century.

They were discovered sometime in 1976 by a visitor named Dan Rohrer. He returned in 1984 with a film crew producing a documentary on rock art for Denver public television station KRMA. On the equinox, the crew witnessed the shaft of light hitting the markings precisely. Among the witnesses was Bill McGlone, a retired engineer and rock art researcher from nearby La Junta who had taught himself Ogam. He translated an inscription on the stone as "Sun strikes on a certain day, Bel"—Bel is the name of a pagan sun god—and another as "People of the sun."

McGlone couldn't raise enough serious scholarly interest in the theory of non-Native Americans in pre-Columbian America, but he wrote several books of local interest: *Petroglyphs of Southeast Colorado and the Oklahoma Panhandle, Archaeoastronomy of Southeast Colorado and the Oklahoma Panhandle,* and *Ancient American Inscriptions: Plow Marks or History?* He died in 1999, and his books are out of print.

The debate over exactly what the markings mean and who made them just adds to their mystery. Soon after the discovery, the Forest Service built an iron cage around the entrance to Crack Cave, with a lock that is opened only for the equinox viewings. If you want to be there for the event, call the Forest Service office in Springfield, Colorado, at (719) 523-6591.

Springfield, about thirty-five miles southwest of the Crack Cave, holds a festival on the autumn equinox every year. To find out when, check the town's Web site at www.springfieldcolorado.com.

A Face of Stone

There are a number of officially sanctioned places where you can see rock art—but you can also stumble across them in previously unknown locations. Mutual UFO Network (MUFON) field investigator Chuck Zukowski, a Colorado Springs resident, has often experienced how research into one anomalous subject will lead to another fascinating discovery of quite a different nature. Here is his account of how a preliminary investigation of a UFO sighting resulted in uncovering a mystery carved into stone in a park near the famous Garden of the Gods:

While I was running my field investigation in Ute Valley Park with my witness, he happened to mention a carved rock face he and a friend had discovered a couple of years back not too far from our present location. The rock carving had no significant relation to the UFO sighting so I treated them both as separate investigations. After completing my investigation for MUFON, I next concentrated on the rock-face carving. Doing a little research of the area, the significant Native American presence in the area was the Ute Indian tribe. The two carvings, which were brought to my attention, did not resemble any type of pictographs or petroglyphs from the Ute tribe but more Aztec or possibly Maya.

Experienced in UFO field archeology, I had some ideas where to go with this. I first contacted a representative from the Colorado State Parks Department and took him to the site. Familiar with what the state parks have to offer, he had never seen anything like this. I gave my report to him, he then took pictures, and I figured I did my best notifying the state about this possible artifact. I haven't heard anything back from him.

Next, I contacted a local group whose members enjoy spending their free time venturing throughout Colorado looking at Native American rock art. I took a small group of their representatives to the site for their examination. Obviously very bewildered and excited, they had never seen anything like this before. The erosion of the patina of the carving itself stated it could have been there a very long time, but how long?

Now, as a UFO investigator I'm quite comfortable seeing things I may not be able to explain, at least right away, so it was interesting watching this group of experienced individuals try to deduce an explanation. Thinking it couldn't be Maya or Aztec, they were thinking it could be a carving done by an early settler to Colorado or an unknown tribe. Still, that's pretty cool. My hopes with releasing this investigation to print is to create a conversation and understanding of what has been hiding in Ute Valley Park all these years. Is this significant to the history of Colorado? Only time and more research will tell.

The carvings are on two rock formations about ten feet away from each other. One depicts a man with a big head, a long nose, and an open mouth with a prominent tongue. The other carving is more abstract and parts of it are worn away so that it's difficult to tell what it may have looked like originally.

"They are definitely carvings, not just the way the rocks happened to form. They don't look like carvings done by Native Americans of this area," says Zukowski. "But they don't look recent either. So maybe this is the work of foreign tribes, passing through. Or early settlers."

Zukowski is surprised the carvings haven't received more scientific attention from state authorities.

"They're interesting and worth attention, so I hope the effort will be made soon. I'd love to know more about them."

Other Places to See Rock Art

Petroglyphs survive the ages better than painted images, but neither form is resistant to destructive humans. That may explain why even known sites on public lands aren't widely advertised in Colorado. Attention, unfortunately, often reaps destruction. For instance, in August 2002, someone carved an obscene word and a drawing over

a petroglyph left by the Fremont People one thousand years ago in Colorado National Monument near Grand Junction. This kind of damage can't be repaired.

Not only vandals threaten ancient images but well-meaning people as well. They might touch them, outline them with chalk for photography, or try to raise faded images by putting a powder over them. So, the following places are pretty well known, and hands-off is the best way to admire them.

Canyon Pintado

There are four hundred known sites for images left by members of the Ute and Fremont tribes along or near Colorado State Highway 139 between Fruita (home of the Mike the Headless Chicken Festival—see Local Heroes and Villains) and Rangely in far-western Colorado. There arc markers along the road for sixteen nearby sites; other sites are unmarked and may take a few minutes or longer to reach. You can pick up brochures in Grand Junction, Fruita, or Rangely that will give more details.

If driving from Fruita, milepost 53.5 will be the first marker. This is Waving Hands Site, a cliff face with a number of images including a pair of hands, horses, and figures.

Dinosaur Diamond Scenic and Historic Byway

You can find rock art at many places along this long highway loop (see the separate entry in this chapter). They're not much advertised because of the possibility of vandalism. However, if you go to Dinosaur National Monument, the visitor center on the Colorado side of the border can direct you to large pictographs and petroglyphs such as those done by Fremont Indians on the canyon walls along the route called Tour of the Tilted Rocks.

Picketwire (aka Purgatory) Canyon

Some of the very old rock art here is so different from the usual Native American styles in the area that it has inspired some interesting theories about their origins—everything from extraterrestrial to ancient Israelite.

Petroglyph Point Loop Trail

This is a three-mile trail that starts at Chapin Mesa Archeological Museum at the famous cliff dwelling ruins of Mesa Verde. It loops around a canyon and mesa occupied by the people formerly called Anasazi. The trail leads to a large rock face filled with petroglyphs carved by the Ancestral Pueblo people some time between 600 BCE to early 1200 BCE. A guidebook is available at the museum.

Dog Mountain

A rock shelter (not quite a cave) here has a six-foot-long petroglyph of a bird chipped into the ceiling, with some additional shamanic elements. The area is a longtime stopover for migrating sandhill cranes.

Fabled People and Places

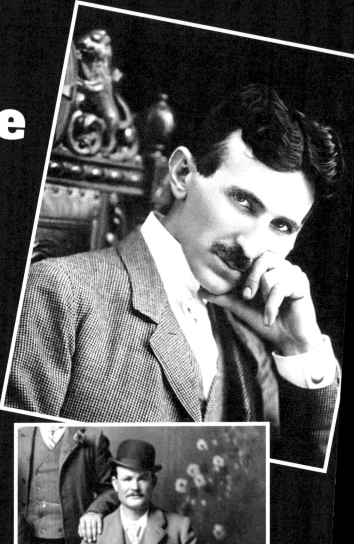

While *fables are morality stories, fabled* is a description of people and things that have an element of the fabulous. The fabled tend to be with us for a brief, dazzling period and then vanish in a way that keeps us wanting to know more.

Their stories are the kind we remember all of our lives, pass on to others, and prick up our ears at a hint that we will learn more about them. Even if we brush off the embellishments, rumors, and legends surrounding the stories, they still have enough fabulous truth in them to remain immortal.

Lost and Hidden Treasures in Colorado

If you believe the stories, fabulous lost mines, secret stashes, and buried caches can be found all around Colorado.

Hidden outlaw loot, Spanish gold heaped into forbidding caves, French gold dug into a mountain, lost wagonloads of money, and an entire railroad boxcar full of vintage French goodies—just to name a few treasure tales—beckon the treasure hunter.

These are the kinds of stories that might make you consider buying a metal detector and a few old maps, and taking a fresh look at Colorado landscapes.

La Caverna del Oro

It's a real limestone cave, thirteen thousand feet high on Marble Mountain to the northeast of the Great Sand Dunes, not far from the town of Westcliffe. Local Native Americans told sixteenth-century Spanish explorers that the place was demon haunted. The Spaniards heard only that there was much gold to be had.

The tale was so enticing that some soldiers, including three monks, left the Coronado expedition and made their way to the cave. By bribery or force, they convinced a number of Native Americans to mine the gold in it. At some point, the Native Americans rebelled and killed several of their oppressors. The remaining monk managed to convince the Indians that he had the power to exorcise the demons from the cave, and the mining continued. When the Spaniards had as much gold as they could safely load onto their pack animals, they killed the Indian workers. Then, they fled back to Mexico.

In 1869, a settler named Captain Elisha Horn (for whom Colorado's Horn Peak is named) claimed that he found a cave with a Maltese cross painted near the entrance. Nearby was a skeleton wearing Spanish armor and pierced by an arrow. There is a faded Maltese cross painted near the entrance of Spanish Cave (another name for La Caverna del Oro) on Marble Mountain, although it shows signs of vandalism.

Somewhere in this cave is supposed to be a wooden door that leads to the gold the Spaniards were forced to leave behind. Experienced spelunkers have been through the cave as far as humans can safely go, and nothing of the sort has ever been reported. Perhaps that's because some say the cross actually marks an exit, not an entrance.

At any rate, if you have any interest in having a go at Spanish Cave, be aware that

La Caverna is reputed by experienced cavers to be the most dangerous and unpleasant site in Colorado and not for any but the most experienced. Of course, those demons remain and the ghosts of murdered Indians as well.

Treasure Mountain

The "bible" of Colorado loot lore is the venerable *Treasure Tales of the Rockies* by Perry Eberhart, first published in 1961 by Sage Publications of Chicago. One of the most enduring stories of this book is of the legendary French gold on Treasure Mountain, a peak just south of Wolf Creek Pass summit in southern Colorado.

As the story goes, a large French expedition of three hundred skilled men and soldiers set out from the Leavenworth, Kansas, area in 1790 to investigate mineral resources in French-owned western lands. They found the best gold deposits on Treasure Mountain in what was then Spanish territory.

Disease, accidents, and other hardships pared the company down to less than one hundred by the time the expedition decided to journey to New Orleans with the gold. Eberhart wrote that most sources estimated the take at around $5 million. Before the French could leave the mountain, Native Americans attacked the group. The Frenchmen hastily buried the gold and made maps of the location. Only five men survived. They decided to return to the nearer French fort in Kansas. The group had to draw straws three times to decide which man would be eaten by the rest. Only two men made it back to the Kansas outpost. One died soon after; the other was the expedition's historian called either Le Breau or Le Blanc.

The man Eberhart called Le Breau made two maps of the treasure location before journeying back to France. One went to Napoléon's government; the other was kept for his family. The story becomes a little hazier after this. While many attempts have been made to find the gold buried on Treasure Mountain, it remains a tantalizing mystery.

Tommyknockers and "Cousin Jacks"

The immigrant men from Cornwall were famous for being excellent miners, and whenever asked by American mine managers whether they had any skilled kin, the miners would usually reply that they had a "Cousin Jack" back home who could be hired for the price of a boat ticket. This is how Cornish miners in the United States came to be known collectively as Cousin Jacks.

Cornish miners refused to work in a mine that didn't have reports of Tommyknocker activity, and Colorado mine managers learned not to laugh at this curious belief. Miners knew the Tommyknockers by the tapping of their little pickaxes coming at inexplicable times and places and by the experiences of other miners.

Tommyknockers are something like elves—cousins of the Piskies or Vogs of the English moors—that hang out in mines. They are supposed to be little, wrinkled men with greenish skin, dressed in miner clothing. They are good luck when pleased with the miners, vital in times of trouble such as warning about imminent tunnel collapse.

If you speak disrespectfully of them, forget to leave a little food occasionally, or whistle in the mines, you might regret it. A mine with a lot of bad luck was supposed to be a sign that the Tommyknockers had shown their displeasure by leaving.

A closed mine was not supposed to be completely sealed, or the Tommyknockers couldn't follow the miners to a new place of employment. The tradition may be why so many old, abandoned mines in Colorado seem surprisingly accessible. This is not an invitation to exploration.

Outlaw Loot
Jim Reynolds

A gang of Confederate sympathizers led by Jim Reynolds robbed and looted the South Park area in July 1864. Some say Reynolds claimed the mission was to rob the gold mines to support the Confederate government. However, the Reynolds gang's attacks on civilian ranches and stagecoach stations, where they stole horses, cash, and other valuables and molested a woman didn't seem idealistic to most area residents.

A posse caught up to them on July 30 in a forest clearing called Geneva Gulch, and a gunfight took the life of one of the robbers. His head was cut off and displayed in a jar of alcohol in nearby Fairplay for some time. The rest of the Reynolds gang scattered, but more men flocked to join the posse, and it eventually caught five of the fugitives. Jim Reynolds, his brother, and another man managed to escape to New Mexico. The estimated $5,000 to $100,000 worth of loot was believed to have disappeared with them. Before he died of gunshot wounds, though, Jim Reynolds gave the real story to a fellow outlaw named Albert Brown. He claimed that his gang buried cash and gold near the site of the first clash with the posse. He even drew a map.

Brown and some partners lit out for the South Park area but found when they arrived that a forest fire had destroyed many of the landmarks for the cache site. They found the skeleton of a horse Reynolds said had become stuck in a swamp, a headless human skeleton, and a hat that supposedly belonged to the decapitated outlaw. That was it.

Before Brown died in a drunken fight in Wyoming Territory, he told David J. Cook, head of the Rocky Mountain Detective Agency and a Denver city marshal, about the buried loot. Cook apparently said he had obtained or had seen the map in his 1897 memoirs (reprinted as *Hands Up; Or, Twenty Years of Detective Life in the Mountains and on the Plains* by University of Oklahoma Press in 1971). As of yet, no discovery has ever been claimed.

According to Cook, the outlaw stash was buried somewhere near Geneva Gulch, just above the head of Deer Creek, at timberline. The loot is described as $40,000 in "greenbacks," wrapped in cloth, and three tins full of gold dust. It's all stuffed in a rock-filled prospecting hole. A butcher knife is stuck in a tree nearby, the handle pointed toward the hole.

The Musgrove Gang

Cook also apparently wrote about another hidden location of ill-gotten gains reaped by the Musgrove Gang in the late 1860s. This gang killed twelve people before Cook's volunteer detective agency caught up with them. The bandits were all arrested or killed. Citizens broke into a Denver jail on November 23, 1868, and lynched the leader, Lee Musgrove, from a bridge over Cherry Creek. As the gang's loot was not recovered, it was believed a fortune in silver and gold coins was buried somewhere along the Cache La Poudre River, just south of the Wyoming border.

The Wild Bunch

Northwest of the town of Maybell in northwest Colorado, Moffat County Road 10N runs through Irish Canyon. The canyon was a popular hideout for outlaws, including Butch Cassidy (shown on page 65) and the Wild Bunch (shown on page 64). Somewhere in the area is supposed to be a cache of $30,000 in stolen silver coins. Cassidy's gang is also said to have buried $100,000 from bank robberies near the town of Monument in El Paso County.

Hidden in Plain Sight

Lincoln County has an intriguing story of criminal fugitives from California who hid out in plain sight here as ordinary farmers and ranchers. The men decided to make one last robbery in 1862 when they learned of a supposedly poorly guarded U.S. Army payroll wagon bound for Denver. The payroll turned out to have good security although not enough to avoid a shootout and robbery. The surviving bandits escaped with a load of gold coins so heavy it slowed them down, so they decided to bury their loot before a posse caught up with them.

In a gulch a few miles east of the town of Clifford, they dug what looked like three shallow graves in a circle with the date of 1847. The gold was put into three dutch ovens and buried in the center of the circle. Then, the outlaws disappeared.

In 1884, a stranger who claimed to be from Chicago found lodging with James Will, a local sheep rancher. The man spent a lot of time roaming the prairie east of Clifford. Eventually, he gave up, but before he left town, he told the story of the stolen payroll and buried treasure to the rancher. In May 1931, George Elkins found a rock inscribed with 1847 and some unreadable letters. The old story was remembered, and treasure hunters hit the area in droves but without luck as far as anyone knows.

Three years later, Tom Hatton found another rock inscribed D. GROVER AND JOSEPH FOX-LOWE, AUG. 8, 1847. This set off another round of treasure frenzy but, again, with no reports of discovery.

There's nothing left of Clifford today, not even a ghost town. It was located about eight miles south of Hugo in Lincoln County at the intersection of U.S. 287 and U.S. 40.

Table Mountain

Another stolen U.S. Army payroll is supposedly buried atop Table Mountain in a location well-named Robbers Roost. Six outlaws waylaid a stagecoach near Virginia Dale Station, a stop along the Overland Trail in 1863. They made off with an iron strongbox holding $60,000 in gold coins meant as back pay for the soldiers at Fort Sanders in Wyoming Territory. The U.S. Cavalry tracked the robbers on the treacherous cliffs of Table Mountain to their cabin at Robbers Roost. The ensuing battle killed the outlaws, and the secret of what they did with the stolen payroll went with them to the grave. The soldiers tore apart the area but found only the empty, bullet-riddled strongbox in a creek.

Virginia Dale Station stands today, and a small, lively community in the area belies the label of ghost town. However, no landmarks have been discovered on Table Mountain that might indicate where the old Robbers Roost cabin used to be.

Lost Money Wagons

In 1858, a wagon full of gold ingots galloped into Chacuaco Canyon in Las Animas County, just ahead of pursuing robbers. Three guards managed to load the gold onto pack animals and moved into hiding behind a rock outcropping near a creek, while the outlaws murdered the rest of the wagon party. The survivors left the gold where they had stashed it and hid in a Hispanic village. When they finally ventured out to pick up their gold again, Ute tribesmen killed them.

In 1907, four wagons carrying six kegs of new dimes from the U.S. Mint at Denver disappeared on their way to Phoenix, Arizona. Years later, the remains of four wagons were found on the dangerous North Rim Road of Black Canyon (so named because it's so steep that the interior is quite dark). Gallons of dimes were picked up along the Gunnison River, and it's thought there are still lots more out there. Those old dimes are worth considerably more than ten cents each today.

Mystery of the Missing Merci Car

Following World War II, American journalist Drew Pearson urged that citizens send donations of food and clothing to help the struggling people of France and Italy. So much was collected that it was shipped abroad in a seven-hundred-car American Friendship Train.

A French veteran named André Picard proposed that French citizens respond with a boxcar full of gifts for the Americans. Again, so much was collected that the single a boxcar wasn't nearly enough. In return for American generosity, one boxcar was sent to every state in the Union, with one to be shared between the District of Columbia and Hawaii.

Every boxcar was a wooden World War I transport model, twenty feet long by eight feet wide, brightly painted, and adorned with shields representing the various regions of France. The gifts inside these boxcars ranged from children's crafts to wedding dresses to a jeweled medal that had belonged to Napoléon. These rolling shipping containers were known as Gratitude Cars or Merci Cars.

Somehow, Colorado became the only state to permanently misplace the one it received. Two other states lost theirs in fires; Rhode Island's wound up in a junkyard from which it was eventually rescued and restored in 2005.

Colorado's arrived in February 1949, was put on tour around the state, and was last seen in the town of Eagle, near Vail, around 1954. Then it disappeared. The Colorado State

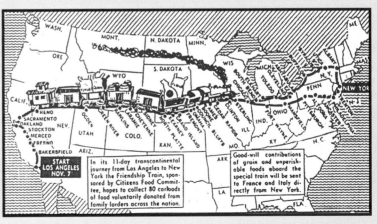

In its 11-day transcontinental journey from Los Angeles to New York the Friendship Train, sponsored by Citizens Food Committee, hopes to collect 80 carloads of food voluntarily donated from family larders across the nation.

Good-will contributions of grain and unperishable foods aboard the special train will be sent to France and Italy directly from New York.

Archives and the Colorado Historical Society have no clues to its whereabouts. The only known surviving object that came with the boxcar is a commemorative plaque that the Colorado Railroad Museum in Golden somehow acquired.

"We don't know how that got here," says Ken Forrest, archivist at the Colorado Railroad Museum's library in Golden. "We figure it was sometime back in the late 1950s, when it was common for people to send or drop off any old railroad-related items for our collections. Bob Richardson [who started the library for whom it is named], was not trained or anything. He'd just accept whatever was given, and if we didn't have room for it, then he'd stick it in a box in one of the old boxcars used for storage.

"Over the years, we've been opening up the boxes when we had time, and it's sort of like Christmas; we never know what we'll find.

"I figure some member of the Veterans of Foreign Wars or something took the boxcar when it no longer seemed wanted and had it stored on his ranch or in a barn until it could be used again. Then maybe he died, and no one else knows where it is or what it is."

That's a more hopeful scenario than the theory that the boxcar wound up demolished for its metal scrap, its plaque the only thing salvaged. What seems equally mystifying is that no one seems to know what happened to the many gifts that came in the Merci Car. According to the Colorado Historical Society, newspaper articles of the day mentioned that the valuable stuff would be put away for "safekeeping" while the boxcar was exhibited in Colorado towns with the less expensive goodies.

No one knows what these goodies were—no inventory has ever turned up, nor any hint of how they were dispersed.

Leadville and the Fabulous Ice Palace

There it sits, a ghost of its past, at an elevation of 10,430 feet above sea level—the highest incorporated town in North America. Its other name is Cloud City, and you can see why when the billowing clouds Colorado is famous for are rolling through.

The story began some time in 1859–1860. A group of prospectors called the Slater party made a good gold strike in the California Gulch—about $8 million worth. The news brought thousands of fortune hunters, who exhausted the gold by the end of 1860. The first boom was over, but a new one sprang up two years later when a couple of veteran miners recognized that pesky black stuff clogging up the gold separators as silver-bearing lead ore.

Alvinus Ward and William Stevens of South Park (a small town that's nothing like the animated television series) bought the exhausted gold mines, and by 1880, the silver boom was on. Leadville became the second-biggest city in Colorado and was seriously in the running to become the capital until it lost out to Denver.

Newspapers called it "the richest city on Earth." Mining camps ringed the town, and when the workday was done, miners swarmed in to take their pleasure in the more than 150 saloons and gambling halls. The most famous was run by Charles "Pap" Wyman. Wyman was rumored to have been a preacher before he set up his drinking establishment in the high Rockies, Wyman's Greatest Saloon. The owner, however, was a man of strict morals who kept a Bible chained to a pulpit for the convenience of itinerant ministers of the Gospel.

Wyman barred married and family men from his gambling tables, posted a clock with PLEASE DO NOT SWEAR written across the face, and would not allow his saloon girls to be groped between the neck and the knees.

He also carried around loose change in a pouch made from a human scrotum. (At least, that's what he told people.)

Leadville attracted many colorful people; some of whom did not intend to ever heft a pickax. Doc Holliday came here after the shootout at the OK Corral. He was acquitted of shooting a policeman in Leadville in 1884 and died of tuberculosis in Glenwood Springs. The Younger Gang lived here for a while. Bat Masterson and the Earps swaggered through. Johnny Brown and his lively wife, Margaret (never known as Molly in her Unsinkable lifetime), were married in a Leadville church.

Huge fortunes were literally made overnight in Leadville. Horace Tabor was the best known of the flock. He invested $37 (a little more than $800 today) as a "grubstake interest" in the Little Pittsburg Mine, cashed in big, went on to own the fabulous and aptly named Matchless Mine, and became a millionaire a hundred times over. He built the Tabor Opera House in Leadville in 1879 with no expense spared for the magnificent three-story structure. Inside, the Opera House is awash in hand-painted scenery, red velvet seats, and chandeliers. It's said that when he saw a portrait of Shakespeare in his new culture palace, Tabor snorted, "Well, what the hell has he ever done for the state of Colorado? Take it down and put my picture up there!"

Tabor was Leadville's first mayor, went on to become Colorado's lieutenant governor, and later served a term in the U.S. Senate. The Tabor story is worth an opera, and one was later composed that centered around Elizabeth McCourt, better known as Baby Doe, Tabor's gorgeous, much younger mistress and second wife after his scandalous divorce.

A domino effect of national proportions finally brought on the Silver Crash of 1893. Tabor lost his entire fortune almost as quickly as he earned it, and wound up as a Denver postmaster who made as much in a year as he used to earn in a day. According to legend, Tabor made Baby Doe promise on his deathbed in 1899 to keep the Matchless Mine for silver's sure-to-come revival some day. Actually, they had lost the mine to creditors. The legend probably sticks because no one really knows why thirty-eight-year-old Baby Doe and her two teenage daughters eventually went to live at the closed Matchless Mine. She could have remarried or lived with relatives. Instead, for the rest of her life, she tried to find investors to help her buy the Matchless again and reopen it.

The mine owners apparently felt sorry for her and allowed her to occupy an old cabin next to the shaft house. Her daughters were eventually fed up and moved out. Baby Doe re-embraced her Catholic faith and became increasingly, quietly delusional. She died of a heart attack in the winter of 1935. Her body was found by neighbors, frozen with her arms outstretched in the shape of a cross. She was buried next to her husband in Mt. Olivet Cemetery in Denver.

If all this sounds like great material for an opera, it is. *The Ballad of Baby Doe*, composed by Douglas Moore with a libretto by John Latouche, premiered in Central City in 1956.

Leadville made one last reach for greatness in 1895 when the town's population was down to 14,477 from its peak of 40,000. The remaining townspeople decided to hold a carnival with a giant ice structure to lure tourists and pump up the economy. By January 1, 1896, the Ice Palace was opened. The ice was mostly for show. The real framework came from lumber, girders, and tresses. Still, the huge blocks of strategically placed ice made the five-acre structure with ninety-foot-tall towers look like an immense crystal fantasy.

Some of the ice walls had whimsical decorations, such as real embedded trout or bottles of Coors beer (filled with water, actually, which thirsty workmen who later broke the ice discovered). The palace also included American roses, a merry-go-round, an ice-skating rink, and electric lights that lit the translucent walls with glowing colors. Even in daylight, the palace glittered with fractured sunbeams.

The Ice Palace's days were numbered by the time an early thaw showed up in mid-March. The building was condemned on March 28. Five thousand tons of ice does take quite some time to melt, though, so there was one last formal skating party on May Day. Ladies and gentlemen skated around a giant maypole for the occasion.

Relative poverty until recent years may have helped save Leadville's wealth of Victorian buildings from being bulldozed in a misguided zeal to "modernize" the city. Today, all of Leadville is a National Historic Landmark

District. The restaurants and places of entertainment are considerably more genteel than during the boom days. There is a National Mining Museum and Hall of Fame, and the Tabor Opera House is still in operation.

Leadville holds a host of festivals annually, including the Crystal Carnival, which today features a skijoring (skiing while pulled by dogs) competition along Harrison Avenue where Wyman's Greatest Saloon used to be. Nothing is left of the Ice Palace—like the fabled Leadville before the crash, it stands alone in history.

Oscar Wilde's Visit to Leadville

In 1881, Oscar Fingal O'Flahertie Wills Wilde set off on a lecture tour of the United States. He was only twenty-seven, but was already a much-quoted wit and had acquired a comic notoriety for his promotion of the "aesthetic" in ordinary life.

He later claimed that when it was learned he would be journeying to "the richest city in the world," the silver mining boomtown of Leadville, a letter warned that he or his manager would be shot if they showed up there. Wilde replied that nothing that could be done to his manager would intimidate him.

Wilde arrived at the Clarendon Hotel on April 13, 1882. He had a spell of altitude sickness but recuperated enough for his first lecture that night at the Tabor Opera House.

He appeared in full aesthetic rig—more than six feet tall in a dark velvet suit, long hair, and knee breeches—and presented himself with the generous remark, "I give myself to Leadville." At which point a stagehand jostled the backdrop curtain and knocked Wilde into the orchestra pit. Nonetheless, Wilde went on to give a nonstop one-hour lecture titled "Ethics of Art."

Afterward, he and his manager were invited to dinner in the Matchless Mine, owned by the reigning silver king, Horace Tabor. They all descended in what Wilde described as "a rickety bucket."

Dinner consisted of three courses of whiskey—"my kind of meal," Wilde remarked.

The next night after his lecture Wilde was carted off to Pap Wyman's Saloon for a determined effort to drink the English "sissy boy" under the table. According to Leadville history researcher Gretchen Scalon, "Much later, local miners reflecting on the event would say, 'Wilde could drink all night and then carry two of us home.'"

At Wilde's third lecture, he read from the memoirs of the Renaissance artist Benevento Cellini. When someone inquired why Wilde hadn't brought Cellini along, Wilde broke the news that Cellini was dead. "Who shot him?" he was asked.

At Wyman's Saloon, Wilde noticed a sign posted over the piano that pleaded, DON'T SHOOT THE PIANO PLAYER. HE IS DOING THE BEST HE CAN, and commented that it was "the most rational form of art criticism I had ever seen."

Wilde said afterward that Leadville had provided his best American audience and insisted, "I found the miners charming and not at all rough."

The Ant People

According to Hopi legend, those of the First People who respected the Creator were saved from the destruction of the first Earth by living in underground kivas with the Ant People. They were told to emulate the Ant People, who were industrious, who gathered food all summer to eat in winter, and who lived in peace with one another. They were also good hosts. In order to keep their guests fed, they kept themselves on short rations—hence those pinched waists.

The Navajo people respect ants as messengers between Earth's surface and the holy worlds below.

Some Westerners have claimed that what may be Native American pictographs portraying Ant People bear a strong resemblance to popular depictions of extraterrestrial aliens—big heads, pinched waists, long spindly fingers, etc. Which has inspired popular theories in some circles that maybe the Ant People are really gray aliens, eh?

Mattie Silks, the House of Mirrors and the Duel

Mattie Silks was a short, plump woman from Indiana, originally christened Martha Ann Norman, who claimed to have gone straight into the business of running brothels at age nineteen without ever having been a prostitute.

Long after a Mr. Silks had faded from the scene, Silks was living up to his name with a wardrobe heavy on fashionable silk attire. In 1877, she moved her operations to the section of Denver's Market Street known as "the Row" where the best brothels were. She quickly became known as a colorful character who packed a gun and claimed to be a crack shot, but who also let her girls keep half of the high prices she charged.

In August of that year, Silks was involved in an event that has gone down in apocryphal history as the Duel of the Madams. The best-known version of it came from a writer named Forbes Parkhill in his 1951 book *The Wildest of the West*. His story had Silks and Kate Fulton, another madam, in an argument over the favors of a handsome fellow named Cortez "Cort" Thomson. They decided to settle it with pistols outside city limits in what is sometimes called "the first recorded duel between women."

According to Parkhill, Silks and Fulton squared off and fired. Both missed, but Silks's shot just happened to nick one of the bystanders—her boyfriend, Cort. He was grazed in the neck but survived. Another version of this

story is that Silks and Fulton decided to strip to the waist for the duel. Each had a boyfriend acting as her second.

The real story was reported in the Denver newspapers at the time. There was a foot race held at a park outside Denver city limits which Silks's beau, Cort Thomson, won. Silks collected on a big bet, and the celebration that followed got out of hand. When she and Kate Fulton scuffled, Thomson stepped in and may have broken Fulton's nose. Her boyfriend came to her aid, and Thomson whacked him too.

Silks and Thomson left in their carriage. Another carriage rolled up alongside and someone fired a gun. The bullet just missed Thomson. (Years later, after they married in 1884, Silks did take a shot at Thomson when she caught him with another woman. She missed, he beat her up, they reconciled, and they stayed together until he died in 1900.)

Silks ran an establishment that attracted the highest-class clientele for twenty years, although she lost her title as queen of the Row when another madam built the fabulous House of Mirrors on Market Street. Her friend, Jennie Rogers, bought the building at 1942 Market Street and had it remodeled into the swankiest cathouse west of the Mississippi.

It's a pity we don't have any photographs. The interior was famous for walls and ceilings covered with mirrors that reflected the crystal chandeliers and other posh furnishings. The girls and their clients could even dance to an orchestra in a ballroom with electric lights.

Silks had to wait until Jennie died in 1909 to buy the

House of Mirrors, so she could finally reign as queen of the Row again. Just to make her point, she had tiles spelling out *M. Silks* installed at the front entrance. However, her second reign lasted only a few years.

Prohibition finally did in the House of Mirrors. Without the fine liquor, the fine ladies couldn't bring in enough customers. The House of Mirrors was sold and converted into a Buddhist temple. Later, it became a warehouse before it changed hands a few more times.

They decided to settle it with pistols outside of city limits.

In recent years, the building was restored into something of its original splendor and is known again as Mattie Silk's House of Mirrors, now a posh Denver restaurant with a bar and a small museum devoted to the building's history. The place once again features large mirrors, and occasionally paranormal activity is reported (like a piano playing by itself—and it's not a player model.)

Silks invested well in real estate and lived comfortably the rest of her days—no small feat for an Old West madam. At seventy-four, she married Jack Ready, a bordello bouncer. Silks had a serious fall in 1929 and died of complications from her injuries. As Martha Ready, she's buried next to Cort, her first husband, in Fairmount Cemetery.

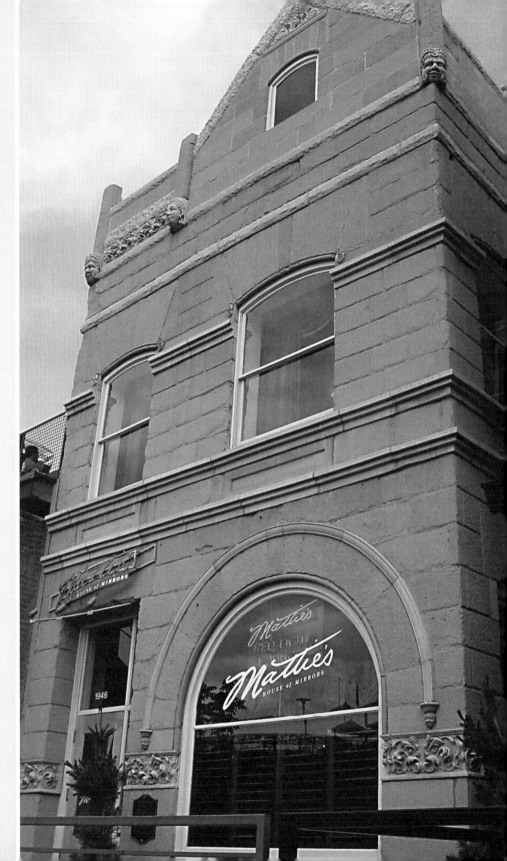

Francis Schlatter the Healer

For a period of about two months in 1895, thousands of people went daily to the yard of a house in a modest Denver neighborhood just to visit one mysterious man. Special trains were scheduled to bring even more crowds from outside the city and outside of Colorado. Streetcars displayed placards to let people know the route would take them to Francis Schlatter's address.

Every description of human lined up for blocks to have a brief encounter with Schlatter as he stood behind a low backyard fence. When he went inside the house for lunch, the crowds sat down and waited. When sunset came and Schlatter went inside again for the rest of the night, people peeked through the windows until chased off.

Why the enormous interest in a bearded, thirty-nine-year-old shoemaker from Alsace-Lorraine? He healed people—for free. At least, many who claimed he rid them of their ailments said so—with no preaching, no request for donations, no selling of anything. People walked up a small ramp and had their hands grasped over the fence. Observers saw a shudder run over Schlatter each time. He would give a mumbled prayer and advise the person to pray to "the Father." Sometimes, he said it might take a few "treatments" of this sort to finally succeed when faith was faulty, and in the end, it was up to God who decide who would be healed.

If Francis Schlatter was a charlatan, it's hard to tell what benefit he gained out of healing people. Newspaper reporters and other observers said that man known as "the healer" appeared to be a quiet, courteous, dignified man with a thick accent. He claimed no particular creed, no ax to grind, no apparent pretensions of any kind. He also generally kept to himself, had few material possessions, and was never seen to flirt, become drunk, or misbehave in any way. Because of his voluntary poverty, his demeanor, and his physical appearance, Schlatter was often described as Christlike.

Schlatter always refused money and other gifts for his service, and if they were pressed upon him, he promptly gave them away. He said that his ability to heal came from "the Father" who guided him on every aspect of his life and spoke to Schlatter in his head. Schlatter advised folks to pray The Lord's Prayer and seek God's guidance, and that was about it for any attempt at evangelizing.

No one knew anything about Schlatter but the little he told about himself. He was born in Alsace-Lorraine in 1856, raised a Catholic, and trained as a cobbler. He immigrated to America in 1884 and moved to Denver to 1892. One day, "the Father" spoke to Schlatter. He was to sell his business, give the money to the poor, and heal the sick. In addition, he was to go on a journey in which he was to trust his every need to God.

Schlatter set out from Denver to walk the West—Kansas, Nebraska, Oklahoma, Arkansas (he was jailed in Hot Springs for vagrancy but managed to escape), Texas, Arizona. For two years, he walked. He went on to Southern California, where he initially attempted healing among Native Americans. However, he first drew crowds in Albuquerque, New Mexico, and his fame spread as *El Sanador*, the Healer.

In 1895, he returned to Denver and stayed with the family of E. L. Fox, a man who had been healed by Schlatter. By mid-September, Schlatter began his healing sessions over the backyard fence. The Fox family supported Schlatter without reserve and acted as his assistants to handle the desperate hordes. The healer seldom went out except to various churches for evening Sunday services. At home, he would swing a long, very heavy, brass rod around vigorously, saying it was something the Father commanded he do to renew his power. He went on periodic fasts for days at a time.

Only one time was Schlatter known to refuse a healing

and that was with a man who became belligerent at the refusal and demanded to know why. Witnesses said Schlatter finally replied, "I cannot treat you. Go! You are a murderer." The man fled.

Two special trains—from Omaha and Fort Worth—were scheduled to bring people to see Schlatter in Denver. There were so many pleas for healing that Schlatter suggested handkerchiefs and scarves be passed to him so he could transmit his healing touch to people who couldn't come to him. Soon, bundles and suitcases of items started arriving, along with barrels of letters. He would sit long into the night to try to answer them all.

Denver newspapers had a hard time confirming people's cures because many people left town as soon as they had their encounter with Schlatter, even though they were told the healing might not take effect for a few hours or days. Other people delightedly demonstrated the things they said they couldn't do before Schlatter touched them, but usually no medical confirmation was made.

Schlatter hinted, then began saying outright, that he wouldn't be staying in Denver much longer. As soon as word spread, the crowds grew. Then one day, it happened. Schlatter's host, E. L. Fox, walked into Schlatter's bedroom on the morning of November 14, 1895 to find a note:

> *Mr. Fox,*
> *My Mission is finished.*
> *The Father takes me away.*
> *Goodbye.*
> *November 13 . . . Francis Schlatter*

FRANCIS SCHLATTER, "HEALING THE SICK." COPYRIGHT 1895, BY W. A. WHITE, RATON, NEW MEXICO.

When Fox broke the news to the waiting crowds, a riot nearly broke out. He was cursed and screamed at when he couldn't say where Schlatter had gone or if he would return. It was the beginning of a sad decline for Fox, who met frequent harassment whenever he went out thereafter. He fell first into a depression, then into a confused and delusional mental state. His family eventually committed him to an asylum.

Imposters had been trying to pass themselves off as Schlatter for some time, and now they popped up around the country. The real Francis Schlatter quietly made his way from one friend's isolated homestead to another, steadily working his way south. He stayed for three months at the ranch of Ada Morley in Datil, New Mexico, where he dictated his life story to her. (She published the memoirs in 1897 under the title Schlatter chose, *The Life of the Harp in the Hand of the Harper*.)

The trail ended in Chihuahua, Mexico, near the village of Nuevo Casas Grandes. A boy looking for a stray cow found a gringo wrapped in a blanket under a tree. He brought the village chief and others to see the man. The gringo was a big, bearded man who had apparently died of starvation. They found a white horse nearby, a fine saddle made in Denver, a Bible with the name *Francis Schlatter* written inside, and a long copper rod in a leather sheath.

When no one came looking for the dead man, he was buried in the local cemetery in a grave whose markings, if any, were eventually lost. The possessions left behind became communal property and used until nothing but the strange copper rod was left.

Word came back to the United States in 1897 that Schlatter had been found dead on a mountainside in northern Mexico. Then in 1922, Edgar Lee Hewett, archaeologist and director of the Museum of New Mexico, confirmed Schlatter's death. Hewett had seen and talked with Schlatter during Schlatter's healing stint in Denver. He recalled Schlatter in his 1943 book *Campfire and Trail*, as "powerfully-built . . . a plain, honest peasant doing something, as he believed, for suffering humanity . . ."

Hewett's Chihuahua guide was the boy who found the dead man. The boy's story convinced Hewett that the man was *El Sanador*. In return for information about Schlatter and a look at the only artifact left, the copper rod, Hewett donated money for the village to hire a schoolteacher. Months later, in Santa Fe, Hewett received the copper rod sent by the grateful Mexican villagers. He donated it to his museum.

Louise Stiver, curator of the Palace of the Governors (New Mexico History Museum), was kind enough to show me a museum photo of Schlatter's copper rod that I'll try to describe here as we couldn't reprint it. As Hewett said, Schlatter's copper rod resembles a baseball bat. The handle end has a brass knob, a short leather strap, and an area with rings mechanically carved around the tube for gripping. The other end appears to be capped with a small hole in the middle.

Ms. Stiver confirmed that she and other researchers have examined the rod and while it was scratched from use, it didn't appear to have any deliberate markings. The rod, like Francis Schlatter, remains an enigma.

He was buried in the local cemetery in a grave, whose markings, if any, were eventually lost.

Nikola Tesla

Nikola Tesla was responsible for a number of pioneering discoveries and inventions: Radar, radio, AC (alternating current electric power), the AC motor and transformer, and the Tesla Coil, a high-voltage generator, to mention a few. He also practically invented the mold of "mad scientist." Tesla's time in Colorado was brief, but the events of the period were so remarkable, they've spawned legends to this day.

Born in 1856, Nikola Tesla was a mechanical and electrical engineer who immigrated to the United States, worked for Thomas Edison for a time, and struck out on his own in 1886. He struggled financially and many of his general plans were pirated.

Tesla needed not only privacy but also wide-open space for his sometimes-powerful experiments. The Colorado Springs Electric Company offered him free land and power, and Tesla liked what he heard about Colorado's dry, pure air and frequent electrical storms. Colorado Springs also had the biggest electrical generator west of the Mississippi. He was going to need it.

Tesla arrived in Colorado Springs on May 17, 1899, and told reporters he was there, ". . . to conduct exhaustive experiments in regard to wireless telegraphy . . ." His home in Colorado Springs was the Alta Vista Hotel. Tesla had a number of personal superstitions and phobias. He deliberately picked a room that had a number divisible by three (207), and despite daily maid service, asked for extra linens and eighteen clean towels a day for additional cleaning.

For his laboratory, he chose a location about a mile east of downtown on Knob Hill and had a fifty-by-eighty-foot barnlike structure built with an enormous antenna (somewhere between eighty and two hundred feet long) on the roof. Signs warned off trespassers. One read ABANDON HOPE ALL YE WHO ENTER.

Tesla didn't just want professional secrecy. Often, these experiments were highly dangerous. Fires were a constant possibility, as the destruction of his New York City laboratory had proved earlier. Once, a barrage of electrical streamers firing across his lab forced him to crawl out on his stomach.

While in Colorado Springs, Tesla realized his hypothesis that the transmission of telegraphic messages was possible without wires. That discovery became known as radio. He also honed his idea that remote objects could be perceived with electromagnetic waves—a little theory that evolved into radar (*ra*dio *d*etecting and *r*anging).

In the most spectacular experiment of his career—the event talked about to this day in Colorado Springs—Tesla discovered that he could deliver a huge amount of electricity to another spot without transmission wires. It happened on a fall night in 1899. Tesla and his assistant put on thick, rubber-soled shoes, stuffed cotton balls into their ears, and set out to create lightning with Tesla's specially designed apparatus featuring the device known today as the Tesla Coil.

The assistant, Kolman Czito, was told to throw open the switch on the apparatus and keep it there until ordered to shut it. Tesla went outside to watch. Inside the lab, the rising snap, crackle, and sizzle grew to a roar. Sparks flew, a sulfur smell filled the air, and a strange blue light expanded. Outside, Tesla watched the surge of energy run up the antenna and into the sky like a lightning bolt—except that the bolt grew steadily—first six feet, then twenty feet, then fifty and eighty. Thunder commenced to rumble.

Tesla's surroundings were lit up by a blue haze like Saint Elmo's fire. The thunder reportedly was heard twenty-two miles away in Cripple Creek. The bolt stretched 120 feet—and suddenly it was gone. The thunder died and the glow dissipated. Tesla ran back into the lab where the assistant denied he threw the switch shut.

Tesla called the Colorado Springs Electric Company with the demand that his power be turned back on immediately. The foreman assured him forcefully that not only had Tesla shut off his own power himself, but also that the electric company's mighty generator was now on fire and likely destroyed.

Oh, and the entire town of Colorado Springs had gone dark.

Fortunately, the electric company had a backup generator, and the town didn't suffer darkness for long. However, Colorado Springs denied Tesla any more power until he replaced the ruined generator at his own expense.

Tesla returned to New York on January 7, 1900. His lab was dismantled, and the contents sold to pay his debts.

Tesla continued to make important discoveries and registered more than seven hundred patents, none of which ever gave him the financial fortune he should have. He was obsessed with the idea of providing free and unlimited electrical power anywhere on Earth, but the idea didn't attracted financial investors.

Tesla died of heart failure in 1943 in New York at eighty-six. His ashes are kept in the Nikola Tesla Museum in Belgrade, Yugoslavia. There isn't much official recognition in Colorado Springs today for Tesla's achievements. A museum run by The Tesla Society went bankrupt in 1999. A small house that had nothing to do with Tesla stands near the intersection of North Foote and Pike's Peak Avenues where his lab once was.

Tesla's sometimes-bizarre claims about his work have given him a sorcerer's reputation in paranormal and metaphysical circles. Rumors said he communicated with extraterrestrials and invented time machines or teleportation devices. Places associated with him tend to attract some very odd pilgrims.

Before Hollywood, There Was Colorado

Seriously. Movies were being shot in Colorado in 1897 when the dusty little Los Angeles neighborhood was still known as Cahuenga. Early film companies, such as Edison and Biograph, sent employees to Colorado to make three-minute movies of such reality shows as *Calf Branding* and *Denver Fire Brigade*.

The railroad companies paid for efforts like these, hoping that visions of the scenic and quaint West would bring out more folks from the East. The Selig Polyscope Company of Chicago had a base in Colorado that by the early 1900s was churning out a number of short films with stories that featured famous mining towns and real Coloradans.

In August 1911, Selig set up a movie studio in a hamlet called American City in the scenic hills overlooking Central City. A company of twenty people arrived to make the new kind of film story called Westerns. Among them were Tom and Olive Mix, a married pair of rodeo trick riders Selig made three one-reel movies of fifteen minutes each before the company moved on to Cañon City. Tom Mix had won the Royal Gorge Rodeo championship there in 1909, so Selig promoted him to share in lead-actor roles.

The company made twenty-five films between June and December 1912. Just about every place it stopped to shoot a scene in has a story about Tom Mix: how he and other actors would visit a bar and shoot lemons off shot glasses; how he hid from his angry wife in the closed-up awning of a BPO Elks' Club window until an employee unfurled it and dumped him at her feet; and many more.

Tom Mix was the biggest star to come out of the fledgling Colorado motion picture industry. Between performing his own stunts at a time when the industry had no safety measures, stints with Wild West shows and rodeos, and his exuberant private life, it's a wonder that he survived to become Hollywood's first cowboy star. By 1935, he had made more than three hundred films, most of them silent. His fame spawned radio shows, comic books, and Big Little Books galore.

For a while it looked like Selig might build a permanent movie studio in Cañon City, but the company eventually decided to stick to its other location in Los Angeles where the weather was more suitable for year-round shooting. In 1914, the Colorado Motion Picture Company moved into Cañon City and produced five to seven movies within a few months. Movies were longer by this time; each ran about thirty-five minutes in this batch.

During the filming of a scene, actress Grace McHugh fell off her horse trying to cross the Arkansas River, and Owen Carter, a cameraman, dove in to save her. They both drowned. The company went out of business later that year.

A number of other small regional companies made films in Colorado until the early 1920s, but by then Hollywood had become the moviemaking capital of the nation.

It was fun while it lasted.

Steve Canyon: The Man, the Comic, the Canyon

In 1947, the Squirrel Gulch district of Idaho Springs decided to rename itself in honor of the patriotic comic strip character Steve Canyon. Three years later, a forty-foot-tall lime-stone statue of Steve Canyon was commissioned, paid for by the U.S. Treasury(?!). What does the formerly named Squirrel Gulch have to do with Steve Canyon or his Chicago-based cartoonist creator Milton Caniff? The answer is—not much. Caniff actu-

ally had little or nothing to do with the odd monument of a fictional, fabled hero.

Steve Canyon was a long-running American adventure comic strip published from January 13, 1947, until shortly after Caniff's death on June 4, 1988. By 1946, Caniff had developed a worldwide reputation for both his writing and art on the syndicated newspaper strip *Terry and the Pirates* for the *Chicago Tribune* newspaper syndicate. Seeking creative control of his own work, Caniff, who was intensely patriotic, approached the *Chicago Sun-Times* with the idea for a new strip. Steve Canyon debuted in 168 nationwide newspapers.

Steve Canyon was an easygoing adventurer with a soft heart. Originally, a veteran running his own air-transport business, the character returned to the U.S. Air Force during the Korean War and stayed in the military for the remainder of the strip's run.

Eventually Canyon developed a sometime-sidekick, a crotchety millionaire adventurer "Happy" Easter. Happy Easter was reportedly modeled after an eccentric who lived near Idaho Springs in Central City—or so rumor has it.

In a post World War II–induced patriotic fervor, Idaho Springs decided to erect the Steve Canyon statue, commissioned an Indiana limestone company to carve it, and somehow convinced the federal government to pay $12,000 for it. The monument was officially dedicated in July of 1950. A plaque on the statue declares, "The United States Treasury salutes Steve Canyon and through him, all American cartoon characters who serve the Nation."

Remembering When Caribou Rocked

Another fabulous Colorado entertainment period unfolded in about as unlikely a place as you could think of. High up near tiny Nederland in Boulder County are the remains of a settlement called Caribou, built for the workers of the Caribou silver mine nearby. It had a church, three saloons, a three-story hotel, a newspaper, and a brewery.

Caribou was once one of Colorado's most important mining sites, but it was dealt a mortal blow by the Silver Crash of 1893. A couple of catastrophic fires beat back attempts to rebuild and keep the town going.

This is one of Colorado's ghost towns that has dribbled away because of neglect and the souvenir hunters, who have taken everything from building stones to gravestones. There's not much left, except the foundation of the hotel and assay office, a derelict cabin, and a small cemetery. On the western end of the site, there is an active mine and a year-round mine caretakers' residence.

Caribou merits the rep of being "fabled" not only because of its mining history but because, for a short time, there was a legendary recording studio that attracted some of the most recognizable names in rock-and-roll music. *Colorado Rocks! A Half-Century of Music in Colorado* by G. Brown, a music journalist, is the best current book about this scene. William Martin, the prospector who discovered Caribou Mine, homesteaded a place he called Tucker Ranch. In 1936, the ranch was purchased by Lynn Van Vleet who established Colorado's first Arabian horse stud farm. It was also a dude ranch and the host site of two early movies, *Arabians of the Rockies* and *Sons of Courage*. For a time, it was also a potato farm.

Music and film producer James Guercio, who deliberately sought a location far from city distractions, bought the spread in 1971 and renamed it Caribou Ranch. He turned a barn into a recording studio and built a comfortable little resort to keep his big-name rock-and-roll clientele focused on making music. Not only was this concept novel, it was even more attractive when word got out that singers could hit higher notes at this elevation of between 8,500 and about 8,769 feet. In a *Rocky Mountain News* interview published January 25, 2008, Guercio recalled that, for reasons no one fully understood, singers could reach an octave higher here than at sea level.

The A-list included legendary bands such as America, Badfinger, the Beach Boys, Chicago, Nitty Gritty Dirt Band, Supertramp, and War. Individual stars included Jeff Beck, Michael Jackson, Elton John, John Lennon, Rod Stewart, Joe Walsh, Stevie Wonder, and Frank Zappa.

According to Brown, other exotic recording studio/resorts sprang up around the world, and Caribou Ranch was no longer the only "it" place. By the late 1970s, economic recession cut back on recording budgets and these working-vacation destinations. But the final track was played in March 1985, when a fire devastated the control room. James Guercio shut operations down and donated the remaining equipment to the University of Colorado in Denver.

He kept the buildings at Caribou Ranch and a little more than two thousand acres as his family home and working cattle operation. He sold the rest to Boulder County and the City of Boulder beginning in December 1996. While Guercio's portion is private, with restricted access, the public share in Caribou Ranch is a seasonally open park and wildlife habitat.

Unexplained Phenomena

This IS The COSMIC HWY.

Unless you've lived in Colorado for some time, particularly the San Luis Valley, you may not notice how much "high strangeness" is in the Mile High State.

The first known recorded sightings of UFOs in Colorado happened in the early 1950s, when thousands of people in southern Colorado and northern New Mexico claimed to see what appeared to be bright green fireballs that didn't act or look like the usual flying stellar material.

Astronomer William K. Hartmann wrote in a famous report that the fireballs might be explained by lunar soil and rocks thrown into Earth's atmosphere when meteors hit the moon. Hartmann's observations were part of a much bigger joint effort. The 1968 *Scientific Study of Unidentified Flying Objects* (better known as the Condon Report) was commissioned by the U.S. Air Force and conducted by the University of Colorado Boulder.

Influential as it was, the study didn't stop more reports of strange things in the skies although it gave the air force, as well as mainstream scientific and academic circles, an excuse to drop attention and cease rigorous investigation.

MUFON (Mutual UFO Network), which calls itself "the world's largest civilian UFO scientific research organization," is today headquartered in Fort Collins in northern Colorado, under the direction of James Carrion.

People flock to the UFO Watchtower near Hooper to search a night sky that one rarely sees in our modern world—one that is free of light pollution. A more unsettling series of anomalous episodes started in the late 1960s and continues to be reported sporadically today. Ranchers and farmers around Colorado reported the strange killings of livestock under circumstances so bizarre they've been loosely called cattle mutilations, also perhaps more accurately called unexplained animal deaths.

The most famous such case took place in the San Luis Valley in 1967. The victim was an Appaloosa named Lady. If you don't remember that one, nudge your memory with Snippy the horse. And if you've ever wondered what happened to that famous carcass, we can tell you.

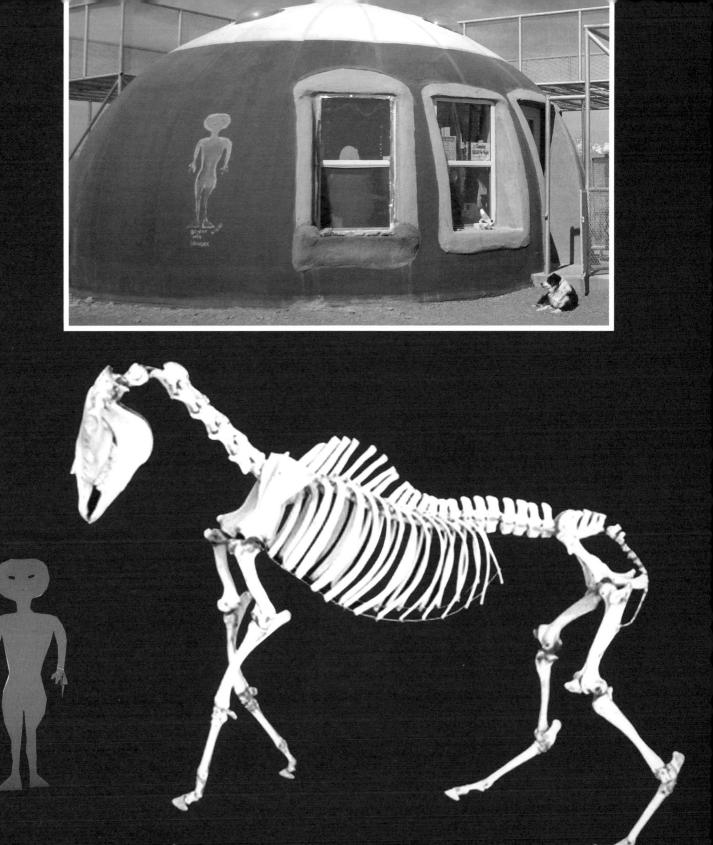

Unexplained Animal Deaths

Around Colorado, particularly in the San Luis Valley and El Paso County, a series of unsettling events erupted in the late 1960s. Ranchers and farmers would find dead cattle, sheep, and horses in their pastures with flesh curiously removed from the bodies. Soft-tissue organs such as genitalia, rectums, tongues, ears, and eyes would appear to have been cut out with surgical precision, sometimes as if done by lasers. The animals would be drained of blood and other fluids but without leaving traces. There would be few or no signs of ripping, tearing, bloodstains, or animal tracks to indicate normal animal-predator activity.

Law enforcement, veterinarians, and others had opinions and guesses, but nothing was ever proven, and speculation has been rampant.

The first widely reported case was of an Appaloosa mare in the San Luis Valley in 1967. While that incident became infamous, there were actually hundreds of similar reports into the early 1970s. A report in the *Pagosa Springs Sun*, on September 25, 1975, said, "The latest animal mutilation in Colorado was reported in the Upper Piedra this week. This is the first such incident in this part of the state, although it is common in recent weeks in eastern Colorado . . . in that part of the state it has been theorized that the mutilations are possibly the work of some weird cult or organization . . ."

Colorado wasn't the only state where this sort of thing was happening. Other reports came from Minnesota and Kansas in 1973, and more incidents were claimed in the East, South, Southwest, and as far north as Canada.

In 1975, Sen. Floyd Haskell made an urgent request to the Federal Bureau of Investigation to investigate these events. He cited "at least 130 cases" reported to local officials in Colorado and verification from the Colorado Bureau of Investigation that such incidents had been reported for the last two years in nine states.

The FBI completed its Operation Animal Mutilation investigation in 1979. The bureau studied fifteen cases of animal mutilation in New Mexico and concluded that while many of the acts could be blamed on natural predators, a fair number of cases were unexplainable. The FBI was unable to identify anyone in particular who might be behind the incidents. You can read the report on the FBI's Web site.

When I asked whether there was a confirmed number of unexplained animal deaths in the state, I was told by CBI's Public Information Officer Lance Clem that the CBI didn't keep records of recent or current incidents and that the older records were in storage. The CBI only becomes involved in such cases if a local law-enforcement agency asks for its help, he added, and only if determination has been made that an actual crime has been committed.

Since the most recently reported rash of episodes in the late 1970s, cases of unexplained animal deaths have surfaced only sporadically. As the *Tribune* (Greeley, northern Colorado) commented in an article about Weld County's history of anomalous activities: "Some say the mutilations continue, but ranchers stopped reporting them because they weren't taken seriously" (Mike Peters, March 12, 2007).

One example of a report that met with such skepticism was part of the same article. On June 22, 1993:

A northern Weld County rancher found one of her horses, named Supercharger, dead in a field not far from the ranch house. . . . The horse appeared to have smooth cutting marks on the head with one eye and ear removed. There were cuts around the jaw, and the tongue was removed. . . . The rancher was angry when told by Colorado State University veterinarians that it was caused by coyotes and birds. "Coyotes with scalpels," the rancher remarked sarcastically.

Mutilations Been Hitting Pretty Hard Lately

Dear *Weird U.S.*,

I have an aunt who lives in a small town in Colorado called Severance. When I was in college, a friend and I took a cross-country trip. Being young and poor and dumb, we figured that anyone we could mooch off of was worth a visit along the way. We planned on a detour through Severance on our way to California.

That area was not the easiest to navigate. We wound up lost, and after a few hours, we were both stressed out. Now, I don't condone drinking and driving, but being twenty-one and stressed, my friend and I were more than happy to stop and have a nerve-calming alcoholic beverage when we passed a lonely bar out in the wilds.

This bar was pretty dismal. The people inside consisted of a bartender so old that he looked like he might fall over dead at any second, a handful of farmers bellied up to the bar, watching a dusty, old television, and us.

At first, we were intimidated by these guys, as they didn't seem the most friendly lot. After a few drinks, though, we all loosened up and began talking. Soon, we were thick as thieves—and once they let their guards down, they told us something that I think you guys at *Weird U.S.* would be very interested in.

These farmers began talking about how their animals had been turning up dead—again. As they put it, "Mutilations been hitting pretty hard lately." We were astonished, and asked them to fill us in. They explained that cows, horses, and other animals on their ranches and farms routinely turned up dead, with strange incisions all over their bodies and, often, with their organs removed.

My buddy and I were listening with our jaws on the floor. These guys were saying this off-handedly, like it wasn't the creepiest, darkest thing they'd ever said. To them, it was just part of the routine.

We asked them why this wasn't bigger news, why they didn't report it. They told us that everyone they've ever known who has reported such a thing has been subject to a campaign of humiliation. Some of them said the public was just disbelieving, but others said that the government intentionally went out of its way to make them look crazy in order to quell any facts about the mutilations from spreading. Either way, the farmers told us, reporting what they found wasn't worth embarrassing themselves and their families as well as risking their businesses.

So I figured you'd like to know that, unless these guys were the best actors of all time, something very odd is going on out there. My night spent with some people who have seen the phenomenon firsthand made me a believer, for sure. —*M. Stevens*

UFO Watchtower

If anything exemplifies belief in the reality of UFOs, it's this place. It doesn't look like much, although it definitely stands out on a treeless plain just off County Road 61 near Hooper. A metal catwalk placed over a short dome glistens silver in the sun. A modest rock garden with a plethora of miscellany is laid out nearby.

My friend Jo and I drive under a hanging sign, past cute cutouts of beckoning space aliens, onto a dirt road. Tires churn up a cloud of dust as we trundle to the building and park next to a camper. No one appears to be home, either in the camper or in the gift shop. A house can be seen in the distance, but no other sign of human life is visible for miles except for a few passing cars on the road.

The sky over us is achingly blue with clouds piled almost as massively as the peaks of the Sangre de Cristos Mountains in the distance. It's so quiet we can hear the rustlings of small critters in the scrub brush. The sign in the window of the shop says we arrived during business hours. Another sign posts the fee to camp onsite, adding NOT RESPONSIBLE FOR ACCIDENTS OR ABDUCTIONS!

A small car drives up, and a woman emerges with a couple of bouncy, medium-sized dogs. Judy Messoline,

the keeper of the UFO Watchtower, has arrived with her companions, Mac and Rowdy. Messoline has the look of a woman comfortable and competent among horses, cattle, children, and anything else you care to entrust her with—despite the fact that she's wearing a sweatshirt stating "I've been probed on the UFO Highway!"

When Messoline and her partner, Stan, moved to the San Luis Valley in 1995, the only thought they gave to the sky was for the beauty of the stars allowed to shine where no light pollution could dim them. Then, they heard about the strange lights and even stranger aircraft that were part of the valley's lore for decades. Assuming that some of the stranger objects were experimental military vehicles made sense to them. However, many of these unusual sightings don't fit the parameters of known human technology. These vehicles are cigar- or saucer-shaped, for the most part. Some are odder, and some are seen only as a few bright lights. Usually, they move unlike anything anyone could even guess was technically possible.

"We don't have just the usual flying saucer sightings out here," says Messoline. "We've had people report things that look like clouds until you look more closely. I saw this cloud thing once that was big and should have moved pretty slow, but it was there one minute and literally gone the next."

Folks talked about those events a lot—and about those truly weird cattle mutilations that weren't anything a normal animal predator could do and might or might not be UFO-related—and Messoline would say, "What we need around here is a UFO watchtower!"

This was an idea that did not take serious form until the year 2000 rolled around, and Messoline and Stan had to face the fact that they had to do something with their 640 acres of arid land besides try to raise thirsty cattle on it. A friend suggested that Messoline make good on that watchtower idea. She came up with a plan for a modest gift shop dominated by a metal catwalk, and campsites for those who wanted a comfortable place to watch the skies. The local planning commission was receptive to the idea of an amusing little tourist attraction, and the proposal caught the attention of local news media and then of national and international news outlets.

For all the initial notoriety, commercial success came rather slowly to the UFO Watchtower.

"After about a month," Messoline says. "I was feeling frustrated and thought I'd holler out at all those UFOs that gave me the idea in the first place. So, I went out and yelled at the sky, 'OK, you guys! I need at least $100 a day in sales to make this work!'"

She hasn't had to worry too much about it since, although the off-season is slow enough that she keeps busy as a substitute teacher. Stan, she says, is thinking about setting up a grill to sell burgers during the tourist season.

Messoline gave us a tour of her Peace Garden. It's the modest rock garden outside the gift shop, done in a rough semicircle with an extraordinary amount of stuff left behind by visitors. People who claim to be psychics have told Messoline that the place has "vortexes"—strange areas of energy.

Messoline invites folks to make a request to the universe here. She doesn't promise anything, but she can recount a number of times when someone claimed to have had a prayer answered, a need fulfilled, a sense of peace restored, even medical healings. For whatever the reason, people have felt touched, inspired, somehow moved enough to leave something behind: ballet shoes (left by a guy who made a special return trip just to put them there), crystals, an electric guitar, a half-slip, cans of Spam and soda, a Native American medicine wheel, and photos of loved ones.

"This garden belongs to the people who come here," says Messoline. And, to whatever forces are attracted to it, apparently. She points to objects that have disappeared briefly only to reappear in a different spot without apparent human intervention.

By and large, Messoline says, her experiences with visitors have been positive. However, one sinister-seeming experience was when a man-in-black type—a character who is often a staple of UFO witness tales—peeled away in a black sedan as she approached the Watchtower one afternoon.

Even worse was the visitor who buried an odd, cone-shaped object in her garden that he claimed would act as a beacon for extraterrestrials. Messoline says at least two people complained of headaches and stomachaches when in its vicinity. After a while, she noticed that reports of anomalies in her area seemed to have stopped. Then, someone told her the guy that buried his device in her garden had a Web site on which he claimed to have invented something that repelled extraterrestrial activity. Not taking any chances, Messoline dug it up and had it hauled away.

Messoline has a lot more experiences recorded in her entertaining book, *The Crazy Lady Down the Road*, first published in 2005. She keeps photo logs of UFOs and guests' written testimony about strange happenings. She doesn't say she believes all of it, but she doesn't discount any of it.

The family with the camper returns to set up folding chairs and make themselves comfortable. Messoline greets them like welcome houseguests; they respond with the same warmth although it's their first trip to the watchtower. She later talks to us about the hundreds of people she has listened to who have claimed to be alien abductees. There are a number of people she has met who also believe they are either of extraterrestrial origin or some kind of hybrid.

One man who looked at her guest logbook asked, "Is there one for *us* to sign?" Messoline says she didn't get the "us" bit until she saw his eyes—quite blue, she says, with no whites.

"I don't judge," says Messoline simply.

What she does do is enjoy. She keeps returning to all the wonderful people she's met and the interesting stories she's heard. She fills herself with positive feelings from the Peace Garden and the thrill of sharing the beauty of the night sky (not just the UFOs) with her visitors. Perhaps the real energy behind the UFO Watchtower is the serene woman offering a welcome and a sympathetic ear to the most fantastic of human experiences.

Great Sand Dunes National Park and Preserve

They look natural from a distance—small mountains bare of vegetation in a sea of grassland, a striking contrast to nearby snow-capped peaks. However, these peaks aren't solid; they're sand—massive piles of it, more than seven hundred feet tall, ever shifting but enduring.

They are not in a desert or near an ocean beach as you might expect but here in the middle of North American wilderness—in the San Luis Valley, naturally. Not that the United States doesn't have other areas with sand dunes—just nothing as tall as these, and no one knows exactly why. To add to their mystery, a number of strange legends are associated with them.

Everything about them is elusive. The dunes shift enough that measuring them is a challenge. The range, or dune field, is about six miles wide at the widest point and about eight to ten miles long. The sands change colors, depending on light conditions—from pure gold to light chocolate in daylight, to purple and nearly black under large clouds, to bright red at sunset, and with a pale and eerie glow by moonlight.

More mysterious are the low rumbles, groans, and booms that can sometimes be heard for miles when strong winds blow or when set off by skiers and snowboarders. Yes, people treat the sandy slopes as if covered with snow, and it's quite a sight to see them sliding down while, far below, spring visitors are wading in Medano Creek, which only forms while snow drifts melt.

As might be expected with such an unusual and mysterious locale, legends make dandy storytelling around campfires as the dunes glow dimly in the moonlight. Wild horses occasionally roam the edges of the dunes, but they avoid the shifting, unsteady footing of the sand. However, it is said that on bright moonlit nights or just before sunrise one can see a very different breed silhouetted on the sandy ridges. No one has ever been able to move close to them, but the hoof prints left behind are webbed.

Tales of sheepherders and their flocks vanishing on their way to pastures past the dunes or grazing near them are common. Some of these could have been incidents of straight banditry, either self-engineered or by others.

Other stories are harder to explain—like the one about the wagon train that bedded down for the night beside one of the dune creeks. The teamsters awoke in the morning to find the mules and wagons gone without a trace. Or, so they claimed.

Then, there's the story about the Mystery Family, settlers named Martinez who homesteaded in a lonely locale near the dunes. One day, the Martinez boy appeared dazed and speechless at a rancher's house. Those that went out to his cabin found the Martinez parents dead of unknown causes. Their son never spoke about what happened. He was taken in by a farmer and became a sheepherder. One day a dust storm arose, and the Martinez lad and his flock never came back. Searchers found a trail that ended at the edge of the dune field.

There are rumors that sometimes the winds will expose the bones of unlucky travelers who tried to cross the dunes and were caught in sandstorms.

The Condon Report

This is the report the U.S. Air Force commissioned that was supposed to be—as its formal name states—*Scientific Study of Unidentified Flying Objects.* It wound up forever identified with nuclear physicist Edward U. Condon, director of the investigative commission from 1966 to 1968 at the University of Colorado Boulder.

It wasn't Condon's finest achievement by any means, and that is not meant as a slight. He was born in 1902 and earned his degree at the University of California at Berkeley in 1926. He was a pioneer in quantum mechanics and helped develop radar and nuclear weapons during World War II. He was a member of the Manhattan Project in 1943, until he clashed with the project's military leader and quit.

Condon was a sixty-four-year-old physics professor at the University of Colorado Boulder in August 1966 when he took on the job of leading an investigation of unidentified flying objects.

Some people thought he was slumming, not the least of whom was probably Condon. The focus of the air force's UFO studies commission revolved around the cases investigated by its Project Blue Book, started in the late 1940s, as well any new cases considered promising. Other universities and organizations had turned down the air force's request, and Condon had to be persuaded to take the job.

It was called the University of Colorado Boulder UFO Project but informally known as the Condon Committee. Dr. Albert Bartlett of Boulder, a physics professor emeritus at the university, was not on the committee but recalled Condon's attitude.

"I think he went into it probably with the idea that 'This [UFO reports] is crazy and I'm going to expose it.' That he would have fun with it. He had a strong sense of humor. He felt that there wasn't any real scientific evidence yet presented, and there wasn't likely to be if it was of the kind of thing he had seen already."

Word was leaked to the public that the Condon Committee was a whitewash job for the air force. John G. Fuller wrote an article called "Flying Saucer Fiasco" for *Look* magazine on May 14, 1968. It detailed behind-the-scene

FOR OFFICIAL USE ONLY

DEPARTMENT OF THE AIR FORCE
HEADQUARTERS UNITED STATES AIR FORCE
WASHINGTON, D.C.
19 SEP 1966

AFRST

Sole Source Procurement for Investigation of Unidentified Flying Objects

OAR (RRG)

1. You are authorized to proceed with a sole source procurement under Program Element 6.14.45.01.4, Project 9730, Research Investigations of Unidentified Flying Objects. The University of Colorado is an approved selection for this procurement. The grant should be implemented in the manner indicated in the Air Force Office of Scientific Research letter of 31 August 1966 to Dr. Thurston E. Manning, Vice President of the University of Colorado.

2. The Secretary of the Air Force, Research and Development, has been apprised of this intended selection and has approved the Principal Investigator.

FOR THE CHIEF OF STAFF

Copy to: AFOSR (SRKB)

SIGNED

EDWARD B. GILLER
Brigadier General, USAF
Director of Science & Technology
DCS/Research & Development

FOR OFFICIAL USE ONLY

events that led to the dismissal of two committee scientists for "incompetence" (psychology professor Dr. David Saunders and Dr. Norman Levine, an electrical engineer) and the resignation of an administrative assistant, Mary Louise Armstrong, who acted as a preliminary case screener.

Saunders collaborated with the Boulder newspaperman R. Roger Harkins to write an exposé published by Signet in 1968: *UFOs? Yes! Where the Condon Committee Went Wrong: The Inside Story by an Ex-Member of the Official Study Group.*

Saunders cited an internal memo written by the committee coordinator, Dr. Robert Low, who was the assistant dean of the university's graduate program. Low had set out to persuade faculty members that then-proposed project was worth the school's time and reputation.

The memo, dated August 6, 1966, was titled "Some Thoughts on the UFO Project." It was addressed to the dean of the graduate school, E. James Archer, and the vice president for academic affairs, Thurston E. Manning. In the memo, Low explained that the project would be achieved by having the committee come to a conclusion that wouldn't hurt the school's

reputation in the eyes of the public or in the scientific community.

Our study would be conducted almost entirely by non-believers who, though they couldn't possibly prove

a negative result, could and probably would add an impressive body of thick evidence that there is no reality to the observations. The trick would be, I think, to describe the project so that, to the public, it would appear a totally objective study but, to the scientific community, would present the image of a group of non-believers trying their best to be objective but having an almost zero expectation of finding a saucer.

He went on to say that a "psychological" focus would be turned on those who made the UFO claims. Low did not deny that he wrote the memo although he claimed the word *trick* was not meant to be a synonym for *deception*. The university officials it was addressed to would not discuss it at the time the book was published.

"Low caught hell for that word *trick*," says Bartlett. "But I know Condon would not participate in anything like a conspiracy to conceal the truth. His integrity was too high, and he had better things to do anyway. He was furious with Saunders, though. I know he said a number of professionally unkind things about him."

Dr. Michael Wertheimer, professor emeritus at CU Boulder, was one of the psychologists on the Condon Committee. He has a PhD from Harvard in psychophysics, and his specialty is sensation and perception.

He recalls going on "quick response team" investigations of purported UFO sightings around the country that he said invariably turned out to be explainable events. He wrote about one such mission for a scientific journal called *Perceptual & Motor Skills* (1968, vol. 26).

"My conclusion was that while, yes, there were quite a few unexplainable cases, reported by credible people, and they were what I call *framasands*. It's a made-up word meaning that just because we don't fully understand something, it doesn't mean there isn't a natural explanation. There were no implications of extraterrestrial origins."

He said he hadn't known what Low's internal memo stated until I read it to him. "I'm surprised to hear that Bob Low was so determined to come to a conclusion beforehand. I certainly did not know of that memo, and I doubt Dr. Condon did, either.

"As far as I and most of the others on the committee were concerned, it was a legitimate, straightforward scientific investigation. Perhaps I was naive, but I really did think a team of experts could find the answers. I would not have participated in any deception."

The Condon Committee's 1,485-page report was released to the air force in 1968 and was published the following year by E. P. Dutton. In a nutshell, the report concluded that those UFO sightings that weren't hoaxes had prosaic explanations. It admitted to a few cases that were, basically, unexplainable and stated that there were gaps in scientific knowledge "that might benefit from further research in the UFO field."

In December 1969, the same month the air force officially terminated its UFO investigations, the American Association for the Advancement of Science (AAAS) held a symposium in Boston to encourage a wider contribution of opinions about UFOs. The event was organized by a committee that included a former student of Condon's, the astronomer and astrochemist Carl Sagan.

Condon spoke little about the committee's findings afterward except to state his regret for involvement in "such foolishness" (*Time* magazine, December 26, 1969).

He died in Boulder on March 26, 1974. The International Astronomical Union named a crater on the moon for him.

Controversy over whether the Condon Report was what it claimed to be—a truly scientific investigation of UFO phenomena—or a cynical waste of taxpayer money lives on. It continues to be one of the most influential documents cited in UFO studies today.

The Long Strange Trip of "Snippy"

Her real name was Lady, but a reporter got the name confused and now she's forever known as Snippy.

On September 9, 1967, Snippy was found in a pasture that was oddly muddy considering the recent lack of rain. Her carcass was stripped of flesh from nose to withers. The heart and brain were gone (other organs were later found to be missing, as well), and the bare bones as pale as if bleached or exposed for a long time.

The carcass itself had a formaldehyde-like smell that could be noticed for days. Cuts made on the carcass appeared to have been done with careful precision, but no blood stains could be found anywhere.

Snippy's owner, Nellie Lewis, picked up a piece of metal with horse hair on it and immediately dropped it, with the exclamation that it burned her hand. Later, she said the burn stayed for some time, and her boots were found to be radioactive. Duane Martin, a U.S. forest ranger, brought his Geiger counter to the investigation and reportedly found considerable levels of radioactivity around Snippy's white bones. Beyond that, Lewis couldn't raise any official interest in the bizarre demise of her horse. The local sheriff and her own husband thought the horse had been hit by lightning and then partially consumed by predators.

Lewis's mother, eighty-seven-year-old Agnes King, had poor eyesight but clearly remembered something that flew low over her house with a loud whoosh the day of Snippy's disappearance. Experiences in the valley with low-flying aircraft were not unusual, but combined with the other odd things found around the carcass, Lewis became convinced that her horse had been mutilated by extraterrestrial beings. Her story was reported under the headline FLYING SAUCERS KILLED MY HORSE! in the local *Valley Courier* and was picked up by the Associated Press almost a month later.

Soon, people were flocking to the ranch to gawk. At least four pathologists were among those scientists who examined Snippy at different times. They came to very different conclusions. One declared the horse had had a severe infection in one leg. He speculated that someone ended her suffering by slitting her throat, and animal predators then did the rest. Another examiner said the cutting and stripping of flesh was done by heat-charged instruments, and nothing he knew of explained the complete lack of blood.

Dr. Robert J. Low (see "The Condon Report" earlier in this chapter), from the University of Colorado Boulder, examined the area around Snippy's body and reported no evidence of any radiation or exhaust marks. Whether he had any expertise in this type of examination is unclear. His degrees were a BS in electrical engineering and an MBA.

That following December, the Lewises allowed local veterinarian Dr. Wallace Leary to take away Snippy's

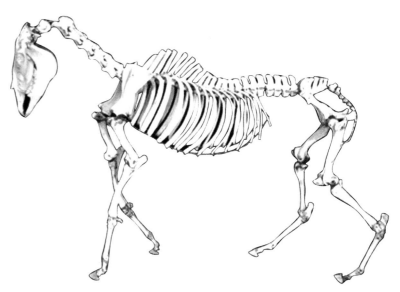

carcass. Leary boiled the remaining flesh off the bones and in the process discovered what he thought were bullet holes in Snippy's left pelvis and right thighbones. He added to the pile of theories with the speculation that someone had shot Snippy, which sent her into a headlong and fatal collision with a barbed wire fence. He assembled the horse's bones with metal rods to keep the skeleton upright.

Leary then placed Snippy's skeleton in front of the pottery shop he and his wife owned, where it stayed until they ended the business. Leary passed Snippy on to Adams State College biology professor Hobart Dixon, who gave her to the Alamosa Chamber of Commerce for display in 1971. When the chamber tired of Snippy, she was given to a local man named Herman Doty Jr., who stuck her in an old boxcar with the hope that he would open a local history museum soon. (He wrote a book about the experience called *Bones in a Boxcar: The Investigation of Snippy the Horse*.)

Doty's ex-wife received Snippy in their divorce and donated the skeleton to the Luther E. Bean Museum at Adams State College in Alamosa. After some time, the museum apparently decided that Snippy was too uninteresting to keep around and allowed Carl Helfin, a local collector of the unusual, to take it. When Carl died, his large and eclectic estate (which included railroad cars, doors, and shower stalls) was inventoried, and Snippy was rediscovered. The Dell Insurance Agency in Alamosa was hired to put Snippy up for sale.

The skeleton went on eBay in February 2007 at a minimum bid of $50,000. No bids were offered, but the insurance agency was swamped with requests for media interviews from all over the world. Relatives of the Lewis-King family said the remains of Snippy were only lent to Dr. Leary, and they wanted them back. Although the family could not prove their case, Snippy was pulled from eBay. The Carl Helfin estate decided to take private bids, with the same minimum of $50,000.

Frank Duran, marketing manager at the Dell Insurance Agency, spearheaded a "Save Snippy" campaign to try to buy the skeleton for the San Luis Valley Museum in Alamosa.

However, as of this writing, the San Luis Valley Museum was outbid by heirs to the Helfin estate and Snippy's skeleton is now awaiting future adventures in a storage unit.

The most tragic part of the story is not well known outside of the valley. Probably the best telling of it is in Christopher O'Brien's 1996 book *Secrets of the Mysterious Valley*. Agnes King, the mother of Lewis, died in 1976 at the age of ninety-seven. Following the funeral, Lewis quietly slipped away from her home. Lewis's body was found in her car at Pioneer Urraca Cemetery, where her mother had just been buried. She apparently committed suicide by running a hose from the exhaust pipe into the interior of the car and closing the windows. No one, including her husband, Berle, anticipated such an occurrence. Lewis had shown an increased interest in UFOs and the occult over the years since Snippy's demise but no obvious signs of depression or anxiety. Her mother's death was not unexpected, and the couple had no overwhelming problems.

An alleged missing journal belonging to Lewis supposedly contained paranormal references, unaccounted-for strangers seen in the immediate area, and other events but nothing that leads to any formal conclusion regarding her death.

It's all terrific fodder for conspiracy buffs and online UFO discussion forums, of course. In the end, however, it's just one more mystery in the riddle wrapped in the Snippy enigma.

The Castle Rock Sighting

People of a certain age in this town between Denver and Colorado Springs have a vivid memory of a bubble-like UFO with a bright light that appeared on the night of January 2, 1968. According to an article in the *Denver Post*, Deputy Sheriff R. S. Weimer said that about a dozen "reliable citizens" claimed to have seen it fly over the town between 6:10 and 6:25 P.M.

People said the thing moved at different speeds, hovered over the Douglas County Courthouse and finally made a spectacular disappearance—it shot suddenly straight up into the sky with a couple of balls of flame behind it. One witness was to have a blood test performed by the Douglas County Civil Defense Agency to determine whether "any radiation or unknown or foreign matter is in his bloodstream," according to the agency director, Morris Fleming.

The sighting was reported to the Condon Committee but before anything happened on that end, news broke that the UFO was a prank built by two high school kids. According to the *Rocky Mountain News* on January 11, the mother of the boys, Mrs. Norbert Dietrich, said that it was the older lad who showed his younger brother how to make the UFO.

They sealed the end of a plastic bag similar to a dry cleaner's cover, braced it with sticks, and tied a small aluminum cup with four small candles to the sticks. When the candles were lit, the bag filled with hot air and lifted it over the town. As the candles burned down, the trapped air cooled and made the cup tip. Hot wax caused the plastic to catch fire, and the thing went up "like a super 1-shot Roman candle."

A lot of sympathy was felt for the adults who had been fooled by a bright, unfamiliar, and oddly acting object in the night sky. After all, said the *Rocky Mountain News*, "When the laughter starts . . . it can cut pretty deep for those who in all honesty reported what they saw, who didn't take fanciful trips into the world of H. G. Wells."

This story, by the way, is not repeated here as some kind of general "debunking" effort. It's simply that whenever a report of a UFO sighting comes up in the Castle Rock area, long-timers are known to roll their eyes.

The Case of the Crystal Skull

In February 1995, a ranch hand discovered a strange crystal skull near Moffat, a small San Luis Valley town. He showed it to his boss, Donna Koch. It was about six inches high, weighed about three pounds and had an elongated, lopsided shape.

Crystal skulls have a legendary status in some new age and occult circles, and this one fascinated many people. Strange things were said to happen in its grimacing presence, and a number of people claimed that energy emanated from it. Psychics warned its new owner that it was not from Earth and should be kept wrapped in silk. One person meditated near it for eight days and claimed to receive communication from "Lemuria" through it.

More than one hundred people reportedly met at Colorado's White Eagle Village Inn, Retreat and Conference Center to meditate around the skull and record their impressions. When an article appeared about it in the *Rocky Mountain News* on November 10, 1996, it sounded an alert with the absentee owners of the land next to Koch's. The *Crestone Eagle* broke the story. Brad Chadez, the son of the property owners, was a glassblower. He created a batch of skulls to sell at a Day of the Dead festival in Santa Fe, New Mexico, and one turned out too lopsided to sell. He gave it to his parents to mark where they planned to build a house on the northeast corner of their property.

Presumably, Chadez got the skull back. As of 1997, it was last seen at the now-defunct Manos Folk Art Gallery in Denver. No word as to whether anyone bought it for near the purported $20,000 that Koch was allegedly offered by a collector of paranormal artifacts.

Of course, once the true origin of the skull was revealed, the only thing left to explain is how so many people could convince themselves that a piece of glass had magical powers.

Where in the World Is Thomas Riha?

On March 15, 1969, University of Colorado professor Thomas Riha disappeared. To this day, his whereabouts remain unknown. Most suspect he was murdered. Some say he was whisked away by the KGB, an organization they suspect he had ties with. Others say the CIA helped Riha disappear, and that they are still hiding him today.

At the time of his disappearance, Dr. Riha was just wrapping up a messy—and strange—divorce. On March 9, 1969, police had been summoned to the Riha home. Inside they encountered Galya Tannenbaum, who claimed to be an immigration official getting Mrs. Riha's signature.

Police found a bottle of ether that they suspected Tannenbaum had attempted to use on Mrs. Riha while she was sleeping. They realized that a love triangle between the Rihas and Tannenbaum was at the root of the mayhem. A week later, Thomas Riha disappeared.

When some fellow professors drove to Riha's home, they were shocked to find a fully set table, ready to hold a meal. It looked as if the professor had left unexpectedly, but without a fight.

Police found out that Dr. Riha had recently named Tannenbaum as the benefactor in his will, an act that gave her claim to his home, car, and even the royalties on all of Riha's writings regarding Russian history.

Apparently Tannenbaum had been arrested earlier for forging the name of another Colorado man—who had been found dead with cyanide in his blood. Two of Tannenbaum's neighbors had also recently died of cyanide poisoning. She was arrested on a slew of charges, but before she could be tried, she was declared insane and committed to a state hospital in Pueblo.

On March 9, 1971, Galya Tannenbaum committed suicide with cyanide and left a suicide note that said, in part, "Everything that made me feel good about myself has been taken away. Life is very cheap."

The press went wild speculating about Riha. A professor of Russian history, born in Czechoslovakia, Riha was cast as, possibly, a double agent. Had he been kidnapped by Russians? Was the CIA hiding him?

An unnamed CIA operative contacted the University of Colorado's president, Joseph Smiley, informing him that Riha was safe, though the professor never did resurface. Though Smiley was allegedly sworn to secrecy, he informed the press anyway, resulting in a mad flurry of correspondence between the CIA and FBI.

What exactly happened to Thomas Riha? Time has yielded no answers, and with each passing year, it becomes even less likely that the truth will ever be known.

Three Good Places to See Anomalies in the San Luis Valley

I like quoting and referring to Christopher O'Brien because of his refreshingly level-headed and sane approach to investigating the strange and weird.

Chris is well known for documenting the history of high strangeness in the San Luis Valley. He now lives in Sedona, Arizona, but keeps a Web site called Our Strange Planet (http://ourstrangeplanet.com) that continues to keep track of anomalies in the valley via local investigators.

Chris has found that being regarded as an expert in San Luis Valley mysteries can have its down side.

> *There are brilliant people who have done an excellent job of researching, like Tom Adams and Gary Massey. But I lived there, and I had those books published, and I'm willing to go almost anywhere and talk about what I've found, so even though I don't claim I have the answers, I'm the "expert," Notoriety compromises any hope of a low-key investigation. I was overexposed, and I had to step out of the way.*
>
> *But before I did, I trained people to follow those rules of investigation. I'm not the only one keeping track of things. The ongoing investigation I hope will shed more light and give us a better understanding of what we call "paranormal."*

Here are some of his favorite places to try to experience anomalies. While none of them are on private land, we remind interested visitors that these areas are meant to be shared and respected.

Christmas Tree Lights in Zapata Falls

Four miles east of Colorado Highway 150, just south of the entrance to Great Sand Dunes National Park, a gravel road leads to a parking lot. From the lot, about a half-mile hike will take you to the grotto with the falls. Just after sunset, stand in the parking lot and look due east to where the road loops near a burned portion of the mountain, or go up to the grotto before dark and wait there. If conditions are right, you'll see what looks like small Christmas tree–type yellow lights floating around. They blink and are usually seen in peripheral vision first. Be calm and quiet, and the lights might become brighter. People have reported a playful quality to the way they move, and the lights are often most visible when other anomalous sightings have been reported in the valley.

Strange Lights in Maxville

Drive north at night on Highway 285 to an area known as Maxville to the locals. It is between Monte Vista and Russell Lakes State Wildlife Area, near roads 4N and 3W. Lots of large, strange lights have been reported in the night sky. O'Brien says, "The best abductee case I'd ever heard" originated from this area.

Backward Gravity at Rock Creek Canyon on Greenie Mountain

Drive south on Rock Creek Canyon Road from Monte Vista and up Greenie Mountain. About five miles up, near Bishop Rock, the second or third hill seems to have unusual gravity. If you turn off your car and place it in neutral halfway down one of these hills, you just might find the car moving slowly backward—uphill.

Curious Creatures

From millennial to mythic, the curious beasts of Colorado are more than meet the eye. Especially all those creatures the state claims don't exist here. People keep seeing them anyway. From the earliest Native American stories to the tall tales of settlers, miners, and lumberjacks, to the testimonies of today's experienced campers and hunters, it's clear that a surprising amount of unnatural wildlife is natural in Colorado.

The GOG Monster

Those who hunt Fortean tidbits and anomalies know that you can stumble across strange stories in the oddest places.

Garden of the Gods Park is one of Colorado's best-known and most-ballyhooed natural tourist attractions. Located near Colorado Springs, it's a spectacular place with enormous, striking rock formations of reddish sandstone. The formations have fanciful names such as Kissing Camels, Tower of Babel, and Sleeping Giant.

You may drive, hike, or bicycle around the park and admire the amazing geology for free, every summer from June to Labor Day (watch out for rattlesnakes). You may even rock climb if the park's history of climber fatalities doesn't faze you (climbers have to register and stay on the established trails for good reason).

Local MUFON (Mutual UFO Network) field investigator Chuck Zukowski was checking into a report of a UFO sighting in this area not long ago.

"I kept running into people who'd say, 'Have you ever heard about the strange creature that lives under the Garden of the Gods?'" he says. "They could never tell me anything more but the same basic version of a story about a couple of high school kids who found a hidden cave entrance near the gift shop. Supposedly, they went in and emerged sometime later with talk about encountering a strange creature. Their hair was shocked white. So, they say."

Coloradans probably wouldn't be surprised to hear that caverns and passages are hidden inside Garden of the Gods. Besides natural caves, hundreds of old mining shafts have been found in this part of the state. However, mining, at least since settlers arrived, has not been recorded in the park area. What is not generally advertised about the park is that Jacob Spaulding, a trapper, discovered a cave here in 1848. Spaulding found a hole in what is called today North Gateway Rock, near the Kissing Camels formation.

He squeezed through the entrance into a passage that went upward about twenty-five feet into a space that ranged from about five to fifteen feet wide, two hundred feet long by one hundred feet high.

Intrepid folks with no claustrophobia visited Spaulding's Cavern for decades. The names of some of these visitors are scrawled on the walls and include some famous people in Colorado history, such as Julia Holmes, a feminist who was the first white woman to climb Pikes Peak. Visitors noted that the smallest whisper echoed amazingly. At some point, stairs were cut into one end of the cavern. However, interest in the cave apparently dwindled long enough to let plants hide the small entrance, and its exact location was lost.

Spaulding's Cavern was rediscovered in 1935, and members of the Civilian Conservation Corps (CCC) went to work to try to open it for public visitation. They soon discovered that the cave was made of sandstone, which crumbles easily. Periodic rivulets of water boosted natural erosion, and falling rocks were a serious hazard. Given the remarkable echo-chamber quality of the place, it was feared that even a raised voice could touch off an avalanche. After one of the CCC workers was nearly brained by falling sandstone, park managers decided that Spaulding's Cavern

was too dangerous to allow access, so the entrance was permanently sealed.

Erosion opened the cave's entrance again in 1963, according to a January 13 report in the *Colorado Springs Gazette Telegraph* (now the *Gazette*). Some Colorado Springs Parks, Recreation and Cultural Services employees crawled into the cave and noted that falling rocks still presented a serious risk. Spaulding's Cavern was sealed yet again. You won't find it mentioned in Garden of the Gods's advertising. You might not even find a park employee who will admit to its existence.

A number of locals think the cavern ought to be reopened for historical investigation—with the appropriate cautions, of course. No encouragement is given here to find a way past the cement seal at Spaulding's Cavern. However, perhaps rumors about a closed cavern have fueled the story about the underground cavern monster. If there can be a dangerous, concealed cave in the Garden of the Gods, what other secrets are hiding behind the park's magnificent landscape?

All a-GOG in the Garden of the Gods

I grew up in Colorado Springs and lived on West Pikes Peak Avenue not far (about one mile) from the Garden of the Gods, where my friends and I liked to hang out at night. This huge, natural sandstone park is full of towering red-rock formations that people like to climb. It was a sacred area to the Utes in the 1800s. During my teen years, we used to ride our bikes and motorbikes throughout the park at night when the moon the only light.

The Garden of the Gods is also home to a legendary Bigfoot type creature called GOG (which stands for the Garden of [the] Gods monster). It stands around seven to eight feet tall and is covered with reddish brown hair, which lets him blend with the natural rock formations. Native legends and a few old-timers who claim to have seen him all said that his eyes glowed a reddish yellow in the dark.

In 1968, three of us decided that we were going to bicycle around the park late one moonlit night. We had been riding around and just acting weird, as teenagers do, when we stopped by a large rock called Balanced Rock. As we were talking and laughing, my friend Dave said he thought he saw something moving in the moonlight about two hundred feet down the roadway. We saw nothing, so we relaxed. About five minutes later, Dave said, "Look!" and pointed down the road again. This time, we all saw this big, shaggy bulk slowly heading in our direction. He was about a hundred feet away, but we could distinctly see the glowing reddish yellow eyes. We immediately let out a yell, jumped onto our bikes, and tore the hell out of there as fast as we could!

We didn't look back or stop until we hit my place, which was a couple of miles from the Balanced Rock. We were so shaken up that my mom asked what had happened. We told her, and of course, she said that we needed to stay away from that place at night. (Needless to say, we went back the very next night with flashlights but didn't see anything.)

Although we'd looked for GOG many times since that night, we never saw it again.

I am now fifty-four years old, and I still can remember every detail of that night. I left Colorado Springs in 1968 to join the army, but I still e-mail old friends to talk about the night of our moonlit encounter with the Garden of the Gods Monster. —*Doc Smokey*

Bigfoot and Kin

Stories of Bigfoot-like critters in Colorado go back quite a ways. Native American stories tell of a hairy guardian being who lives in the sacred Sangre de Cristos Mountains, on holy Mount Blanca. Some traditions say this being has been known to eat humans, others say it is an "elder brother" and spiritual helper.

The Bigfoot Hunter

Keith Foster is a veteran bow hunter and bow maker, wildlife artist, and plant scientist. The last thing he probably thought he'd ever be was a Bigfoot researcher. However, a strange close encounter in 1993 set him on a path of inquiry that has associated him with Sasquatch studies ever since.

Foster lives in western Kansas, but he and his family have vacationed in Colorado for years.

"I had never before heard of anybody having a Bigfoot sighting in Colorado," he says. "We had a family cabin in a complex of other cabins near Lake Fork Ranch in the southern San Juan Mountains. My parents, Maurice and Sarah, always went out there in early spring to open the place up, turn the water on, that kind of thing.

"In 1990, my parents drove out to this place and as they approached someone's A-frame cabin, they saw what they thought at first was a bear standing on the porch. When they got closer, my dad said it was actually a big, furry, hairy, man-thing standing in front of the porch. Its head was level with the eaves of the cabin, and those eaves were about eight feet high off the ground. It looked at them, turned, and ran off on two legs across open ground, across a stream, and into the forest. They didn't see its face, but they otherwise had a pretty good look at it."

Three years later, Foster was fishing with his two young sons in the same area on a branch of the Lake Fork of the Conejos River.

"There was a stand of willows about 100 to 150 feet away," he recalls. "Something started screeching at us from behind the willows. . . . The closest I've ever been able to describe it is that it was a long, drawn-out noise, kind of like tires squealing in a drag race. It was sort of like an elk, but this was five times louder. And, it sounded deeper, with reverb. Ever hear an African lion roar with that deep-throated vibration you can feel in your bones? Like that."

Without firearms, Foster thought it best to get his sons out of a potentially dangerous situation. He came back with a pistol at dawn the next day.

"Found older tracks about a quarter-mile away," he says. "In a line, one foot in front of the other. Not like a bear. It had rained some so the tracks were blurred a bit around the edges, and I couldn't make out the toes. But, the footprints were about four feet apart, and each was about sixteen to seventeen inches long."

Foster went home and logged onto the Internet.

"I sent out about thirty e-mails to all the hunting guides doing business in the area, asking if they had ever experienced something similar. I received three positive replies, and a bunch of answers saying they had heard of someone else having that kind of experience."

One bow hunter said he had had a close encounter in 1975 near Lost Creek Wilderness, north of Pikes Peak:

"He'd been bugling for elk. He was wearing camo and hiding in the brush when something entered the meadow he was watching. . . . It looked like a very big, powerful man covered in dark-brown fur with a reddish tinge. It came within thirty yards of him and then seemed to sense or smell him. It turned around and walked away."

Another guide told of two clients—a father and son—who came across what they thought was a bear feeding on an elk carcass:

"They wanted a closer look at the bear, so they crept up to about thirty yards of it. . . . It stood up and walked away,

walked like a man, they said. It resembled a gorilla and had a gorilla-looking face. The guide said he knew these two and believed them."

The third report came from a man who hunted with a pack of trained dogs: "They came across a set of very, very large tracks," says Foster. "Not a mountain lion, not a bear. The dogs acted confused, then scared, and refused to hunt."

About a year or so later, Foster heard about an unsettling encounter from a cousin who had vacationed in the same family cabin complex.

"One night something started shaking the RV and woke my cousin up. Rocked it, then picked it up and let it drop, shook it again. My cousin got his pistol, but the RV was shaking so hard he could only sit on the floor. He saw a big, tall, upright figure pass in front of his windows. He didn't dare move out of there. Sat up with the gun all night."

When morning dawned, the cousin ventured out and discovered a box of apples had been removed from under the RV. Keith's other relatives nearby hadn't heard a thing, but all involved agreed there had been a memorably rank odor.

"They described it as a blend of rotting flesh and the monkey house at the zoo," Foster says. "Really smelled up the neighborhood."

A year or so later, Foster met some people staying in the same cabin complex.

"We were talking about bear sightings. They brought up what they thought was a bear that attacked their RV one night. It sounded a lot like my cousin's experience, down to the rank smell."

Foster continued to collect Bigfoot stories in the Colorado–New Mexico region that go back to ancient days. He learned that the Pueblo tribe of New Mexico has traditional tales of hairy beings eight to ten feet tall who live in the mountains from north-central New Mexico to southern Colorado.

In 1900, workers at the Independence Mine near Crestone reported giant tracks in the snow near the mine entrance. A lifelong resident and hunter told Foster about sightings in the 1920s, including one by his own granddad, of a hairy man-beast locals dubbed Boji.

Foster found a kindred fellowship in the Bigfoot Field Researchers Organization. In early August 1998, he participated in a field-research study in Conejos County that was reported on the BFRO Web site. He once worked with a wildlife biologist to figure out where Bigfoot might live in Colorado.

"Remote wilderness, forest, water, and a stable elk population are key," he says. "Given that humans and development keep encroaching, these areas are shrinking back."

Colorado game hunter and guide Jeff Dysinger has had two encounters, according to Foster. The first came in

September 1998 when he and a colleague were guiding a group of clients. They were on a trail with a drop-off on one side when a large animal on two legs jumped down in front of Dysinger's horse, ran down the hillside, and vanished.

A year later, Dysinger was bow hunting when a look through binoculars revealed a reddish brown apelike creature, about seven feet tall. Dysinger was able to watch it for several minutes until it moved out of sight. Foster painted a portrait based on his description. He says Dysinger has approved its accuracy.

Foster speaks about Bigfoot as a scientist and experienced hunter.

"Trying to find a Sasquatch in a forest is like trying to find a highly trained military sniper who wants to hide in that forest, nearly impossible. Essentially, a Sasquatch is like a very stealthy puma with reasoning powers that may dwarf the reasoning ability of a chimpanzee. Sasquatch are ideally suited for the night, the deep forest, cold weather, and a lonely existence, whereas man is suited for the warmth of the day, open places, and a gregarious existence. Man and Sasquatch, though similar in form, are nearly complete opposites in regards to ecological niche. I think that is interesting and even perhaps enlightening. There is an environmental and historical niche available for just such a creature, and if it is not filled by a species we now call Sasquatch in North America, it should have been filled by nature at some point in Earth's past. Even if all the sightings are false, the physical evidence of the tracks indicates that just such a creature still walks Earth."

Miscellaneous Sasquatch

There's no guarantee where to see Sasquatch in Colorado, although Pike National Forest is listed as number seven of the twenty best sites by crypto-zoologist Loren Coleman in his book *Bigfoot! The True Story of Apes in America*.

A couple of old Colorado Bigfoot stories tend to have a life of their own. In 1881, a story about a mysterious half-man–half-beast appeared in the Leadville Chronicle. It stated that a humanlike creature with long, shaggy fur was seen several times by miners near Lake Creek in the Grizzly Peak area.

The reports were usually laughed off. One day, two miners heard a strange moaning sound. They split up to investigate, and one miner claimed he encountered a huge creature that glared and made the moaning sound. It was covered with long, brown hair and had a pair of long tusks.

The original tale appeared in the *Leadville Chronicle* when the editor was Orth Stein, a man legendary for his storytelling, He came to Leadville in 1880 as a young reporter and pretended to be one of the many quack "Indian doctors" that infested just about all of Colorado's mining boomtowns. His exposé in the *Leadville Chronicle* was credited for the sudden departure of most of the quacks.

Stein liked to keep his readership entertained with some of the most colorful tales that have ever come out of the Old West: the ancient ship found in a cave, the immense underground cavern with a crystal-clear lake, and the discovery of a fifty-foot serpent skeleton unearthed near Leadville.

Stein gave realistic details to these stories, which were reprinted by newspapers across the United States. In the 1880s, vast tracts of the country were still pretty much terrae incognite to civilization back east.

The "Lake Creek Monster" may well have traded on the tales of the Himalayan Yeti just then filtering into the West, although the terms *Abominable Snowman* or *Sasquatch* were unknown. Lake Creek is a common stream name in Colorado, and the state has four mountains named Grizzly Peak.

Then there's the story from October 1904 of a hunter in the mountains near Buena Vista who fled from a creature he described as a huge orangutan. Harry Pritchard must have seemed credible because a group of hunters set out to capture the primate. They found only a few large footprints. Calls to Buena Vista area historians have yielded no clues as to the tale's origin.

Just What Waz the Wazooey Man?

One of Colorado's most unusual encounters with a cryptid, known locally as the Wazooey Man, was reported in author Jim Brandon's book *Weird America*. The incident allegedly took place around May 15, 1973, on Red Creek Road, located four miles south of Pueblo. According to Brandon, "Two boys who were plinking with an air pistol in the arroyo one evening gradually became aware, in the fading light, of two huge red eyes. They looked like bicycle reflectors, and with a jolt of youthful ebullience, one of the boys took a shot at them. The next thing they knew, both youths had been picked up and dumped unceremoniously into a nearby ravine by some unseen force."

The book goes on to tell how the boys were then hit in the head with a fencepost before they fled to their truck, where they realized that they had lost their keys. They were forced to flee on foot, menaced for some distance by the accosting entity that looked like a "mobile haystack" with two huge, red eyes.

The Slide-Rock Bolter

Lumberjacks in the nineteenth century had a tradition of telling tall tales featuring fearsome creatures. Some of the critters were animals, birds, and insects behaving bizarrely; others were original creations.

William Thomas Cox, Minnesota's first state forester, collected many of these stories from all over the lumberjack spectrum. He had his collection published in 1910 by Judd and Detweiler, Inc. of Washington, D.C. *Fearsome Creatures of the Lumberwoods: With a Few Desert and Mountain Beasts* is now in the public domain.

The lumber industry is not what it was in Cox's day, and the old lumberjack tales just aren't being told around campfires as they used to be. Here, then, in Cox's own words, is the story of Colorado's unique, fearsome critter— the Slide-Rock Bolter, aka *Macrostoma saxiperruptus*.

In the mountains of Colorado, where in summer the wood are becoming infested with tourist, much uneasiness has been caused by the presence of the slide-rock bolter. This frightful animal lives only in the steepest mountain country where the slopes are greater than 45 degrees.

It has an immense head, with small eyes, and a mouth somewhat on the order of a sculpin, running back beyond its ears. The tail consists of a divided flipper, with enormous grab-hooks, which it fastens over the crest of the mountain or ridge, often remaining there motionless for days at a time, watching the gulch for tourists or any other hapless creature that may enter it.

At the right moment, after sighting a tourist, it will lift its tail, thus loosening its hold on the mountain, and with its small eyes riveted on the poor unfortunate, and drooling thin skid grease from the corners of its mouth, which greatly accelerates its speed, the bolter comes down like a toboggan, scooping in its victim as it goes, its own impetus carrying it up the next slope, where it again slaps its tail over the ridge and waits.

Whole parties of tourists are reported to have been gulped at one scoop by taking parties far back into the hills. The animal is a menace not only to tourists but to the woods as well. Many a draw through spruce-covered slopes has been laid low, the trees being knocked out by the roots or mowed off as by a scythe where the bolter has crashed down through from the peaks above.

A forest ranger, whose district includes the rough county between Ophir Peaks and the [Lizard] Head, conceived the bold idea of decoying a slide-rock bolter to its own destruction. A dummy tourist was rigged up with plaid Norfolk jacket, knee breeches, and a guidebook to Colorado. It was then filled full of giant powder and fulminate caps and posted in a conspicuous place, where, sure enough, the next day it attracted the attention of a bolter which had been hanging for days on the slope of [Lizard] Head.

The resulting explosion flattened half the buildings in Rico, which were never rebuilt, and the surrounding hills fattened flocks of buzzards the rest of the summer.

For the record, there isn't any place today officially called Ophir Peaks. Vanished place names in Colorado, however, are nothing new. Often, they're associated with what once was a bustling mine and a nearby settlement. When the mine panned out, usually so did the residents. The names they gave to local sites either evaporated along with most of the population or were changed by later residents.

On the other hand, Lizard Head is an ancient eroded volcanic neck in Summit County, within the Lizard Head Wilderness Area of the San Juan Mountains. It's one of Colorado's Fourteener mountains, attracting climbers because of its distinct challenge.

And there really is a mountain village called Rico. It's an old gold mining town, with a population of about two hundred in the winter that more than doubles in the summer. No word as to whether part of it was ever suddenly flattened.

THE SLIDE-ROCK BOLTER

Local Heroes and Villains

Maybe it's the altitude.

From saints to sinners—and a fair number of enigmas in-between—it's a challenge to come up with just a few folks who reach the Pikes Peak, as it were, of the unique.

In this case, what looks like a cast from a Western movie—a shopkeeper, a preacher, a flamboyant prophet, a farmer, a bounty hunter, a mountain guide, and some scene-stealing animals—has the quality that proves that life trumps fiction.

Suelynn Gustafson, aka Grandma Goth

Once upon a time, a little girl was doted upon by her family despite her oddness. Her mama would painstakingly dress her long hair in curls. The little girl hated it. She hated all the cutesy-sweet things a pretty little girl supposedly loves.

Suelynn Gustafson much preferred the company of her pet skunk to dolls and much preferred being with her eccentric Uncle Harold, who taught her how to skin goat carcasses and remove hides in mere seconds.

When she was about twelve, Suelynn's momma gave her a funeral card expressing the mournful sentiment of someone's passing. Suelynn was fascinated—she loved the feeling of sadness, the sense of death's mystery and darkness, the grandeur of a proper funeral.

"I *liked* to feel sorry, I thrived on it," says Gustafson today. "I loved 'ugly things.' Fortunately, my parents weren't as educated as parents are today, or they might have been worried for me."

Gustafson grew up, married, divorced, had a son, and moved back to Denver, where her family had a business that dealt in antique hardware. For years—coiffed and dressed to be both businesslike and alluring—she traveled around the country setting up pubs for a restaurant chain.

Finally, she decided to open her own store called Flossie McGrew's, two blocks from the family store known as Grandpa's Snazzy's Hardware on south Broadway. Gustafson intended for Flossie McGrew's to be an upscale thrift shop, but it turned out there was more of a demand for the same kind of kitschy, imperfect, and morbid things that Gustafson preferred.

She became known as a purveyor of the bizarre, the strange, and the hilariously outdated. Halloween props, theater makeup, and new costumes added to the inventory.

When the store next to Grandpa Snazzy's moved out in the late 1990s, Gustafson was prompt to move lock, stock, and weirdness to a space considerably smaller but a lot more convenient. A couple of years later, she bought a small former Congregational church, circa 1885, nearby and began renovating it for her future home, a project she's still working on.

"I got a load of unused metal coffins from a place that was going out of business," she recalls. "And I didn't have anywhere to put them except over in the yard of the church I bought, so there I was arranging 'em, when the neighbors started coming by and asking, 'What you doing?' I said, 'I'm moving in!'"

Gustafson flashes a row of gold front teeth at the memory. She discarded the conventional garb of her restaurant past and wears whatever she durn pleases, which today tends to be holey, knee-length jeans, tops with spooky graphics, and socks of strange patterns.

When her hair skipped the graying stage and went straight to white, she sought a new color for it, which has become her trademark.

"I didn't make a good blonde," says Gustafson. "But there was this purple shampoo I liked the look of in my hair, so I found a nice shade of fuchsia dye and started using that. Men love it. Kids, too, especially kids."

The purple hair, the strange clothes, the contented absorption with all things weird and dark (she founded the Society of Funeral Coaches to celebrate the hearse industry), all gave rise to the local moniker of *Grandma Goth* for Gustafson.

For all the eccentricity (and the traffic-stopping storefront of Flossie McGrew's), Gustafson is not a high-profile person. She neither courts personal attention nor shuns it, although her friend Deborah Hiestand produced and directed a short documentary about her called Grandma

Goth, which appeared at the Starz Denver International Film Festival in 2006.

Strolling about her shop, pausing now and then to give a story about this or that merchandise ("Those are my favorite items," she says, looking up at the prosthetic leg suspended from the ceiling), it's plain that Suelynn Gustafson has found her niche in life.

"If you're truly an individual you're on your own, and that may mean you're alone on a dark path. But if it's something you love, and you're not afraid to do that, then you'll be happy," says Grandma Goth.

She became known as a purveyor of the bizarre.

Rattlesnake Kate

When Katherine McHale Slaughterback heard hunters' gunfire on October 28, 1925, she knew there was a chance there might be some wounded ducks at the pond near her corn farm, outside Ione, Colorado.

She and her three-year-old son, Ernic, mounted her horse and headed out to look. When Slaughterback dismounted to open a gate, she realized they were in a heap of trouble.

Normally, rattlesnakes will go out their way to avoid humans, but they are also critters of habit. They have their summer feeding areas, their winter hibernation dens, and a migration corridor between the two that they prefer to stick to even when other creatures (such as humans) move into the area.

Slaughterback, a divorcée, hadn't had the farm for long and was probably unaware such a corridor was nearby. At any rate, Slaughterback, her son, and her horse now found themselves in the middle of a rattlesnake commute. She shot three with her Remington .22 rifle, and then more began to appear out of the undergrowth. Suddenly, there were rattlesnakes everywhere: full-grown poisonous snakes on a mission, and the nearest hospital was miles away.

Slaughterback told her son to stay on the horse and slapped it on the backside to make it move quickly to a safer distance. To save her ammunition, she pulled a "No Hunting" sign out of the ground and started whacking.

A couple hours and 140 dead rattlesnakes later, Slaughterback managed to clear a path to her horse and son and went home.

After she cleaned up and rested, she decided she couldn't let all those snakes go to waste. They could use the meat and could turn those skins into something useful. Slaughterback, who had taken a course in taxidermy, recruited a neighbor to help harvest the massacre.

News of this woman's gritty feat spread fast, and reporters were driving to her barn while she was still hanging snakeskins on a line to dry. From the start, some doubted that this ninety-pound woman could actually do what she did. So, she made a fashionable dress out of fifty skins. The rest became a headband, a necklace, and a pair of shoes. She wore the outfit to parties and other events where she was invited to tell her story.

From then on, Rattlesnake Kate was in the business of harvesting rattlesnake venom, skins, and rattles, and preserving rattlesnakes.

Slaughterback is buried in Mizpah Cemetery in Platteville, near Greeley. The gravestone she chose before her death reads: "Rattlesnake Kate, daughter of Wallace and Albina McHale, July 23, 1893–October 6, 1969."

Her rattlesnake outfit and other memorabilia are exhibited at the Greeley History Museum. Her small farmhouse can now be found in Greeley's Centennial Village, an outdoor museum of historical buildings.

Bishop Frank H. Rice

Frank Hamilton Rice could be considered an incarnation of the "holy fool"—a person devoted to God who uses absurdity like a living sermon. Or maybe he was just a crackpot.

Rice was born in 1881 in a Presbyterian parsonage in Danville, Illinois. He spent a stint studying for the Methodist ministry at Epworth University of Oklahoma City and wound up as a parole clerk for the Oklahoma State Penitentiary.

When a violent prison break erupted on January 19, 1914, the three escaping convicts took several people as human shields, including Rice. The convicts put up a battle that cost them their lives and those of four hostages. Rice survived by pretending to be dead.

The resulting publicity gave Rice a taste of what it meant to be in the spotlight. He was hired as a solicitor for the Colorado Prison Association the following year and moved to Denver with his wife and daughter. He left that job to be editor of a trade publication.

As a popular Sunday school teacher for the Grant Avenue Methodist Episcopal Church, Rice convinced the church to sponsor weekly dances for teens, until church elders accused him of corrupting the youth. The resulting crusade and public debate got him ousted.

Rice was a natural-born crusader who loved attention even though it kept getting him into trouble. What he needed was his own church.

Back in the day, all the State of Colorado required to incorporate as a church or a university was a few correctly filled-out papers and $3.50 (about $45.00 today). Rice decided to go for both.

The Liberal Church of America, Inc., was incorporated on February 23, 1923. Rice followed up by establishing a board and consecrating himself as bishop. He declared P. T.

Barnum to be the church's first saint.

The mission of the Liberal Church was ". . . to help folks keep themselves out of hospitals, jails, and insane asylums and to assist them to live in the here and now and let the universal law of nature and God care for the future life."

Rice was constantly in the newspapers because of some stunt. His services, held in a hall on Skid Row, were lively, to say the least (he often smoked a stogie at the pulpit), and he refused to pass a collection plate or charge for marriages and funerals. (His marriage ceremony consisted of pronouncing the word *married* in front of the couple.)

His protest against "mechanical" prayers was to publicly use an adding machine to produce "petitions" that the God of Mathematics would someday translate.

Rice declared Pabst Blue Ribbon beer to be a sacramental beverage, but when he couldn't afford alcohol for communion, he made do with buttermilk. For the big Thanksgiving and Christmas church dinners, he made sure anyone who asked received a shot of hard liquor (one per customer).

At Easter, he would ceremoniously transfer the sins of his congregation onto a literal scapegoat. He repeated the act with some flourishes on behalf of the late cannibal legend Alfred Packer and his five victims, who had died without being absolved of their sins. (See "Alfred Packer, Man-eater," in this chapter.)

Rice gave out academic degrees and ordinations to almost anyone who asked and to quite a few who didn't, such as Robert Ripley of *Ripley's Believe It or Not!* fame, who was made a Doctor of Divinity and a Universal Fact-Finding Doctor. The degrees helped many a bum escape being hauled in for vagrancy because a "doctor of divinity" could legally beg without having any visible means of support.

The bishop once ensured that a murdered prostitute

would be given a nice funeral by having the word spread that he had passed on himself. Denver florists and undertakers donated flowers, a casket, a vault, and mortuary equipment. The presumed "corpse" then preached the service.

All the shenanigans aside, Rice was a man who truly believed in helping the downtrodden and making the world a better place. He supported labor unions, promoted sex education, spoke out against the Ku Klux Klan at its height of power in Colorado, and ran for every office from senator to dog catcher (he never won).

He said the true holy trinity was "food, clothing, and shelter" for everyone who needed it, and through both sensational antics and dogged soliciting, he provided for the needs of many who didn't qualify for help from the usual agencies.

By 1945, however, Rice was wearing out. He never achieved the big church of like-minded humanitarians. He didn't make a salary and could barely provide for his own family.

Twenty years after the founding of the Liberal Church, Rice wrote,

> *"I freely plead guilty to the charge of being a 'crackpot.' . . . Only crackpots undertake to alleviate the poverty of others and to remove the limitations on Liberty. If I appear to be unorthodox, I trust I shall be forgiven because operating in an institution for Public sinners, the worthy and unworthy, without endowment is not susceptible to too much formality, dignity and conventionality."*

On February 26, 1945, Bishop Rice, sixty-four, died at Denver General Hospital of a heart attack. Possibly aware that his days were numbered, he had taken out a life insurance policy only two months before. Three thousand dollars (about $90,000 today) and some office furniture was left to his family.

Rice's funeral was reported as modest and tasteful, but the turnout was one of the most impressive in Denver's history. Newspapers reported that the mourners included derelicts, Supreme Court justices, professors, cops, legislators, and people from "every segment of Denver life."

The Liberal Church was one of those institutions that could only exist with a charismatic leader, and it did not long outlast its bishop.

Frank Hamilton Rice is buried in Denver's Fairmount Cemetery.

Brotherhood of the White Temple Church and Amazing Stories

In a secluded canyon near the small town of Sedalia, south of Denver, is a community founded on a fantastic belief system by a man who called himself Dr. Maurice Doreal.

According to an interview he gave to *Time* magazine in September 1946, his original name was Claude Doggins and he was born in Sulphur Springs, Oklahoma. He said he was part Choctaw Indian, born on a reservation, and had served in the U.S. Army Signal Corps during World War I.

That's about all that's known publicly about him, before and after Claude Doggins was transformed into Dr. Maurice Doreal, the mystic who held the key to Life, the Universe, and Everything.

According to the *Time* article and an interview he gave *Life* magazine that same year, Doggins became Doreal at some point after military service when he met with the Ascended Masters of the Great White Lodge, in a secret location seventy-five miles underneath Lhasa, Tibet.

Doreal built his revelations into a congregation called The Brotherhood of the White Temple, first in Oklahoma and then in Denver by 1929. His followers called him the Voice, which spoke for the twelve-man Supreme Council back in subterranean Lhasa. The Voice kept in communication with the council, he said, by astral projection. He claimed to have met with the Dalai Lama.

When Doreal revealed to his followers that atomic war could be imminent, he also said he had a plan to escape the coming chaos by moving the church to a secluded area. There, the lead deposits in the canyon would protect members from radioactive fallout, and the church would emerge when all was clear to lead survivors into a new age.

He posed for news photographers dressed in gold Chinese robes while seated on a throne he claimed was once that of the ill-fated Maximilian I of Mexico. Magazines and newspapers from coast to coast covered the story with a great deal of glee.

The congregation worked feverishly to build Shamballa Ashrama, the "center of occult wisdom in the West" that Doreal said could turn into a summer resort if the apocalypse did not materialize.

Instead, it became home for a small following and a correspondence school that sold Doreal's mystic teachings in a long series of mimeographed booklets.

As little as any outsider knows about the inner workings of the Brotherhood, only hard-core fans of science fiction might know that Dr. Maurice Doreal was a minor character in one the most colorful hoaxes in literary history.

In March 1945, the pulp magazine *Amazing Stories* began printing stories it claimed were the "racial memories" of Richard Shaver, former artist's model, Communist Party member, and welder. The editor of *Amazing Stories*, Ray Palmer, rescued a letter from a wastebasket, opened a correspondence with the obviously delusional author, and turned the man's ravings into a story that he published as "I Remember Lemuria!"

Not only did that issue sell out, but also letters poured in asking to know more about Shaver and his purported memories. Readers claimed to have had similar experiences inside a hollow Earth, with strange dreams, visions, and unusual sightings, and particularly with the descendants of advanced extraterrestrial races, the evil Dero and the noble Tero.

Shaver seemed delighted at the interest in his wild tales, even if Palmer and his stable of writers had to rewrite them into readable versions. Palmer constantly stoked fan interest, pro and con, in the Shaver Mystery by insisting it could all very well be true. Shaver Mystery Clubs sprang up around

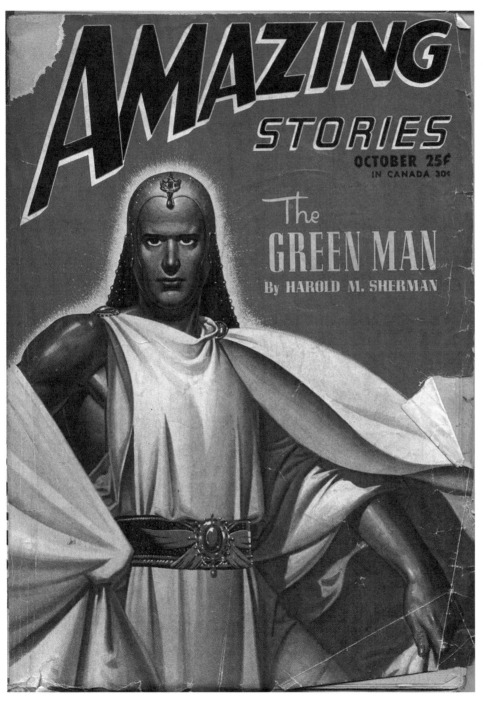

the United States. From 1945 until 1948, most of the content of *Amazing Stories* was stories written under Richard Shaver's name.

In the August 1946 issue, a letter from a reader brought Doreal's writings up as something that augmented the Shaver Mystery. Editorial response was both encouraging and slightly skeptical about the Ascended Masters thing.

Doreal responded in the following October issue with a lengthy letter in which he said that many of the claims of Richard Shaver were indeed true, that he personally knew the Dero under another name, had visited the secret caverns himself, and warned people against trying to find the hidden entrances to the hollow world (one of which he claimed elsewhere was in the Cathedral of St. John the Divine in New York City) unless they were spiritually prepared.

"The underground cities and caverns are, in most part, protected by space warps, a science known to the ancients but only touched on by modern science," Doreal wrote.

Outside the Shamballa Ashrama, it's not known when Doreal's Theosophy-flavored pamphlets started to take on an even more exotic flavor. However, he was an avowed and avid science-fiction fan and claimed to have more than ten thousand books on subjects related to the Shaver Mystery.

Several Internet Web sites and forums devoted to UFOs and conspiracy theories today use quotes from Doreal's works without question. Most appear to be unaware of any connection between Doreal and the Shaver Mystery hoax or science-fiction history and its trends.

Ray Palmer never admitted to publishing a hoax, although he claimed to having written many of the Shaver stories based on Shaver's incoherent ramblings. Palmer also proudly quoted a charge that if the Shaver Mystery was a hoax it was "the biggest ever attempted in modern science-fiction history." By 1948, a reader rebellion helped boot Palmer out of his position at *Amazing Stories* and into publishing the first of several magazines of his own—*Fate: True Stories of the Strange, the Unusual, the Unknown.* He died in 1977.

Richard Shaver's stories continued being cleaned up and published, and he became known for what we'd call today outsider art—stones with innate pictures he claimed he developed rather like photography. He died in 1975.

Doreal died in 1963. The remaining Brotherhood in Sedalia prefers to keep a very low public profile and refuses to give any interviews on the life, death, and work of their leader. It discourages outsiders from entering its property and has little interaction with the surrounding community.

The correspondence school is still in operation, although the pamphlets about Atlantis, how to achieve astral projection, and understand the *real* teachings of Jesus come in slicker bindings. The Brotherhood's Web site

speaks of its leader in the present tense and says Doreal is "an agent for the foundation of the Great Spiritual Kingdom of the coming Golden Age."

No word on who is keeping the Brotherhood in contact with the Ascended Masters these days.

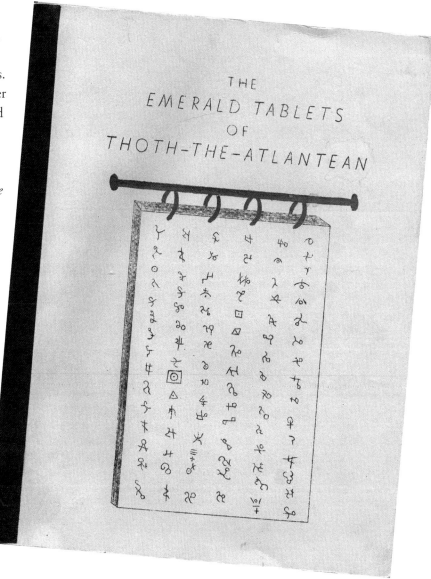

Tom Tobin and "The Terrible Espinosas"

Thomas Tate Tobin was illiterate, modest, possibly half-Indian, and ignored by a territorial government reluctant to admit that he had shown up the U.S. Army.

All he did was track down and kill the first known serial killers on U.S. soil.

Tobin was considered second as a scout and tracker only to the legendary Kit Carson, a fellow Missourian and relative by marriage. No one was interested in chronicling Tobin's adventures into the stuff of dime novels, so his story is rarely known outside of southern Colorado.

In the spring of 1863, two Hispanic men were on a mission from God—or the Virgin Mary. The mission was to kill as many Anglos as possible.

Two years before, President James Buchanan had officially declared once-Spanish Colorado a free (non-slave) territory. In the intervening two years, some violence may have erupted between the Espinosa family and some of the Anglo settlers and prospectors. On the other hand, the Hispanic men's fury may have arisen from the deaths of family members, a land grab, or other injustices committed during the U.S.–Mexican War that ended in 1848 and ceded Spanish territory to the United States.

All that has ever been confirmed was that two brothers, Felipe and Vivian Espinosa, felt both aggrieved and divinely inspired enough to go on a campaign of murderous Anglo bushwhacking.

The bodies started showing up near Cañon City, south of Colorado Springs—ranchers, settlers, miners, travelers. The Espinosas' method was to shoot one or two people at a time on lonely roads and at isolated sites. Some say victims were mutilated. Their heads were struck with axes or even cut off or their hearts were removed.

The Espinosas evaded both soldiers and civilian posses in the rugged mountains and went unidentified for some time. One man was mistaken for one of the killers and strung up by an excited crowd before more deaths proved him innocent.

At some point, the Espinosas sent a letter to Colorado Territory governor John Evans that claimed he would join their list of twenty-two gringo deaths if he didn't give them five thousand acres in Conejos County with a promise of amnesty. By some accounts, Evans responded by posting a $2,500 reward for the capture of the brothers, dead or alive, a small fortune for that time.

Eventually, a witness survived an attack and identified the brothers. A posse killed Felipe at what is now called Espinosa Peak, near Cripple Creek. His sibling slipped into the crowd and passed as one of the posse.

According to some stories, Felipe's head was taken and pickled as a souvenir. Found on his body was a handwritten manuscript in Spanish—the first revelation that the brothers believed themselves on a mission of divine retribution.

Meanwhile, Vivian escaped, recruited a cousin or nephew who may have been as young as twelve, and the killings resumed.

As the body count mounted, people clamored for the army to do something. By September, the commanding officer of Fort Garland, Col. Sam Tappan, turned to the veteran scout, tracker, and occasional bounty hunter Tom Tobin, then about age forty.

Years later, Tobin told a grandson, Kit Carson III, that he agreed to help track down the Espinosas for humanitarian reasons, although it was also said Tappan offered him the governor's reward if successful.

Tappan insisted that an officer and a detachment of fifteen soldiers go with Tobin to make it an official military action. Tobin ditched the men two days into the trip because the contingent could be heard for miles. He waited until the soldiers had camped for the night and then slipped off with a Mexican boy from his ranch.

Tobin found evidence that the Espinosas had rustled a couple of oxen to feed themselves. When he saw a large flock of crows wheeling around an area, he correctly guessed that the Espinosas had found a place to butcher one. The boy was ordered to stay behind a short distance. If Tobin didn't reappear in a couple of hours, he was to ride back to Fort Garland as fast as he could.

The Espinosas were making camp near La Veta Pass when Tobin surprised them with gunfire. Vivian fell headfirst into the campfire but came up with a gun before Tobin finished him. The Espinosas' partner was shot down as he fled. Tobin and his young assistant cut off the Espinosas' heads for proof of their demise.

Tobin found a journal and letters written in Spanish on the bodies. He had a Hispanic wife and probably could speak some Spanish, but he was illiterate. Possibly someone read passages aloud to him. Tobin later said the journal entries claimed at least twenty-five gringo deaths, with intent to kill many, many more. (It's generally believed the Espinosas were responsible for at least thirty-two murders. At least one source says it was many more. See "Cano's Castle" in Personalized Properties and Innovative Environments.)

The writings had many pious invocations and claims that the Virgin Mary had directed and blessed the murderous mission. Revenge for various injustices inflicted by Anglos seemed to be the motive, but the details were sparse.

The soldiers arrived in time to bury the bodies. That night, Tobin slept with the heads under his saddlebag to deter their theft.

Colonel Tappan, his officers, and some of their wives had just returned from a ride and were gathered in a room at

11950. Tom Tobin Ranch, Blanca, Colo.
Published by C. J. Young, Blanca, Colo.

Fort Garland when Tobin strode in a few days later with a sack. Tappan asked how the manhunt went, and Tobin replied, "So-so."

Then he opened the sack and let the heads roll across the floor as people screamed and scattered.

Governor Evans may have stiffed Tobin on the reward but did present him with a handsome buckskin coat, much like one presented to Tobin's more famous frontier pal Kit Carson. The army gave Tobin a Henry rifle, one of the top firearms of the day. The legislature wrangled over the reward for years.

Colonel Tappan eventually paid part of it to Tobin, and over time, Tobin received more from the Colorado government but never the full amount allegedly promised.

According to a January 13, 1980, article in the *Denver Post*, the heads of the Espinosas may have turned up in 1979 when a basement cleaning of the Colorado State Building unearthed a couple of skulls wrapped in cloth in an old wooden box. No one seems to know how the skulls were disposed of although there are rumors they were thrown in the building's furnace incinerator.

Tobin died in 1904, at eighty-one, and was buried in a small private cemetery near his ranch in Blanca, north of Fort Garland. His tombstone is inscribed *Thomas T. Toben*. (The cemetery is on private land, and permission is required for access.)

In 1946, Kit Carson III gave an interview at his trading post in Sanford, Colorado, in which he said Tobin showed him the spot where the Espinosas' bodies were buried. Tobin advised against ever showing the burial site to anyone else. Because of the missing heads, he said, the killers' spirits would float in limbo around there forever.

Alfred Packer, Man-eater

When a self-styled mountain guide walked into the Los Pinos Agency (Ute reservation government) in Colorado Territory, April 1874, minus the party of prospectors he was last seen with in February, folks started to ask questions. To which Alfred (or *Alferd* according to the rumored tattoo on his arm) Packer replied that he had suffered frostbite and had been left behind. He didn't know what happened to his clients. Eventually, he walked out on his own.

Speculation over the fate of the missing men followed Packer from saloon to saloon, where he exhibited several wallets. The talk grew louder from men who had entered the San Juan Mountains with Packer a few months before. They remembered Packer as incompetent, badly provisioned, and having no cash or rifle when they started out.

On May 8, under pressure from the Indian Agency manager Gen. Charles Adams, Packer confessed to a dire turn of events that befell his party. Starting with the oldest, Israel Swan, sixty-five, the men succumbed one by one to exhaustion, cold, and starvation and were eaten by the survivors until only Packer remained. He confessed to eating human flesh until the snow melted enough to find his way out of the wilderness. Sure, he took the dead men's valuables —they didn't need them any more.

A pack of concerned citizens forcibly escorted Packer to the fatal site but found nothing. Packer was arrested anyway on suspicion of murder and jailed in nearby Saguache. The following August, an artist sent out by *Harper's Weekly* magazine to illustrate the fabled West came across a gruesome scene in Slumgullion Pass, overlooking the Gunnison River. John A. Randolph carefully sketched a group of five hacked-up corpses. His report brought the coroner and and many locals running.

After burying the bodies, the crowd returned to

Saguache to find that Packer had managed to escape the jail and frontier justice. He wasn't arrested until nine years later, when someone recognized him in a Wyoming saloon.

"Emergency cannibalism" was no crime then or even today in the United States. What the people of Packer's place and time could not forgive was that he had presented himself as an experienced mountain guide and led trusting men to their doom. The question was whether Packer had done so deliberately in order to enrich himself.

By the time the trial took place in newly established Lake City, near the fatal scene, Packer was formally accused only of the premeditated murder and robbery of one of the prospectors, Israel Swan. Swan's relatives claimed that their kinsman had carried about $6,000 plus an expensive Winchester rifle—more than enough motive for his murder. That was thought enough to hang Packer.

Alfred G. Packer was born in 1842 in Allegheny County, Pennsylvania, to James and Emily Packer. He enlisted for the Union in 1862 in Company F, Sixteenth U.S. Infantry Regiment, Minnesota. He was honorably discharged shortly after for epilepsy. He enlisted in an Iowa regiment and was discharged again for the same reason. He decided to try his luck out west.

In 1873, Packer cited his value as a mountain guide to gain entry for a group of prospectors into a larger group headed for Breckenridge, Colorado. Whether Packer had ever been in the area before is unknown.

With or without Packer's help, the group became lost. The men were half-starved when they stumbled across a winter camp of the Ute tribe in January 1874. Ouray, the Ute leader, advised them to stay put until spring.

Gold fever won over prudence. Two smaller groups decided instead to head for the Los Pinos Agency between Saguache and Gunnison, along a path detailed by Ouray. The first group's leader, Oliver D. Loutzenhizer, was

fed up with Packer and threatened to shoot him if he followed.

As snow fell, Loutzenhizer's group fashioned skis and eventually made it to the Indian Agency. Packer and five of his clients trudged behind at a safe distance. That was the last anyone saw of Packer's group.

Packer took the stand in his own defense. He said he led the five men away from Ouray's recommended path to higher ground where the snow was lighter. They took shelter in a wooded area overlooking the Gunnison River. Stranded by a blizzard, provisions ran out and despair turned to madness.

Packer told of leaving the camp to look for landmarks to civilization. When he returned, four of the men had been slain and the killer, Shannon Wilson Bell, was roasting human meat over a fire. The crazed Bell attacked him, they struggled, and Packer killed Bell. He admitted to only minimal cannibalism. To no one's surprise, Packer was convicted (see courtroom, above) of premeditated murder on Friday, April 13, 1882.

According to Larry Dolan, a saloon owner who was a witness against Packer, Judge Melville B. Gerry pronounced judgment in colorful frontier vernacular.

Stand up yah voracious man-eatin' sonofabitch and receive yir sitince. When yah came to Hinsdale County, there was siven Dimmycrats. But you, yah et five of 'em, goddam yah. I sintince yah t' be hanged by th' neck ontil yer dead, dead, dead, as a warnin' ag'in reducin' th' Dimmycratic populayshun of this county. Packer, you Republican cannibal, I would sintince ya ta hell but the statutes forbid it.

Packer's hanging was set for May 19, 1883, but legal appeals won him a new trial. The Colorado Supreme Court set aside the murder conviction because there had been no state murder statute in 1874, when Colorado was still a territory.

Packer was retried in 1886 in Gunnison, this time on the charge of voluntary manslaughter of all five men. He was sentenced on June 8 to forty years in the state penitentiary in Cañon City. He was then forty-three years old.

Packer was a model prisoner who kept busy with woodworking. A magnificent dollhouse he crafted is displayed in the Hinsdale County Museum in Lake City.

After sixteen years, Packer's bid for parole was rejected. His case came to the attention of *Denver Post* reporter Polly Pry. With the support of her paper, she appealed to Gov. Charles Spalding Thomas for Packer's pardon. Thomas refused and cited threatening letters—"the foulest compositions that I have ever read"—from Packer to his unsupportive relatives back east.

The *Denver Post* campaigned to free Packer, and in 1901, Packer won conditional parole. The owners of the *Post*, Fredrick Gilmer Bonfills and Harry Heye Tammen, reportedly had plans for Packer to join a traveling circus they also owned. Governor Thomas thwarted that idea by requiring Packer to stay in Denver for at least six years.

Packer worked as a security guard for the *Post* and later as a ranch hand. Neighbors knew him as a kindly storyteller, popular with children. He never won the official pardon he hoped for.

Packer died at age sixty-four, on April 24, 1907, following a stroke.

He is buried in Littleton Cemetery under a modest military grave marker with the spelling Packer himself sometimes used: "Alferd Packer, Co. F. 16 U.S. Inf."

Posthumous Doin's

Neither Packer nor his alleged victims were allowed to rest in peace. Packer's gravestone has been stolen and replaced at least once, and the Littleton Cemetery Association eventually covered the grave in cement in 1973 to discourage ghouls.

Superintendent John Houser says the cemetery association believes Packer's body to be intact. Others claim that Packer's head was separated from his body before the burial. It was then dissected and sold to a traveling sideshow until it wound up in the hands of an oddities collector who sold it about ten years ago to the famous curiosity exhibitor Ripley's Believe or Not!

"It's true, we have Alferd," says Edward Meyer, vice president of exhibits and archives for Ripley's Entertainment, Inc., headquartered in Orlando, Florida. "He was on exhibit in our New Orleans facility until Hurricane Katrina hit."

Packer's head was reassigned to the Ripley's museum in San Antonio, Texas, in 2008.

Myers would not disclose how Ripley's was able to determine the authenticity of the relic, except that the seller's

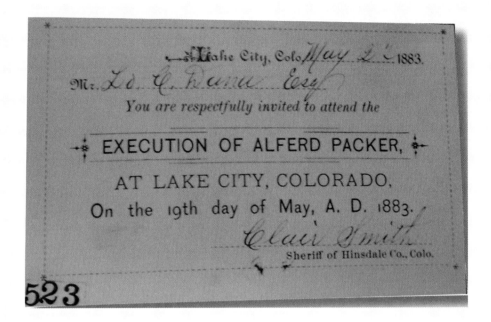

information "was enough to convince us." He did admit the purchase price was "Well in the neighborhood of $20,000."

"Mummies don't come cheap."

Technically, Packer's head was not mummified. Meyer says the separation and preservation "as an educated guess" took place shortly after his death. Arsenic was probably to used to preserve the skin, a method common in embalming until banned in the early 1900s. However, before that happened, the head was neatly dissected and the brain removed.

"All that's holding everything together are a series of little metal hooks," says Meyer. "People in those days were interested in knowing if there was anything unusual about a famous criminal's brain."

The bodies of those Packer was convicted of killing were also disturbed for the purpose of science. They were disinterred in 1989 when forensics law professor

Dr. James Starrs of the George Washington University in Washington, D.C., obtained permission to lead an archaeological dig with a team of experts. The bones were dated and identified in the anthropology labs at the University of Arizona in Tucson and the Smithsonian Institution in Washington, D.C.

In a 1990 article titled "Victims Exhumation Project, Lake City, Colorado, July 17, 1989," for the quarterly journal *Scientific Sleuthing Review*, Starrs stated that the results proved that Packer was, indeed, a murdering cannibal and a liar.

The bodies were re-interred under a cement slab on the spot of their original burial on August 15, 1989. A large plaque, a smaller memorial stone, and five small plain white crosses mark the spot where the remains of Shannon Wilson Bell, Israel Swan, James Humphrey, Frank "Reddy" Miller, and George "California" Noon are buried.

The Absolutely, Positively True Story of How the UC Boulder Student Cafeteria Came to be Named for a Cannibal

Toward the end of April 1968, the United States reeled from the assassination of Dr. Martin Luther King Jr. College campus unrest had spread across the United States. Administration buildings were occupied in protests against the Vietnam War, racial discrimination, and violations of civil rights.

Recently elected to head the new Student Assembly about this time, two graduate students at the University of Colorado, Boulder, discussed a plan to submit both serious and frivolous resolutions to engage their constituents. As they talked, they happened to walk by the student cafeteria, then undergoing renovations.

"The food's so awful there they should rename the place for Alfred Packer," commented Paul Talmey, Student Assembly president.

Visualize a light bulb springing on over the head of Talmey's vice president, Paul Danish. Danish's interest in journalism was inspired by a book he read in high school, *Timberline: A Story of Bonfils and Tammen* by Gene Fowler. *Timberline*, about F. G. Bonfils and H. H. Tammen, the colorful men who owned the *Denver Post*, related the tale of Alfred Packer. (See the section devoted to Packer.)

A resolution to rename the student cafeteria something fittingly hilarious, Danish urged, would bring refreshing frivolity to the tensions of more serious issues, and show fellow students that their elected campus representatives really could accomplish some things. His co-conspirators, notably Talmey and Bob Ewegen, a former editor of the student newspaper, the *Colorado Daily*, agreed.

Such a resolution was sure to win overwhelming approval at the upcoming Student Assembly, no question. However, how could they ensure it would survive the real power on campus, the Colorado University Board of Regents?

Ewegen, then on hiatus from graduate school, had a plan: It involved revered television journalist Walter Cronkite, anchor of the *CBS Evening News* since 1962 and universally popular for his air of avuncular integrity.

"I was working for UPI (United Press International)," says Ewegen. "I knew Walter Cronkite was an old UPI man. I said I'd write the story, and the minute they gave me the results of the vote at the meeting, I'd send it over the wires as the students having approved the name change on the cafeteria. (I was shamelessly ethically-challenged in those days.) I knew Cronkite would read it, and if he reported it on the evening news, well, it had to be true."

The plan went off without a hitch. Cronkite covered the story the next day. Ewegen's report rippled across the nation. Such was the overall positive response that the campus administration didn't wait for an official blessing.

The Alferd G. Packer Memorial Grill (with the slogan "Have a friend for lunch!") was dedicated on May 14, 1968, with the throwing of a raw hamburger patty against a wall. It stuck with a loud smack, to the cheers of attendees, reported the *Denver Post* and *Rocky Mountain News*.

A meeting of the UC Board of Regents was scheduled within that month, and approval of the new cafeteria name was on the agenda. Clerks at the regents' Denver office say no record exists as to the discussion, unfortunately.

"I'd say they were just pretty relieved this was normal student high jinks," says Danish. "Considering we could have been burning down the ROTC building."

Shortly after, UC Boulder began holding Alfred Packer Days every spring.

J. C. Ancell of Longmont helped set up the cafeteria for its 1968 dedication and went on in 1972 to become associate director of the UC Boulder University Memorial Center (which houses the cafeteria) until his retirement in 2002.

"The seventies were the heyday," recalls Ancell. "We had a week with an event going on every day—a contest for the best motto and artwork to go on the T-shirts and programs, a daily cafeteria 'special,' that kind of thing. Friday would be the big day."

Free beer ensured high attendance but there were also rib-eating contests, raw-meat tossing contests, and rock bands. Sometime around 1975, a ceremonial version of the grill's "Packer Smacker" sandwich featured a live "scantily-clad coed" according to Ancell, between bread covers and presented on a coffin-shaped board.

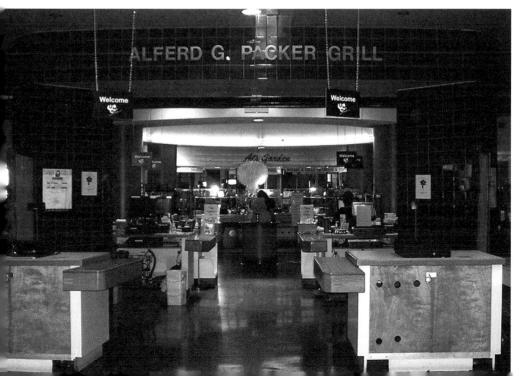

All living things evolve, for good or ill. The guilt of an awakened political consciousness (and limits on beer service) sounded the death knell for the Packer fest, leading to its demise by 1999.

Danish became a journalist and politician in Boulder County, still something of a gadfly. Talmey, semiretired CEO of a market research firm, now lives in Telluride.

Ewegen, now deputy editorial page editor at the *Denver Post*, summed up their memories of "the Packer Caper": "We all had a good laugh. The whole country had a good laugh. And we sure needed it then."

Mike the Headless Chicken

Tiny Fruita (population 9,416, as of 2005) lies in the heart of Colorado's Banana Belt region, known for its magnificent scenery, dinosaur fossils, agriculture, and wineries.

However, the memory of a former sideshow attraction, Mike the Headless Chicken, has the power to make its townspeople run about like—well, you know—every third weekend in May.

The saga of "Miracle Mike" began on September 10, 1945, when Clara Olsen asked her husband, Lloyd, to harvest one of their poultry for dinner. Olsen swung his axe and decapitated a young rooster called Mike. The critter picked itself up and went on scratching and bobbing as before.

Such a reflexive action is not unusual as poultry beheadings go, but this time it appeared to continue longer than usual. Olsen decided to let Mike's reflexes stop firing in their own good time. He was surprised to see Mike still on the go the following morning. Anything that determined to live, Olsen figured, should get its chance.

Using an eyedropper, Olsen put grain and water down what was left of Mike's gullet, which seemed to suit the chicken just fine. After about a week of this, Olsen took Mike to the University of Utah in Salt Lake City for some answers.

Scientists determined Olsen's axe had missed Mike's jugular vein, leaving most of the brain stem and an ear intact. A brain stem is all the mentality a chicken really needs, and a blood clot kept Mike from bleeding. Apart from decapitation, Mike remained a healthy fowl.

The Olsens took Mike on the road and exhibited him for twenty-five cents a gawk. People from Atlantic City to San Diego flocked to see "Miracle Mike." Magazines featured him, as did *Guinness Book of World Records*. Mike was insured for $10,000.

Eighteen months later, Mike suddenly began choking and his owners were unable to find the eyedropper fast enough to clear his esophagus and prevent his demise.

Gone but certainly not forgotten, Mike was immortalized by sculptor Lyle Nichols with a much-larger-than-life metal rendering of his headless form on Fruita's Mulberry Street. In 1998, the city's Parks and Recreation Department initiated Mike the Headless Chicken Days.

Events vary from year to year, and there are always unique features, such as the 5K Run Like a Headless Chicken, the Chicken Dance Contest (at which scores of citizens pour onto a field to perform to a live polka band), marshmallow peep and chicken wing eating contests, and a game of flag football with a greased rubber chicken.

Fruita's relationship with unusual creatures goes way back—way, way back. So far, it is the only town in the United States with an official dinosaur—the Ceratosaurus. That and a small museum of distinction, Dinosaur Journey Museum, reflect its link to a scenic regional byway called the Dinosaur Diamond (see the section on it in Ancient Colorado).

In April 2007, *Science* magazine published a study revealing that the protein in *Tyrannosaurus rex's* bones is closely related to the collagen in today's chickens—perhaps a clue as to Mike's remarkable ferocity for life—bringing to full circle, like the Dinosaur Diamond, Fruita's fabulous fixations. For more information: www.miketheheadlesschicken.org.

I Believe in Mike!

Everyone in small town Fruita, Colorado, has heard the story of Mike the Headless Chicken. I learned the story, which I couldn't believe at first, when I first moved there with my family. A man chopped the rooster's head off so his family could have it for dinner when something went wrong, and the chicken didn't die. The man fed and watered the bird with an eyedropper. Mike, the bird, lived for eighteen months before his life gave out. Every year Fruita holds a Mike the Headless Chicken Festival in his honor. I now believe the story and an elderly friend of mine claims to have held the famous Mike. —*Hay Hay*

Lost Your Mind Yet?

Have you ever felt like you have lost your mind? Well, Mike did. It all started on September 10, 1945. Fruita, Colorado, farmer Lloyd Olsen sized up one of his roosters (Mike) for a Sunday dinner. Within moments, Mike had become part of Fruita's history. A misguided blow from the axe left Mike's brain stem and jugular vein intact, resulting in an extraordinary year and a half of travel and exhibition. That's right, Mike lived without a head. Mike's life was supported by eyedropper feeding through his esophagus. He was first taken to the University of Utah for a short scientific checkup, and then went on a road tour through Atlantic City, New York, Los Angeles, and San Diego. Mike was insured for $10,000, which is no chicken feed, and was recognized in *Life* and *Time* magazines and continues to hold the world record in the *Guinness World Book of Records*. Rumor has it that Mike succumbed in a small Arizona motel when food lodged in his esophagus. Mike's will to live remains part of Fruita's heritage. In fact, every year we celebrate with a festival—Mike the Headless Chicken Days.

We hope to see you there. And, next time you're feeling stressed, just remember, you can live a normal life even after you've lost your mind. —*Christine Gilbert*

Political Animals and Uncommonly Faithful Companions

Shep

If you're driving north along U.S. 36 from Denver toward Boulder, take a look over at the sloping area between the eastbound highway and the 121/128 Broomfield exit. You might see a little fenced grave with a couple of markers for the late Shep the Toll Road Dog, "Part Shepherd. Mostly Affection."

In 1951, when U.S. 36 was a country toll road, the toll collector's job was often quite boring. When a stray pup showed up, he was welcome relief to the staff and became their official mascot. Drivers came to know Shep and would leave treats and spare change for his care. When Shep died in 1964, the Colorado Department of Transportation decided he rated a real grave site and gave him one near the former toll collection area.

Because of the high-traffic risk, anyone wishing to visit the grave is advised to park at the Regional Transportation Department's Park-n-Ride site on U.S. 36 at Wadsworth Boulevard and cross the ramp to reach the embankment to Shep's grave.

Cats and Chickens

In 1988, the picturesque town of Guffey (population about fifty in town, about one thousand scattered nearby), elected a cat as its mayor. This former lumber-and-mining town has had a cat or dog as its official leader ever since.

The current mayoral occupant is the big black feline Monster, who conducts business at the Guffey Garage, owned (as are most of the restored antique buildings) by Bill Soux, electrician and local history buff.

Guffey offers rustic lodging and camping, food, a Post Office, and the only other services for twenty-five miles to the people of who live, drive, hike, and bike the area around Colorado Highway 9 near Mile Marker 21 and the Adventure Cycling Association's TransAmerica Bicycle Trail.

What Guffey's really known for is the annual Fourth of July fund-raiser called the Chicken Fly. For twenty-two years, folks at this fest have enjoyed good eats, live music, and various entertainments.

The highlight involves ascending the Chicken Tower (an old drilling rig) to toss live chickens and see which one flies the farthest. Competitors are gently shoved out the "chicken launcher" (a velvet-lined mailbox) with a "chicken plunger" (toiler plunger).

Paco Bell

Florissant has a small petrified forest and the Florissant Fossil Beds National Monument, which preserves some of the best prehistoric remains of animals, plants, and insects in the world.

It's a scenic little town full of pioneer spirit that doesn't mind admitting its mayor is a party animal (which party he refuses to say)—a real jackass named Paco Bell.

Paco Bell is the latest in a line of burros chosen to officially head Florissant's community by a group of locals fed up with being ignored by the county commissioners and other authorities.

The first election, held in 1996 on Heritage Celebration day, pronounced the burro Birdie to be Hizzoner. Birdie was succeeded four years later by a miniature donkey called Dillon. In 2004, Milo the llama made a bid for equine diversity, but lost to Paco Bell, who was duly sworn in by Sheriff Kevin Dougherty.

Paco Bell has made a few national appearances, including a clip of Hizzoner on Martha Stewart's TV show. His handlers are Celinda and Harold Kaelin, of the Pikes Peak Historical Society.

Prunes and Shorty

Burros have an honored history in the former boomtowns of Colorado. Fairplay, for instance, has memorials to two at the corner of Seventh and Front Streets—Prunes, a miner's hardworking pal who died in 1930 and Shorty, a lazy but loveable mooch who passed in 1951.

Donkeys on the Run

Hundreds of mines in the vicinity of Cripple Creek used to run on donkey labor, and their descendants now have the run of the town. They wander and eat where they will. (An area group looks after their welfare.)

The donkey packs provide endless amusement for the locals when tourists invariably roll down their car windows to pet the cute critters and give them treats. Once the donkeys push their heads into a car, it's about impossible to convince them to pull out.

Cripple Creek has been holding the annual Donkey Derby Days for more than seventy-five years. The Western Pack Burro Association holds races (professional and amateur) over ten miles of rugged mountain trail between the cities of Victor and Cripple Creek during the last week of June.

Personalized Properties and Innovative Environments

There's nothing more human than our desire to control our personal space, whether our environment is fixed or mobile, manufactured or natural, given or taken, isolated or crowded, transitory or permanent. A well-controlled environment brings a kick of satisfaction akin to being masters of the universe.

There's something powerful about meeting others who are masters of their own universe. No matter how kooky, high-minded, esoteric, or quirky they are, a visit to their world, to see their dreams realized, inspires us to reach for our own.

Cano and His Castle

The neighborhood knows it as "Cano's Castle." Sprouting from the corner of Tenth Avenue and State Street in Antonito, it's been called outsider art and a folk religious shrine. Not one photo I've seen of the place does it justice.

The original modest frame house is topped with two hand-built stories. Vines grow over what looks like the original front door. A rough staircase descends from a door at the back of the second story.

There is a separate, split-level structure in the backyard; a shorter and a taller building stuck together. The taller end has two towers that can be seen for blocks, not just because of their height but because they are covered with glittery objects—hubcaps, embedded bottles, flattened cans, bits of mirrors and reflective tiles. An old wooden shack with another do-it-yourself story, covered with yet more shiny stuff, stands nearby. Here and there are hand-painted placards proclaiming the love of God and the evils of alcohol and drugs. Bottles hung as windchimes clink gently all over the yard.

The door at the back of the house opens, and a man comes down the steps. I call out, and he heads over. He says he's too busy to chat.

"I'm working over there today," he says, gesturing across the street at a wide lot where junk has been cleared to expose a small brick floor. A tall arch where a basketball net hangs has a sign proclaiming that JESUS ES AMOR. "I'm trying to make a place for the neighborhood kids to play."

I ask for five minutes of his time, and he agrees. We sit in the shade. Dominic Donald "Cano" (from *Chicano*) Espinosa is lean and bronzed, with two short, grizzled braids and a necklace of chunky turquoise.

After he was discharged from the army in 1970, Cano lived with his parents in the house until they died in the 1990s. He is the fifth eldest son out of thirteen siblings.

Cano says he participated in antiwar protests when he returned from Vietnam, and some of his military medals were rescinded as a result. He couldn't find a job and fell into drugs and drinking.

"My mother, she'd say, 'You were born with a bottle at your lips and you'll die with one in your mouth!'" Cano says. "I wanted to control my mind. I prayed for help. I think I was inspired by Jesus to start doing this because I needed a hobby."

He began building the split-level Castle with the towers in the backyard in 1980, using whatever he could find, whatever people gave him. Style-wise, he says, the Buddhist temples of Vietnam, Cambodia, and Thailand inspired him.

"That's the Palace." Cano points to the expanded house, then to the split-level structure. "And the Towers on the Castle, I call 'em the King and Queen. The little building on the side, that's the Rook. The shed with the casita [a small house] on top, that's the Knight's Horse. I'm gonna put a dragon on it, with hubcaps. Make it so that when the wind blows or you pull on a rope or something, it'll rattle! I want to put a gazebo on the top of the Palace, and put a winding stair all down the side."

He tells me the place is dedicated to his mother, Margarita, and a friend from the army who died. I gladly accept his invitation to see more of his home. The Palace's back stairs are really a steep ladder with ropes for hand rails. Cano stands at the top and gives me a hand up.

Past a storm door, a short hall opens into a small room painted deep blue. The windows are lined with open shelves filled with empty bottles (nonalcoholic). The furniture is shabby and comfortable. Pictures of family and religious figures, books, and knickknacks form a shrine against one wall.

"I like to sit here and think," Cano says as he takes a seat in a recliner.

A photo of Cano, a few years younger, is part of the shrine. He's bare-chested and wearing feathers and braids.

"My father was half Indian," he says. "My maternal grandmother was full-blooded Indian. The rest is Spanish. I like to dress up like a warrior for the town parades sometimes. I wear a leather breechcloth. I ride my horse."

Yep, he has a horse, stabled elsewhere. I ask him about the stories I've heard about his racing the local sightseeing steam train on his horse.

He grins and says, "The train people, you know they asked if I'd do it all the time, but I just like to do it once in a while. I like to entertain the kids. I won't take money for it. Wouldn't be right."

Cano says his Spanish side comes from a family that once owned one-tenth of Conejos County, where Antonito is located. He says his great-uncles were the notorious Espinosa brothers, the nineteenth century serial killers that Tom Tobin hunted down (see Local Heroes and Villains). What really inspired the brothers (and a cousin or nephew) to go on their murderous campaign has always been a mystery—except to Cano.

"Those brothers, they bushwhacked like ninety Anglos," Cano says. "They were hired guns. The Spanish landowners hired them to kill Anglos, scare 'em, keep 'em away from their lands."

The Espinosas' youngest brother, Francisco Espinosa,

he says, was murdered as an old man in the 1920s, allegedly by the local sheriff who changed courthouse documents to take his lands. He shows me Francisco's portrait. Cano's mother told him the story in whispers.

To be called an outsider artist means little to him. "It's all about Jesus," he says. "If I can get one, ten, a hundred people to be inspired enough by the Castle to do something to snap out of their negative lives, that's enough. We're all messengers of God."

As I leave, the setting sun turns the Castle's glittering towers into gold.

Sleeper House

Looking at it today, it's hard to believe this house once sat derelict after being used in a classic Woody Allen film. *Sleeper*, the 1973 comedy, is about a man awakened after being frozen for two hundred years. And who wouldn't want a fantastic, one-of-a-kind Modernist showplace like the *Sleeper* house, complete with an "Orgasmatron"?

Lots of people, apparently.

The house sits on Genesee Mountain overlooking Interstate 70, on the south side of the highway about fifteen miles west of Denver. It's clearly visible to thousands of motorists every day.

Because of its unique design by architect Charles Deaton, it's also known as the "Clam Shell House" and the "Flying Saucer House." Deaton called it the Sculptured House, and his family reportedly called it the Apple Turnover. He told *Art in America* magazine: "On Genesee Mountain I found a high point of land where I could stand and feel the great reaches of the Earth. I wanted the shape of it to sing an unencumbered song." Or put another way, "People aren't angular. So why should they live in rectangles?"

Deaton was a self-taught architect and industrial engineer-designer, born in 1921 in Clayton, New Mexico. He earned more than thirty patents for inventions ranging from board games to the first modern single-use sports stadium. His last patent in 1987 was for a dual baseball-football stadium with moveable seats.

Deaton originally meant to live here, in the only residential project he designed, but by 1963 he ran out of money and never completed it. Woody Allen is said to have paid $20,000 to use it in his film.

Deaton sold the house in 1988 to a financier. But after vandals broke every specially designed window in the place,

the new owner boarded it up and left it. Animals turned it into a de facto wildlife refuge.

In 1999, John Huggins, an Internet millionaire and native Coloradan, bought the house for about $1.3 million, then spent millions more to repair decades of neglect. The house was added to the National Register of Historic Places in 2004.

In 2006 Huggins sold the house, with a fraction of the original property, for $3.45 million. At the time of this writing, Michael Dunahay—the founder of a business called Vacation Solutions—owns it.

And the "Orgasmatron" from the film? It's really just a circular elevator that provides access to all the floors.

Colorado Chautauqua

When walking through the rolling grounds with its cluster of quaint, old buildings today, you may find it hard to tell that this historical landmark was part of a cultural revolution. The Chautauqua in Boulder, Colorado was one of hundreds of Chautauquas throughout the country that drew thousands of people every summer to live communally and become more enlightened. If that sounds new age, it isn't.

In 1872, the concept of a place where ordinary adults could spend the summer to be educated, entertained, fed, and housed in a beautiful outdoor setting was both radical and appealing—even the idea of summer camps for kids wasn't realized until 1881. This was an era when news, education, and professional entertainment could be in short supply outside larger towns.

John H. Vincent

The radicals who started this new movement were John Heyl Vincent, a Methodist minister, and Lewis Miller, an inventor. They organized a camp for Sunday school teachers on the shore of Lake Chautauqua in New York State. It later became known as the Chautauqua Assembly, and then the Chautauqua Institution.

What seems more like a retreat to us today became so popular that it was copied in locations across North America—although the organization, focus, and offerings varied. What people came for was an array of classes in everything from elocution to dance, mandolin playing to botany. Some Chautauquas offered home-study materials and lecturers that spoke on every topic of the day, plus entertainment from brass bands to vaudeville acts.

Living at a Chautauqua was communal. Families were the best repeat customers, and many returned to their own place year after year—they often went from a tent to a cabin that grew to a small house. But most people continued to share meals in the site's Dining Hall.

In its heyday of the 1920s, hundreds of independent Chautauquas were in operation. However, automobiles, movies, radio, and other inventions provided more options at more convenience. The Great Depression also made the experience less affordable for many, and fewer people came every year.

Eventually, most Chautauquas closed, the buildings were bulldozed, and the land was converted to other uses. A revival of some aspects of the old-time Chautauqua Institution has occurred around the country in recent years; however, four have stayed in continuous operation, including the Colorado Chautauqua in Boulder. Opened in 1898, it operates year-round today, with the old auditorium still hosting a range of entertainment, the former Academic Hall acting as headquarters, and the original Dining Hall operating as a restaurant. An Arts and Crafts–style Community House was added in 1918 for smaller events, and it remains a popular gathering place.

The park surrounding the place is still intact and includes a small neighborhood of old cottages, some of them kept available for short- to long-term rentals.

The Tao of Community

About seventy miles south of Manitou Springs is Custer County, a region known today for cattle, horses, and "dry farming," a technique of raising crops without irrigation in areas with less than twenty inches of annual rainfall. It remains the second least-populated county in Colorado, making it a good place for a Taoist hermitage, established by Chinese philosopher and classics translator Gia-fu Feng.

Gia-fu, as he's usually known, was born into an upper-class family in Shanghai in 1919 and came to the United States in 1947 to study for a master's degree in international finance. The communist takeover of China and the outbreak of the Korean War kept him here, and he decided to hit the road and see America. His wanderings eventually brought him to the West Coast, where he connected with writer Jack Kerouac and the other "Dharma Bums" who founded the Beat movement.

Gia-fu was bearded and sometimes spoke "crazy wisdom," so he was tagged as a guru and became well known within 1960s counterculture circles. He was part of the development of the Esalen community in California. He studied with and translated classic Chinese works for the philosopher Alan Watts at the American Academy of Asian Studies in San Francisco.

Gia-fu started a center based on Taoist principles in California's Santa Cruz Mountains called Stillpoint. In 1972, Gia-fu, along with his partner, Jane English, and the community moved into a house near Pikes Peak, which became the transplanted Stillpoint.

Gia-fu added to the local color when he became known as the Chinese master who would hike along the Pikes Peak Cog Railway track every day. It was a form of meditation for him, but the area was too populated to provide the solitude he wanted. In 1977, he found another place: a 160-acre farm near the town of Wetmore in Custer County.

It was mixed terrain—a mountain property with a meadow, a forest, and the Middle Hardscrabble Creek running through it. The property had a barn and a shed but no other shelter, so Gia-fu and friends found materials to build cabins by tearing down an old two-story military administration building on a closed air force base.

Stillpoint was incorporated as a nonprofit religious organization and became known as Stillpoint Hermitage. The idea of a hermitage and hostel appealed to many Europeans who made the pilgrimage over the years that Gia-fu lived there.

Gia-fu died in 1985 of emphysema. His grave is on the property, marked by a marble headstone and a small figure of a laughing Taoist man with a gong. He left his share of the property to Margaret Susan Wilson, a friend and legal advisor. She died in 1991 and left it to her sister, Carol A. Wilson.

Stillpoint: A Center for the Humanities & Community was incorporated in 1995. As Carol explains it, a board of former Stillpointers and friends "sponsors poetry and prose readings, musical programs, conversations, and other forums for experiencing and understanding the meaning of community in our lives."

Carol's struggle to keep the property whole and protected from development is related in her book, *Still Point of the Turning World: The Life of Gia-fu Feng.*

The property became forever preserved through a conservation easement with the San Isabel Land Protection Trust, and about twenty cabins and the barn—renovated as living and meeting quarters—are allowed to remain. Their condition ranges from near-ruin to restored to original condition, and each reflects the personality of its builder and has its own name.

The Dragon Cabin, for instance, has a dragon painted on a back window. Gia-fu's weathered-wood, two-hundred-square-foot cabin is designed to resemble the huts of Taoist hermits in China. People have adopted individual cabins to restore and maintain them. School groups, organizations, and individuals put in repair and restoration work on the grounds when they come for a stay.

For more information, contact Carol Wilson at cwilson387@earthlink.net.

Individuals put in repair work when they come for a stay.

Guffey's Historical Hostels

Yes, Guffey is the place with the feline mayor, Monster, and the annual July 4 Chicken Fly in the Local Legends chapter. However, the habitats owned by Monster's second-in-command, Bill Soux, deserve their own mention.

Guffey, located along Colorado Highway 9 at mile marker 21, is tiny, with a population of about twenty-two year-round. It's between Cañon City and Cripple Creek. Guffey is also on a scenic road through beautiful mountain country and a favorite stop for those traveling the Adventure Cycling Association's TransAmerica Bicycle Trail about a mile away.

Bill Soux has taken some of the remains of this former mining town and turned it into part community center, part quirky lodging. His small cabins mostly date from the 1880s and are spruced up with salvage and imagination. The cabins have electricity but no running water except for the hot showers, although plenty of bottled water is provided for washing and drinking.

Some of the cabins are just big enough for fold-down bunks; others are roomier and fancier. The bathing and toilet facilities are on the primitive side but clean and as whimsical as the rest of the lodgings.

Everything has an eclectic, Old West charm. Other interesting stuff to look at is plentiful, such as Soux's own art works, his collections of everything—a lot of which is for sale—and his string of vintage vehicles (don't let their rather derelict exteriors fool you).

Guffey has a post office, a library, a restaurant or two, and a bar, and a number of artists live in the area. It offers the only services around for twenty-five miles, as Soux's Web site states (www.guffeycolorado.com), but while Soux maintains a repair garage, there's no gas station, so fill up if you're going to drive there. And call ahead if you're thinking of an overnight stay: (719) 689-3291.

Bishop's Castle

Not many areas of Colorado can be called lush, but CO-165 west off Interstate 25 near Pueblo passes through rolling countryside that is unbelievably idyllic. This is the road that passes through Rye.

Fifteen miles past Rye, deep in the lovely San Isabel National Forest, a building out of a fairy tale appears. It's several stories high, made of stone and extraordinary ornamental ironwork, with turrets piercing the sky, and a dragon's head perched like a ship's figurehead at the edge of the metal-and-glass roof.

All around the place is evidence of ongoing building, including the fellow with the thick shock of silver hair who is working on a Bobcat as I trudge toward him.

Jim Bishop is a hardy man with piercing eyes and strong opinions. He can launch into diatribes against the government, "the Infernal Revenue Service," and various state officials at the drop of a hammer. Visitors can read various large signs posted around the place with his hand-lettered warnings, screeds, and requests for donations.

Bishop is a kinder, gentler man when he's just talking about the Castle and his plans for what he's going to build next. The way he outlines things, you can see they could easily become as much reality as what he's done so far.

"I'm gonna put an inner and an outer wall around the place," he tells me. "With rooms inside that people will be able to stay in, hold workshops, whatever. A gatehouse over there. A drawbridge with a moat. A dungeon."

It all started more than forty years ago with his parents'

mountain acreage and the desire to build a sturdy cabin. "We didn't have much money for materials so I used the stone that was around here," he says. "It was just a one-room cottage, but then everybody kept saying how much it looked like a castle. And I thought that if I could make something that small and simple look like a castle, what could I do if I built a real one?"

Bishop had dropped out of high school to work in his father's metal shop, and learned the art of ornamental ironwork, which he put to good use along with the painstaking masonry. Despite initial official resistance to his appropriation of local stones, the project just kept getting bigger.

"I read a lot of *National Geographic*," he says. "I loved those pictures of cathedrals in Europe. And castles, of course. I like skyscrapers, too."

"I had the idea I could turn this into something that would make this into a livelihood. It hasn't happened yet, but I'm gonna see how far I can get with it before I get too old to work any more."

He does it all himself. It's a point of pride—a lasting monument to one's man's vision, talent, and grit.

Bishop, his wife, and their four kids never lived in the castle. They have an old house in Pueblo. His wife has a job in Pueblo, Bishop does his commercial ironwork there, and it's where he can "go get cleaned up, take a break from all this."

"It's a balancing act. I kind of have the best of both worlds. 'Specially now that I have my sovereignty." Sovereignty apparently has to do with learning how to work within the system and still get what he wants, mostly. Something about getting his enterprise declared a nonprofit charity.

A cabinlike building nearby is Bishop's gift shop and mountain home. Someday, he'd like to install a hot tub and an elevator. Maybe his wife would spend more time with him here if he did, he says.

She's supportive of his dream castle, but she doesn't like to come out much. Their son Roy died here, he says, looking away. Roy was four when a tree stump on the

property fell on him, decades ago. It's obviously still an aching wound for the family.

"We still have his ashes," Bishop says. "We need to do something with 'em, I guess. We don't have closure. I named the back tower on the Castle after Roy. I'll finish it someday."

Their other kids bring their children out on weekends now. They have cookouts and hang ropes from the arches of the Castle so the grandkids can swing.

Bishop will talk to groups, classrooms, and clubs. About the Castle? Politics?

"Well, I'll go speak about anything people are interested in," says Bishop. "If I didn't, people would say, 'That guy's in love with himself.'"

He's opened his beloved Castle to other people's celebrations. At last count, he says, there've been 110 weddings, several marriage-vow-renewal ceremonies and even a few funerals held there. "Maybe there'll be a gay wedding someday, who knows," he says.

There's definitely a spiritual aspect to the Castle. The great hall on the second floor has the soaring ceiling of a Gothic church, and the stained glass windowpanes bear the names of people in memoriam. Bishop says he's a Christian.

What does he want people to take away with their visit to his Castle? "I hope I've inspired them to try to do things with their hands. Create things, make things," Bishop says. "And freedom; I want them to appreciate the freedom we have to come and go."

And if his message is blurred by the perception that he's, well, just weird?

"Some people just can't be inspired," he says. "And I'd rather be a nutter than be normal. It's no fun being normal." For more information or to rent the Castle for an event, call (719) 485-3040.

Betty and Rolland's Place

You'd have to have a reason (and an invitation) to visit Betty Wall and Rolland Fischer, or you might never see their off-the-grid, Chinese-inspired, camp-style homestead hidden in the mountains above Boulder. It's located off Lost Angel Road in the small, informal community known as Sugarloaf.

All you might see initially are a couple of unusual red-tile roofs because the homestead is built on a slope, just out of sight from the road. One of the roofs has a small tower on it with a clock on each of its four sides.

The generally Asian look of the buildings has nothing to do with Wall's Chinese ancestry. Fischer was inspired by a story in an issue of *Scientific American* about traditional Chinese architecture.

Fischer grew up in Boulder in the 1950s when, he says, building one's own home was nothing unusual. Fischer bought the patch of land with an aspen grove and an artesian spring in 1974.

"I like the tile-covered curved roof," he says. "It's harder to do, and it makes absolutely no sense. But it's memorable and has aesthetic appeal. I was fighting what I saw happening down in Boulder—all those people coming in off the plane and flooding the place with ticky-tacky sameness. I wanted a greater standard. I wanted deeper roots."

He decided to stay small, to avoid having to get a mortgage, and to split the home into separate little buildings to avoid partitions that take away living space.

The couple's main living space is a cottage with a guest room upstairs. Separate buildings are the bathhouse/laundry/sleeping loft, the outhouse, Wall's massage studio, Fischer's workshop, his watchmaking shop with the clock tower, and a garden shed.

Wall was a biologist from Massachusetts who met Fischer in 1980 when she came to a Boulder Rolfing school to learn a new trade. Fischer was in the process of building while he lived at a neighbor's place. At first, Wall didn't know what to make of this proposed homestead.

"It was so different," she says. "But I've always enjoyed camping and dreamed of living in a little cabin in the woods, so it wasn't hard to make the move."

The site is on a fairly steep slope, not usually the most ideal building location. However, with an artesian well on the place, which Fischer dug himself, he was able to put a cistern with a solar pump above the main property so that there would be enough water pressure, and water would flow to the appropriate areas easily via "gravitational plumbing."

Solar panels provide all the electricity they need for lighting, their computer and printer, and an old 1930s wringer washer. A septic system takes care of sewage, and propane gas is brought in for heating and cooking. The refrigerator is actually an outdoor cellar, built into the side of a hill.

Wall spent the summer of 1981 putting in raised beds and terraced gardens for vegetables. She built all the stone retaining walls herself. She had never done this type of work before, but "Fischer explained how to do it so well."

And then on July 9, 1989, during a record heat wave with no rain, someone apparently tossed a cigarette stub into dry brush. A stiff wind blew fire up Black Tiger Gulch and across Sugarloaf Mountain, where the couple lives. No one was killed, but within six hours, forty-four houses and other structures were consumed, including about everything the couple had except for the small stone building with the clock tower.

That's where they lived for a time. They had no insurance, and they were determined not to go into debt to rebuild. Fischer turned his equipment and skills as a road grader and excavator to help his neighbors clear their property of charred buildings. As he did, he noticed a difference in smell: the burned wood in older homes smelled of "temple incense"; the "plastics, plywood, timbers made of modern, treated wood to repel insects, all the stuff full of formaldehyde and glues" used in the newer homes smelled like "toxic waste."

It was clear which materials would provide a healthier environment, and Fischer's new rule for rebuilding was to use nothing that smelled bad when burned. He salvaged tiles from condemned buildings to replace those lost in the fire. He made his floors from heartwood cypress planks reclaimed from old vats.

Of course, they appreciate even more what they have today and the impermanence that comes with it. Fischer said something else was also learned.

"It's not a totally bad thing to be totally dispossessed, if you're determined not to be a victim and to do better. For the rest of your life you'll have a reference to draw strength from."

Boulder Kinetics Race

The Boulder Kinetics Race is a springtime tradition that hit the ground running, as it were, in 1980. It gained its inspiration from the late, great American sculptor and gallery owner Hobart Brown, who in 1969 started Kinetic Sculpture Racing in Ferndale, California. What started as drag-race challenge between a small group of local artists turned into annual event involving a forty-two-mile course over multiple kinds of terrain between Arcata and Ferndale. Ten years later, Rick Hartner, a visiting Boulder firefighter, witnessed the racing sculptures and got the itch to start such an event back home.

In a search of sponsors, Hartner looked up regional Coors beer distributor Ray Imel. Coincidentally, Imel had read a recent *Smithsonian* magazine article on the California Kinetics Race, so he was up to speed by the time Hartner pitched his idea. They weren't able to acquire a beer license in time, but they did obtain radio station KADE/KBCO as cosponsor and by the race day, May 3, 1980, they had sixty entries.

The rules for kinetics entries were simple: All sculptures had to be capable of traveling by land or water, powered only by their riders. Each vehicle required working brakes, life preservers, and all other necessary equipment to be kept aboard the craft.

The event grew bigger and rowdier every year with a new set of human-powered sculptures to wow the crowds each time. The Kinetics Parade was instituted in downtown Boulder on the Saturday before the race, so the vehicles could strut their stuff in advance. Pancake breakfasts were held, the Elks sold the Coors, concessionaires sold everything else, and TV news helicopters buzzed around Boulder Reservoir constantly. For a while, a kinetic hot-air balloon rally was also held, with twenty or more balloons (some with unusual shapes such as a

shopping cart) on the morning of the Kinetics Race.

People came out in droves, bringing everything needed for a beach party, including only the minimal amount of clothing. As Ray Imel recalls, "Suntan lotion was plentiful, and if you brought binoculars you would see several acres of bare skin."

"Only in Boulder!" chortled all the people who didn't know Kinetics Races were in several cities by now. As many as forty-five thousand people attended; what kept them coming were the incredible inventions, many of them by repeat contestants who wanted to outdo their previous years' entries.

Award categories also increased. It wasn't enough now to complete the race in the fastest time or to have the best costumes, engineering, style, or sculpture. The "What Were They Thinking" award was added for a design better in concept than realization, a "What's in a Name" award for a sculpture title such as Robin Hood: Men in Kite, and an award for the best bribe given to the judges (yes, that's encouraged).

However, beyond all this cleverness and innovation, the surrounding environment suffered. Expenses mounted.

Parking fees and space were issues, and so was the traffic jam at the end of the event. Drunkenness and acting up became more of a problem. Insurance became an issue, and simply keeping up with organizing the race became a year-round job. In November 2007, KBCO discountinued its sponsorship, and other sponsors faded.

Fans of the race banded together as the Boulder Kineticists and vowed to keep the tradition alive. As organizer Paul Bailey explained, "It's tradition, it's creative, it's goofy. It keeps Boulder interesting."

The newly built Twenty-Ninth Street mall agreed to allow the race to take place in a parking lot. Some new sponsors came up with basic funds, local musicians provided live music, and Ray Imel came back as one of the judges. The race took off again on May 3, 2008.

Though the event didn't draw thousands of spectators as it had in the past, its new organizers know that sometimes less is more, that the creativity and fun of these sculptured vehicles are what drew people together in the first place, and sometimes people have to go in reverse to make real progress.

The Creations of Charles Haertling

A number of buildings in Colorado—especially in the town of Boulder—are so unusual they're nearly impossible to forget once seen. People who brake, gawk, and marvel at these buildings may not know one architect is behind them all—Charles Haertling.

Haertling earned his architecture degree in 1952 from Washington University in St. Louis, Missouri, and moved to Boulder the next year to teach at the University of Colorado. He opened his own practice in 1957.

Haertling's buildings swoop, crouch, hug, and cling to their environments as if arrested in motion only for a moment. They have curves where you might expect angles and angles where you might expect curves. They may offer open-armed welcome or throw up an imposing protectiveness like a pulled-up drawbridge.

The designs also depend on the location, which frequently is somewhere with a great view that should be maximized but also has factors such as privacy, steep slopes, deep snowfalls, wildfire danger, or fierce winds that require consideration.

Haertling's work extended beyond private homes. As a member of the Boulder City Council from 1967 to 1973, he was a driving force in establishing the city's famed open space around the town and the greenbelts within it. The local Carnegie Library houses his drawings, sketches, and photographs, and the Haertling Foundation preserves his memory and works. The city-owned Charles A. Haertling Sculpture Park downtown features a diverse number of works by various artists.

Too many of his buildings have been altered over the years, but several can still be seen with their original design, at least as exteriors. Haertling died of a brain tumor in 1984, but one of his sons, Boulder filmmaker Joel Haertling, has a Web site (www.atomix.com) with more than fifty of his designs featured. Each building is named after the client who commissioned it. We've included a short house tour of his work here for you.

The Brenton House (1969)

Probably the most famous Haertling design is this house located in Boulder, and better known as the Mushroom House. It was featured in the same 1973 Woody Allen film as the Sculpture House on Genesee Mountain.

Dr. R. Stanley Brenton and his wife, Barbara, a pianist, commissioned the design of this home for a slope that was exposed to Colorado's famously ferocious winds.

Haertling designed what he called a uterus house, says Barbara. Like a womb, its curves are meant to feel warm and protective with no angles inside or out.

It was Boulder's first foam house—a steel-frame grid supported by cinderblocks and covered with polyurethane foam protected by weather coating. The design was so unusual, some neighbors protested to the city that it would become a traffic-stopping nuisance, and Haertling lowered the height to make it less obvious.

In front, the house has the famous mushroom shape. The top floor held Dr. Brenton's study. The back looks completely different with a main level that stretches across five podlike structures that frame the great views. Haertling said the pods reminded him of the barnacles he had to scrape off ships during his stint in the navy.

The Brentons raised four daughters here. Barbara says, "It very much still works for us. It's inviting and comfortable, and we've never had any problems with it. The strongest wind just flows over and around it."

The Volsky House (1964)

Haertling designed the 1964 Volsky House early in his career for a university professor. The building is on a steep hillside, with much of the back end sunk into the ground and the front jutting out like a ship's prow. It has a circular floor plan, an interior garden, and a 360-degree view from the living room.

According to *Dwell* magazine's retrospective on Haertling in its July–August 2008 issue, one of the irked neighbors who protested the design's "sheer grossness" was George Gamow, the scientist who helped develop the big bang theory. In 1966, a year after the house was finished, *Life* magazine had a six-page spread on the structure.

The Noble House (1958)

This is another striking house in Boulder, built on a lot on which Haertling had to incorporate a stream and several trees. The result was something he described as "a wigwam structure using structural form to economic advantage." The roof, he said, was composed of identical "leaves," which kept building costs down because they also acted as walls, none of which are straight. Everything tends to be pointed and triangular—windows, beams, staircase, fireplace, and even the driveway. It's been called the Tee Pee House, Umbrella Home, the Pyramids, and even the Bra. When it was finished, the *Denver Post* called it the Space Craft Home.

The Warburton House (1963)

Gold Hill is home to this house, built at a nine-thousand-foot elevation with humongous winds but great views. The clients had a budget of less than $25,000. Haertling took inspiration from a yucca pod and designed a low, curved, loglike building sunk a bit into the ground to reduce wind exposure. He put a turret on the top where the clients could enjoy the view. The spiked ends on the turret act as lightning rods.

St. Stephen's Lutheran Church (1964)

Located in Northglenn, a suburb of Denver, this church has been called the Flying Nun Church after the 1967 television comedy starring Sally Field as a nun whose distinctive headgear made her able to fly. It's situated on a high, exposed lot and has a roof with swooping curves that end in gigantic, tusklike peaks.

The Denver Hearse Association

Car clubs are nothing new, and plenty celebrate all things cool in automobiles. But how many clubs do you know of that are into hearses—and not just for that final road trip?

In Colorado, there's only one club for those who love hearses—the funeral vehicle of the modern Western world. Jeff Brown and Zachary Byron Helm started The Denver Hearse Association in 1996. Brown owns a 1973 Cadillac Superior 3-Way named Charlotte and a nameless 1960 Cadillac Superior Combo; Helm owns a 1964 Oldsmobile hearse called Abby, a 1973 Cadillac Superior known as Savannah, and a 1975 Cadillac S&S that goes by Alexi. Yes, most of their hearses have names.

A gallery of members and their prized vehicles can be found on their Web site, www.hearseclub.com, and two members graciously consented to tell *Weird Colorado* about their prized rides.

Helen the Hearse

Traveler Willowyn Hawk's first hearse was a 1975 Cadillac Superior. It wasn't running, and a previous owner who planned to make a limousine out of it had gutted the interior, but it provided valuable experience for Hawk.

"I bought it for $1,000, fixed it up and got it working, and sold it for the same amount," says Hawk. "Then I bought a 1960 Cadillac Superior from a gentleman out in Yoder who kept it in his barn. He wasn't really a hearse fan; he just used it to haul his motorcycle to Sturgis [South Dakota]. He was the third owner, and it's supposed to have originally been used by the Evergreen Mortuary.

"It was a steal at four grand 'cause it was in really good shape; running well with the original casket lifter still operational and all. Just needed a paint spruce-up and some interior work. And it's a mountain model, which means it has a leveler, too. Fifty-year-old hydraulics, and it still keeps the interior level when you're driving on a slant!

"I called my first hearse Niobe, but this one is Helen. My mom and I decided on it. All cars have a personality once they reach a certain age, and this one is just classy."

Hawk at this writing is a part-time bartender and full-time anthropology student at Arapahoe Community College with a view to studying mortuary science, possibly for a career in forensics. It's less a choice about indulging morbid interests and more about being "Right here and now, helping people."

Hawk keeps Helen at a friend's garage, and has no desire to trick the hearse out. "You don't mess with a Helen. The

holy grail of vintage hearses is a 1959 Cadillac, and even when they're inoperable, they'll sell for at least ten grand. Helen is as close as I'll get for the money. I'd like to give her a new paint job, redo the old leather seats that have dry rot; that's about it. All I want to do is keep a great old car from heading to the junkyard."

About the only challenge with Helen is finding a parking spot. It isn't easy for a "whole lotta classic car twenty-one feet long," so it's not as if Hawk can do much errand running.

"I can park at the far end of a supermarket parking lot, but by the time I get back there's a crowd of cars parked around her, like a magnet. And I've gotta be so careful getting out of there 'cause the newer cars are like plastic."

However, Hawk does manage to take Helen out for more than parades and car shows.

"She's wonderfully convenient for camping. She fits in a RV parking spot just fine, and I can throw a queen-size mattress over the casket rollers for sleeping."

Helen has a fifteen-gallon gas tank and gets eight to twelve miles per gallon, "fifteen on the highway, after some tinkering." She can move faster than 85 miles per hour, but Hawk won't push her. "She starts to float, and that makes me nervous."

Flora and Selena

Ron Walker of Lakewood says he always wanted a hearse but never found his dream vehicle until he saw one parked at a Sonic Drive-In with a FOR SALE sign.

It was 2002, and Walker was then driving a 1967 MG. He sold it to Jeff Brown, co-founder of The Denver Hearse Association, and got the hearse in exchange—a 1968 Pontiac Bonneville Superior Coach.

Walker did a lot of mechanical restoration, from a new engine to transmission, brakes, and springs. Then, he found another hearse for sale, a 1971 model.

"This one had all the glass broken, the interior stripped and all," says Walker. "I got it for $200."

Walker and his girlfriend, Hali Sechrist, separated the vehicle in two and made a utility/camping trailer out of the back end.

"I put in an air compressor and a generator for my work," says Walker, who works as a boiler installer and handyman. "It has the original casket lifter, and I wanted to put an air mattress in there for camping but I've never gotten around to camping in it, yet."

He named the full hearse Flora after his paternal grandmother, and the trailer Selena after his mom's mom. Walker has taken the pair to several car shows and Denver Hearse gatherings.

"Everybody who knows me says these vehicles fit my personality," says Walker. "I like being somewhat unique, not a part of a crowd. And it's just a pleasure to drive. Heads turn, and I get ninety-nine thumbs-up kind of reactions to every one flip of the bird."

Roadside Attractions and Oddities

Colorado abounds in human-created tourist attractions that are off the beaten track, not always ballyhooed by the local chamber of commerce or visitors' center, and often nothing like what you might imagine.

Many people who have lived their whole lives in Colorado have often heard of only two or three of them. These attractions usually don't advertise much, and may not have a Web site. They're tucked in odd corners of the state, on private property, or off country roads.

They may have faded into the background of forgotten history after a period of fame and glory—or were always known only by word of mouth. Behind each one is a story and people who are remarkable in very different ways, particularly among the caretakers of these odd establishments. These folks like their niches, and they like talking to people about them.

Whether they were started as someone's private whimsy, an attempt to preserve history, or a flat-out desire to reap the rewards of tourism, these attractions have at least one common denominator . . . they're truly unique and special. They can sometimes be hard to find for yourself (the state of Colorado discourages billboards and other signage on open roads), so we've assembled some of our favorites here. So sit back and enjoy the ride!

SWEET SKIN, symbolic of purification. Hot Springs bubbling from the mountain side heavily laden with four of the most essential body elements—Sodium for digestion; Potassium for energy; Magnesium for sweetness; Calcium for Bone and Nerve, then Carbon Dioxide for elimination and purification.

RADIO-ACTIVE
HOT SPRINGS
Ouray, Colo.
Natures Health Resort
Owned by C.W. KENT
of the ELECTREAT MFG. CO.

SWEET SKIN

rampa Jerry's Clown Museum

Coulrophobia is a fear of clowns, often triggered in childhood by some trauma associated with these jolly folks. Jerry Eder of Grampa Jerry's Clown Museum in Arriba obviously doesn't have that phobia, although he does admit that he has a clown-related "disease." In his case, it was triggered by a penchant for putting on clown makeup for children's birthday parties and small-town parades.

"I'm a hambone, not a clown," he says. But when he sold his commodities brokerage business in 1987,

Eder needed a hobby and clowns filled the gap. Friends started making and giving him clown objects, and pretty soon his collection ballooned. He reckons he's got about four thousand items on display in an old building on his property, and about as many more packed away. Eder rotates things occasionally, especially as he's always getting more clown-related items from friends, family, and complete strangers who have heard about his museum.

"We're looking to put up another building for more stuff," he says.

"The stuff" is organized by category—music boxes, whiskey decanters, cookie jars, books, banks, you name it. His oldest items are clown dolls dating from the 1920s and 1930s, and the oddest is a clown made from a cow's hairball. (Eder had a friend who worked in a slaughterhouse.)

In a town with a population of only about 222, it's pretty amazing that Grampa Jerry's is actually one of two museums here. The Arriba (locally pronounced *AIR-a bah*) Museum has to be one of the world's smallest civic attractions. It's a teensy cabin built around 1900 and full of local history, located in the town's civic park on Lincoln Avenue.

Grampa Jerry's Clown Museum is conveniently nearby, which makes a stop off I-70 even more worthwhile. Word of mouth attracts even international visitors who have a personal or professional interest in clowns. And Eder regularly gets tour bus groups and gaggles of schoolchildren.

So he keeps the area around his museum park-like and neat, with playground equipment. And occasionally he breaks out glasses of iced tea or lemonade for a group if given sufficient advance notice. He's nearly always around, but wise visitors give him a call before showing up.

As with most diseases, there is some risk of infection if you visit Eder's clown collection.

"Hopefully," says Eder. "It's the kind that will add years to your life."

For more information, call (719) 768-3257.

Prison Museum

"Cañon City—Prison Capital of the World"—
not exactly the kind of advertising a chamber of commerce
likes, but there it is. With the addition of the Colorado State
Penitentiary II, Cañon City holds nine prisons.

This used to be an isolated site in rugged country, a plus
to deter and thwart prison escapes, but the town has slowly
grown up around it. The Museum of Colorado Prisons is
housed on the grounds of the first prison, dating back to
1871. (You can still see the old, handsome, but forbidding
stone walls and towers peeking behind the grim modern
buildings.)

Enclosed by a tall fence, the museum looks like
someone's large cottage, maybe a warden's, raised so that you
enter it at the top of a flight of stairs. Built in 1935, it used
to house up to forty-two women prisoners. It had a staff of
mostly women, a first for the prison system, but it moved
elsewhere in 1968. Then the place housed men in protective
custody for the next decade, and then became the Museum
of Colorado Prisons in 1988.

Outside on the neatly maintained grass is a defunct gas
chamber sitting in its own shed. Inside is a history of the
prison, from its debut as the Colorado Territorial Penitentiary
to the modern era when the Colorado Territorial Correctional
Facility was built on the same grounds.

The two women taking admission are the kind of
savvy people a researcher hopes to meet. Sarah McCullar
has worked several summers at the museum, and Victoria
Newman is a seasoned pro (thirteen years as a correctional
officer before going over to the tourism side) who has
written a couple of books—*Prisons of Canon City* and
Woodpecker Hill (about the old prison cemetery).

The main floor opens into a single-wide corridor
flanked with small cells. Each cell is open and has some
displays of a specific theme, including famous and infamous
prisoners (Alfred Packer did time in the men's prison),
executions, corporal punishment, prisoners' crafts, past
wardens, riots, officers killed in the line of duty, and more.

Among many other things, here is a display of
"disciplinary paraphernalia" that is scarier then the array of
inmates' confiscated weapons and other contraband, the
noose from the last prison execution by hanging (in 1933),
and the Old Grey Mare, over which a prisoner was folded to
be whipped.

The mannequins in vintage prisoner or guard uniform
tend to look rather grotesque. One has a beard and
resembles Fidel Castro. Another is of a female guard, a
dummy from the 1950s or so with an immaculate coif,
exaggerated eyelashes, and bright red lipstick and nail polish.
(Nobody's gonna call *her* "butch"!)

There is a cell devoted to movies made at the prison—
The Big House (1930), *Canon City* (1948), *In Cold Blood*
(1967), *Scarecrow* (1973), and *The Women of San Quentin*
(1983).

The museum is a fascinating revelation about law and
order in quite a different era. It's hard to believe the youngest
inmate was an eleven-year-old boy, or that misbehaving
prisoners were flogged with wet lashes until at least the
1940s. Or that dead prisoners were routinely sent to Denver
for medical research until the 1960s.

Downstairs are the old facilities for the laundry, medical
clinic, dining hall, and the prisoners' law library.

Back upstairs I ask the women about unusual
phenomena.

"I've heard my name whispered twice when I was alone,"
says McCullar. "Spooky. If I have to go downstairs, I yell,
'Hello!' I'll even sing or whistle."

"I've heard my name called," says Newman. "I thought
my daughter had dropped by and was calling me. She
wasn't."

Cell doors have been known to slam on their own, though they are extremely heavy and impossible for a draft to move in the slightest—and furthermore, they've been painted open. The cash register has been known to slam shut by itself, too.

The prison has become a popular place for ghost-hunting groups in recent years. And not just during the last two weekends in October, when the museum dresses up as the Haunted Prison Museum.

"Once a group took out the lightbulbs in the exit sign so it would be darker for filming," says McCullar. "I saw them put those bulbs aside, and that sign went on later, with the bulbs back in, all by itself."

"We've heard the recordings, the EVPs, they call 'em," says Newman. "One was 'Release me,' repeated three times. There was, 'Hey, you!' which is exactly how prisoners call guards, and another was someone saying, 'The cops came and got me.'"

Even if they're not precisely comfortable there, McCullar and Newman are not scared away. Perhaps that's an attitude shared with the spirits of former denizens.

For information, see www.prisonmuseum.org.

Buggin' Out at John May Museum

You get an idea of what's in store at the turnoff to this museum in Colorado Springs. There's a giant scale replica—ten feet tall, sixteen feet long—of a West Indies Hercules beetle. His name, says one of his caretakers, is Herkimer. The closer you get, the more Herkimer looks like something from an old sci-fi movie.

If you experience any significant unease around the usual bitty creepy-crawlies, this place could seriously haunt you. It could also enchant you.

Who knew that African locusts had sherbet-colored wings that Pre-Raphaelite fairies would envy? Or that there were Brazilian butterflies so luminescent the reflection off their wings could be seen for miles? Or that a collection of vibrant little beetles could look like fantastic brooches in a jeweler's case?

The museum is home to more than 100,000 preserved invertebrates (a group that includes worms, insects, arachnids, and sea creatures). Only about 8,000 can be displayed at any one time, so the exhibits are rotated periodically.

What you do get to see is the best of the best in terms of biggest, strangest, and most rare bugs. There's also a trio of tall tiki figures at the entrance to the May museum's exhibit hall.

"My father carved those himself," says Lynda Senko, a retired teacher and one of the daughters of John May, who built the museum in 1947. "We had a second museum in the 1950s in Florida, but it didn't last long. The humidity was bad for the insects."

It was John May's English grandfather Edward who start a family tradition when he acquired insect specimens for the British Museum in the late nineteenth century.

His son, James, and grandson John in 1929 began a tradition of exhibiting tropical insects at shows all over North America. They settled in Colorado Springs in 1942, and in 1947 they built a permanent home for the collection on the family ranch with an RV campground next door. James May died in 1956; John died in 2007 at the age of ninety-one.

John's three daughters and a granddaughter run the museum today. They're the ones who dubbed the giant model insect "Herkimer."

Admission into the John May Museum also gets you into a set of mobile homes nearby that houses his collection of videos, print articles, and photos about space exploration. For more information, see www.maymuseum-camp-rvpark.com.

Brothel Museum

Its actual name is The Old Homestead House Museum, which gives the impression of it being one of Colorado's living-history attractions devoted to wholesome pioneers or staid Victorians. But there was never anything wholesome or staid about it—or its original proprietor.

Originally from Indiana, "Pearl de Vere" sashayed into the boomtown of Cripple Creek in 1893 after a short but very successful career in Denver as "Mrs. Martin." She was thirty-one, beautiful, red-haired, and one heck of a businesswoman. She plowed her earnings into a small frame house and a stable of "soiled doves" said to be the most beautiful of the red light district.

De Vere married a mill owner in 1895, but when a fire destroyed most of the businesses in Cripple Creek shortly thereafter, the husband had to accept work in Mexico. Plucky Pearl stayed behind to rebuild.

By 1896, de Vere presided over the most elegant establishment in town. The Old Homestead was furnished in the finest Victorian style with costly wallpaper from Paris in the parlor (a Parisian wallpaper hanger came just to install it),

crystal chandeliers, leather-topped gaming tables—the works.

The most modern conveniences of the period were there: electricity, telephone, intercom, and two bathrooms. There were only four working girls, chosen for classiness as well as looks, and examined by a doctor every month. They were well paid, and de Vere, by all accounts, was a good boss.

Patrons couldn't just drop into The Old Homestead, they had to make appointments. First-timers had to have letters of recommendation. De Vere wanted to be sure her clients could cough up the then huge sum of $250 for an evening's entertainment.

After a particularly spectacular private party on June 4, 1897, a tipsy de Vere took some morphine to help her sleep and never woke up. When her family discovered de Vere hadn't really been making a living as a dressmaker, it disowned any responsibility for her burial. More shocking to her friends, the high-living madam left no money. An unknown Denver admirer sent $1,000 and instructions that she be buried in the fabulous Parisian gown she died in.

Pearl de Vere's grave is in Mt. Pisgah Cemetery on the town's outskirts. Tourism revived interest in de Vere's story, and her shabby old wooden grave marker was replaced with a heart-shaped marble tombstone in the 1930s. (The original marker is at the Cripple Creek History Museum.)

The Old Homestead operated as a bordello until 1917, became a boardinghouse, and then an illicit casino. In 1958, the place got a massive overhaul and reopened as a museum with many of the original establishment's items still intact, miraculously preserved in storage all those years at the house.

It's the only "parlor house" of Cripple Creek's red light district to survive, and its two stories are dwarfed by the larger brick buildings that went up in Cripple Creek's revival. The exterior style is simple—discreet, you might say. The Parisian wallpaper has also survived pretty well. So have the butler's uniform and a small number of elegant women's outfits, from a fur coat to nightgowns. The overall effect of the furnishings is very elegant and quite tasteful.

There are a few photographs of some of the girls, but only a colored painting of Pearl de Vere and her sister as very young women. The rooms are surprisingly small—entertaining must have been intimate in more ways than one. Madam Pearl had the smallest bedroom, although it is situated so she could keep an eye on things.

One of the few things that hint of the house's shady past is the Viewing Room. It's a bathroom off the second floor with a window on the hall. Here a girl could step inside and strip so as to help a gent decide if she was to be his companion for the evening. The window was hidden by wallpaper long ago, but tour guides are sure to point it out.

One of those guides is Lodie Hern. She and her late husband, Harold, purchased the building in 1968, ten years after it was first made into a commercial museum. Harold was a longtime Cripple Creek School principal who used to joke that he was "the only educator he knew that owned a bar, a restaurant, and a whorehouse."

When legal gambling came to Cripple Creek in the late 1990s, Hern says few tourists came for anything but the casinos, and the Herns were unable to keep up with the taxes. For awhile, the museum was owned by a casino.

The museum is now owned by The Old Homestead House Foundation. Love for history and proprietary interest keeps Hern going today as a guide there.

You can get a thirty-minute tour of the place daily from Memorial Day to September. For information call the Cripple Creek History Museum at (719) 689-2634.

Washing Machine Museum

The humble laundry appliance might not strike some as worthy of a museum, but consider the logo that graced a line of washing machines made in the early 1900s: SAVE WOMENS LIVES (sic).

That's no hype if you consider that for centuries laundry tools were nothing more than water, a cake of handmade soap, and something hard to pound, scrape, and press against the clothing. Plus a person, usually female, who did all the manual labor.

Against this dreary, inevitable, back-breaking chore, scores of inventors have tried their hands at lightening the load with mechanical assistance. By the 1920s, there were at least seven hundred manufacturers of washing machines in the United States.

That makes for a huge and fascinating variety of invention—at least Lee Maxwell thinks so, and he ought to know, considering he has amassed hundreds of washing machines and related items dating back to the 1800s (not counting the oldest item—a big, round rock, perfect to pound with).

You can see much of this on Maxwell's colorful Web site, but to get the full bodacious impact of the collection you'll have to round up at least nine other people and make the pilgrimage to his homestead, an old farm with a lovely Victorian house next to the Eaton Grove Nursery in Eaton.

As a one-man operation, Maxwell can give limited time to playing museum guide, as well as curator. In most cases, he requires a small admission fee and a minimum of ten people to give a tour. It's well worth it, with twelve thousand square feet of gleaming, fully restored examples of human invention, set out by period and maker in pristine warehouses. The earliest Maytag line alone has eighty-two models in a chronological array of polished cedar wood tubs and shining copper parts.

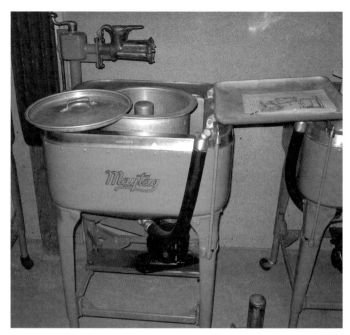

Maxwell is not a talky guide, preferring to stop and point out the details for a relatively few select items. One wooden model was made by a husband as a wedding present in 1932. There's a photo of the couple posted on it.

"I'll bet any bride would've been thrilled down to her heels to receive this," says Maxwell.

It's even more fascinating to see the machines in operation. Early carnival-ride inventors may have gotten ideas from the way these things swing, revolve, tilt, shake, twirl, and bounce—some of them so aggressively I am advised to stand back on a couple of occasions when Maxwell turns one on.

"One lady," he says, deadpan, "was standing too close when the tub broke free and cut her in two where you stand."

Why would this retired electrical engineering professor take up this odd hobby, and even write a book called *Save Womens Lives: History of Washing Machines* (available through his Web site)?

"Don't like to fish, not good at golf, and I hate bungee jumping," says Maxwell. "I've always been interested in old things. And I just don't want to see this history lost again." For information, visit www.oldewash.com.

Wonder Tower

There are a lot of directions that begin or end with the words, "You can't miss it," but with the Wonder Tower of Genoa you really can't. Drive east of Denver on Interstate 70 until the Rocky Mountains have receded to a dim haze in your rearview mirror, and there's nothing but the road through rolling farmland. Drive some more. You are now in eastern Colorado, which looks a lot like western Kansas.

Nine miles past Limon just before the hamlet of Genoa, look to the left and you'll see a very tall, odd structure and a long, rambling building attached to it. Painted on the side of the tower in letters you can see a mile away, it says SEE SIX STATES!

The last paint job on this place is peeling, revealing a few decades of past color choices. A couple of cars are parked out front, vintage junkers full of old bottles—props to help the place look busy from the roadway, like the motionless observers way up in the tower windows that are makeshift dummies.

The Genoa Tower and Museum (formerly The World's Wonder View Tower) is every bit worth the trip as one of Colorado's oddest historical landmarks. In 1926, railroad engineer and entrepreneur Charles W. Gregory teamed up with silent business partner Myrtle Le Bow to build what the tourism industry of the time called "a one-stop"—a roadside amusement with multiple attractions to bring in the

motorists off U.S. Highway 24. Besides the tower, the place had a motel, gas station, dance hall, and restaurant—twenty rooms in all.

Sixty feet high, the tower was once the highest point between New York City and Denver (confirmed in 1934 by the U.S. Geological Survey). Investigators from Ripley's Believe It or Not! determined you really could see the landmarks of six states from the tower's summit on a clear day.

The current owner, Jerry Chubbuck, is a seventy-ish man with guileless eyes and a perennial grin. He bought the Wonder Tower in 1960 and has been adding everything from arrowheads (twenty thousand at last count) to an old

zither. Every available surface is crammed with what looks like heaps of garage sale leftovers.

"See that?" says Chubbuck, nudging a box on the floor with his foot. "That's the rib cage of a bison. Look close, there's an arrowhead embedded in there."

It really is the remains of some long-ago hunter's kill, excavated from an ancient camp he found near the Big Sandy River. The place is now known by archaeologists as the Olsen-Chubbuck Site, named for Chubbuck and the family of fellow artifact collectors who helped him uncover several finds.

It's the first indication that I'm dealing with more than just a simple packrat. Chubbuck sells a pamphlet that will tell you the whole story. And he's happy to show you the mastodon tusk and other fossils he's found, too.

"Guess what that is!" he crows, plopping a hard chunky object in my hand. "Well, put it this way—if a dinosaur were headed north, this would be what would come out the south end!" (I fail to guess the nature of other objects that turn out to be rooster glasses, a walrus penis, camel nose bells, and a tool that rids raisins of seeds.) Nearly everything is for sale, which supplements his income from the $1 site admission.

All of this nearly overshadows remnants of the old Wonder Tower attractions—at least two two-headed calves, a few other animal oddities preserved in jars, and the old rock-encrusted rooms where dances and food used to be served. Here and there are Native American–style "pictographs" and small rustic murals painted back in the day by a Sioux woman who called herself Princess Ravenwing.

And, of course, there is the tower. Chubbuck invites me to make the trip up on my own. There are three landings, each a progressively smaller room with a lot of windows, painted in bright colors, and packed with yet more stuff.

The staircase finally turns into nothing more than a stepladder embedded into the wall with very narrow treads. At the top is a hatchway with a wooden box covering it. The walls are so close at this point that I have to sling my equipment bag around to my back, gingerly turn sidewise, and shove the heavy box aside with one hand while I cling to the ladder.

It is truly a spectacular view at the summit of the tower, though because of the clouds, the most I can see is a lot of Colorado in all directions. There is an old broken telescope-like device on the platform and a couple more dummies.

In its heyday, the Wonder Tower never closed. It was a Greyhound bus station, a truck stop, and a hangout for locals who came by to grab a burger and listen to live bands. Then came Highway 24's replacement, the new Interstate 70, which shunted vehicles away at a distance with ever-increasing speed. Combined with Colorado's stringent limits on advertising signage in rural areas, it meant a downturn in fortune. The gas station, café, and motel faded away.

In 1960, then owner Bill Bonner was ready to retire and remembered a young cattle rancher who had hung around as a curious kid and brought dates to the café as a teenager. It was a drought year, and Bonner made an offer that Chubbuck thought just might be what he needed to save the family farm and support his wife and kids.

As it turned out, Chubbuck was eventually able to sell the farm and raise his family at the Wonder Tower site. He and his wife, Esther, still live in comfortable quarters there today. We make the rounds so Chubbuck can be sure I've got good pictures. He offers, twice, to put on a cowboy outfit for posing.

"Nope," I say to the guileless eyes. "You're perfect the way you are."

For more information, call (719) 763-2309.

Kelloff's Best Western Movie Manor

Drive-in theaters have disappeared all over the United States, but in Monte Vista there's one that manages to keep going because of a unique concept. You can watch the movie on the big screen from the bed of a motel room next door. This is the brainchild of George Kelloff, who still takes tickets on summer nights, although these days it's George Jr. and his wife, Judy, who run the show otherwise.

It started when George Sr. and his wife, Edna Mae, built the Star Drive-In in 1955 with a small residence next to the projection booth. Edna Mae's parents were visiting one week in 1956, so she and her husband slept on a sofa bed in the living room with a picture window that faced the outdoor movie screen. It was the perfect place to view movies in real comfort, the Kelloffs agreed, so the next day George installed a speaker in their room so they could get sound as well.

After several months of enjoyment, George suggested to his wife one night, "Dear, wouldn't this be a helluva place for a motel?" His wife responded kindly, "You're nuts. Besides, you're broke. Go to sleep."

George did sleep on it, but he didn't give up on the

idea. He eventually got a loan and a franchise with the Best Western motel chain and opened the Movie Manor on July 1, 1964. The property was on the site of the defunct Monte Vista Airport, so there was even room for folks to fly in on the old runway. He also opened the still-running Kelloff's Restaurant next to the motel and furnished it with a movie theme. It closes around dusk in time for the shows to start.

Each motel unit is named for a film star (a friend and I stayed in the Charlton Heston room), and most have a big window that faces one of the movie screens. Speakers pipe in the sound. Expect family-friendly flicks only.

The Kelloffs spend winters elsewhere, but they return in the summers to visit with their family and enjoy the drive-in. George helps out with ticket sales at the drive-up box office. It especially gives him a kick to meet visitors who came as children and now bring their own kids.

"I'd rather do that than anything else," he says. "I enjoy meeting people."

If you want the original drive-in movie experience you can also bring your own car and view a movie on the second screen. Each screen runs a different film at the same time. But I have to agree with George Kelloff. There's nothing like watching a drive-in movie from the comfort of one helluva motel.

For more information, call the motel at (719) 852-5921 or the drive-in at (719) 852-2613.

Colorado Gator Farm

No joke, the alligators at this attraction are real and quite comfortable in Mosca, Colorado's non-tropical climate because of the geothermal pools they get to laze around in. The gator chow—little balls of fat kept in small buckets that visitors are encouraged to toss—also probably keeps 'em mellow. And if the pair of copulating tortoises we see on first entering the place are any indication, the other critters down on the farm are pretty laid-back, too.

My friend Jo and I get the tour with Mike Price, a guide who introduces us to a runt gator called Ted, and goes through a little spiel by which we get a photo of us handling Ted, plus a "certificate of bravery" punctured with Ted's ferocious little teeth. After that we get to tour the place on our own. The farm is also a garden nursery, commercial fish producer, reptile refuge, and exotic-bird hangout. Goggling at gators that aren't doing anything much besides snapping at food could get old rather fast.

Erwin and Lynne Young started the tilapia farm in 1974 and brought in baby gators in 1987 to take care of the dead product. As the gators grew they became a local attraction, and soon people decided the eighty-acre reptile park was the perfect place to drop off unwanted exotic pets.

The Youngs operate programs to educate

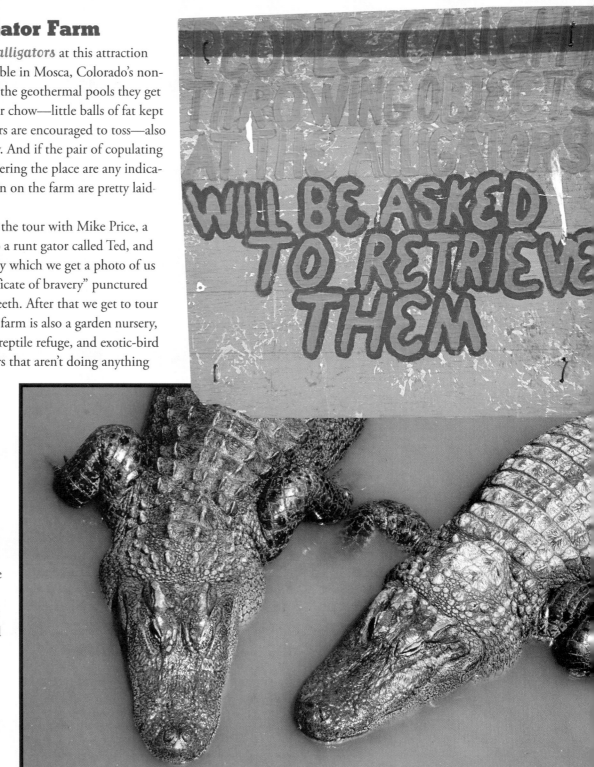

the public about the risks and needs of these imported guests. But running this no-kill shelter can be expensive. While the place is reasonably clean and surprisingly low on unpleasant odors for the number of critters it hosts, it looks frankly funky.

Inside it's a steamy barnlike place full of tropical plants and fish tanks. Outside, it's a series of animal pens, large and small, surrounded by fields. It turns out nobody doesn't like gator chow, including the ducks and various members of the ostrich family. The farm also attracts more than 125 species of wild native birds, including the rare Great Egret.

It's early in the season when we visit, so there are no gator-handling classes ($150 for the course, in which you go from little 'uns to eleven-footers) at the moment. The husky young guys in dirty T-shirts and bare feet doing general cleanup chores have time to chat.

For all their casual ease, the guys say being mindful of anything that could go wrong is what keeps them out of the hospital, or worse.

We tell them about a rumor we heard that an illegal alien, a Hispanic laborer, was eaten at the farm. He was completely devoured;

the unfortunate incident "covered up." Price and the other guys grin.

"First off, didn't happen," says Noah Mather. "Second, it's not like everything just disappears into those jaws. The gators will leave bones and big pieces. We've fed 'em dead goats and deer and things, and there's always stuff left over."

So, have they ever found anyone, um, unaccounted for at the end of a tour?

Pause. "I found a ladies' shoe once," says Mather. "Right among the gators. Nobody was reported missing. And I didn't remember seeing a woman walking out with only one shoe so I can't figure that one out, except that maybe someone brought it just to throw it at the gators. That's about it." For more information, visit www.gatorfarm.com.

Swetsville Zoo

The Swet home would stand out anywhere. On the outskirts of Timnath, named for a city in the Old Testament, it's a real traffic stopper. A modified castle facade in yellow and white, its cheerful turrets would beckon even if there wasn't a bigger attraction next door on the same property—the Swetsville Zoo.

Like many farmers, Bill Swet acquired quite a lot of metal odds and ends from all the cars and equipment he's collected over the years. He also got pretty handy with welding. So one day in 1985, just for fun, he put together a large, whimsical bird with a shovel for a beak and a bicycle-frame body. He stuck that on his front lawn and got a bunch of compliments, which encouraged him to convert a pile of junk into a line of wacky critters. Pretty soon people were stopping by just to see what was new.

There are now dinosaurs of all heights, and more fantastic creatures such as dragons and giant insects playing instruments, what may be the world's largest wind chime and a few kinetic sculptures that whirl or rock in the wind, and a real Volkswagen Bug up on humongous legs. There are about two hundred creations along the meandering paths on the Swets' former farm, so there's plenty to gawk at and enjoy. And Swet has more stuff in storage buildings to avoid the vandalism that occasionally rears its pin-headed nastiness.

The Swet family seems to like being in local parades. There are several human-powered and motorized vehicles that are meant for it, such as a bicycle built for ten, a

throne on wheels, an enormous rodent that pulls a Cinderella coach, a dinosaur-shaped car called the Autosaurus, and what looks like an elegant restored antique auto that was actually pieced together from things like bus parts.

Swet and one of his young grandsons take me around and point out the features and origins of the parts that have managed to find a new and wacky harmony together. Asked about his favorite sculpture, Swet says promptly, "The last one I just finished!" And I take a picture of him next to it—gigantic metal flowers. As with all his sculptures, it has the patina of rust.

"I like experienced steel," he says.

Swet did the castle facade in 1997. It was destroyed in a fire, so he rebuilt it in 1998. Besides being a metal sculptor, a retired farmer, and one of the founders of the local firefighting unit, Swet is married to his high school sweetheart, Sandy. Sandy is obviously pretty tolerant of her husband's tastes in outdoor décor.

"She does the landscaping," he says. Sandy was very ill with cancer in 1996 and was given only a short time to live—"But I've still got her with me!"

I congratulate him, and when his grandson runs into the

"My whole life is here."

house I ask who's going to take over the zoo someday when Swet is no longer around. Swet smiles. "Oh, a lot of these pieces are already spoken for. There's going to be a Walmart across the street soon—they've bought a few and they're

going to put them in a park around the store. I've also got some things like antique tractors, those'll go pretty fast. Other people want certain sculptures. But I hope the bulk of it will stay here. I've made arrangements." He pauses. "I was diagnosed with cancer two weeks ago."

Of all the things in Swet's gently zany kingdom, his diagnosis seems suddenly the most surreal and certainly the least welcoming. I express my hope for his better health, which he accepts with the same calm and easy grace as my compliments on his work. As we wrap up the tour, I ask how it's been to open his property to strangers.

"Ninety-nine percent of the visitors have been great," he says. "There's a one percent that have been rude or intoxicated or something, but then you find that anywhere."

The grin broadens. "One day it was pretty slow, and I noticed a car with a moon roof had pulled into the parking lot but no one came out. I didn't have to get very close before I realized the

people inside were having, an, ah, romantic interlude. I brought Sandy out without telling her exactly what I saw, and she caught on real quick—high-tailed it back into the house!"

Heavy equipment is operating with a continual roar on the other side of the Swet property. Swet sees me glance at it.

"There's a Costco going in there," he says, without further comment and no apparent pain. Plainly, changes are coming to Swetsville in more ways than one.

"This is an incredible legacy. I hope you're able to keep everything together here for the future," I say, as I prepare to leave.

"Me, too," Swet says, still smiling. "My whole life is here."

For more information, call (970) 484-9509.

Really Hot, Hot Springs

The first uranium, which radium is found with, found in the United States was a type called pitchblende ore, discovered in a goldmine in Central City. There have been booms and busts in uranium mining ever since, but Colorado has always been one of the country's major sources for radium.

And at one time, the many natural hot springs in this state boasted of their "healthful" radioactive content.

In the early 1900s to late 1920s, before the dangers were not yet widely recognized, radium was thought to have the potential to cure everything from cancer to acne. Denver was an important radium-processing center in the early 1900s. The Home Products Company is an example of the industry that once flourished there. It was the manufacturer of Vita Radium Suppositories for, among other things, "restoring sex power."

As it happens, one of the many trace elements in some natural hot springs is radon, the gas that emanates from decaying radium. Once that was discovered, "radio-active water" was touted over the previously advertised benefits of "magnetized" water and the presence of lithium salts.

Of course, radon disperses once it hits open air, so the savvy health seeker of that era knew that the really effective place to seek that miracle radiation cure was to sit naked in a cave where radon was contained and potent. Taking a "vapor bath" was what that was called. If you could take the waters in an enclosed area, then you supposedly had the benefits of both.

Once the dangers of radiation poisoning became more obvious in the 1930s, radium advertising dropped like, yes, a hot rock.

"Radium" remains the name of a small, scenic ranching settlement near Kremmling in the northwestern part of the state, across the Colorado River from Radium State Park with its Radium Wildlife Area. And the town of Ouray still has a Radium Springs Swimming Pool. But those are about the only exceptions to the R word.

Thousands of tourists continue to hit Colorado roads with a hot springs destination in mind. Claims about radioactive water aren't even a dim memory, which is just as well because it's unlikely that anyone is ever going to emerge from the soothing waters of a hot spring glowing with more than good health.

Here are a few existing springs that once touted radium content, in name or advertising or both.

"Sweet Skin" Radio-Active Hot Springs and Vapor Cave Baths, Ouray

In 1929, Charles W. Kent bought a sanitarium started in 1925 and invented a legend about an Indian maiden named Sweet Skin who benefited from the spring's radioactive waters. "Room, Meals and Bath, $4.00 a day" included a stint in the "vapor caves," where "you drink and pour the Radio-Active Hot Water over your body as long as you can stand the heat. . . ." The place changed hands (and names) a few times, and was at one time owned by the St. Germain Foundation, a quasi-theosophical group called I AM. Today it is known as the Box Canyon Lodge and Hot Springs (www.boxcanyonouray.com).

Waunita Hot Radium Springs, Gunnison

Now known as Waunita Hot Springs Ranch (www.waunita.com).

Radium Hot Springs, Idaho Springs

Now known as Indian Hot Springs Resort (www.indian-hotsprings.com).

Hot Sulphur Springs Mineral Baths, Hot Sulphur Springs

Once advertised "Naturally heated mineral water, high in Radium content, very beneficial for Arthritis, Rheumatism, etc." Now known as Hot Sulphur Springs Resort and Spa (www.hotsulphursprings.com).

Eldorado Springs

As late as 1928 it was advertising "Evening Swimming Every Night, Warm Radium Water, Pleasing Lighting Effects . . ." The swimming pool and resort of the same name as the town, once considered the Coney Island of Colorado, are gone, but the bottled spring water (www.eldoradosprings.com) is big business today.

Roads Less Traveled

t is often said that the road to hell is paved with good intentions. Some of the most popular routes to hell in Colorado, however, aren't paved with anything at all—save a few good tales of death and destruction. It could be a treacherous mountain road high above rushing water, a spooky old railroad tunnel, or the many natural places in the landscape dubbed with sinister names.

However, the places to really watch out for are those of beauty in which evil has entered: a ghost-ridden river where people have dissappeared, a canyon turned into an intstrument of mass death.

Go forth now, if you dare, on some of Colorado's roads less traveled, but don't say you weren't warned.

Hellish Highways

There's something about a narrow, isolated country road with challenging aspects that seems to invite legends of ghosts and violence. In Colorado, it's often a stagecoach or railroad route high on a narrow shelf blasted into a mountain that started out dangerously enough as it was, and continued over the decades to accumulate colorful legends and spooky tales.

Gold Camp Road

Of all the Colorado roadways with a reputation for scariness, none is like Gold Camp Road. The challenging terrain of the road isn't the problem. The tunnels, reputed to be haunted, are.

Gold Camp follows the roadbed of the Short Line Railroad built in the 1880s by the Colorado Springs and Cripple Creek District Railway Company. The defunct railroad grade was converted into a single-lane dirt road for cars in 1922. A private tollway for sometime, it became known as Gold Camp Road in 1939 and came under ownership of the U.S. Forest Service in the 1940s.

Today, Gold Camp Road is still a single-lane dirt route between Cripple Creek and Colorado Springs. In some places, the road passes snugly between canyon walls. In others, it offers incredible valley views—some of them a long way down. The road has no lights and no guardrails, but there are some turnouts where you can enjoy the view. An eight-and-a-half-mile stretch is not open to cars, which has made it popular with dirt bikers, ATVers, bicyclists, runners, and hikers.

The tale that frightens so many travelers is about children, a school bus, and a cave-in. Gold Camp Road originally passed through three tunnels dynamited through rock. One of the tunnels partially collapsed in 1988, which prompted the closing of this section to automobiles.

Sometime after the collapse, rumors that the tunnels were haunted began to materialize—screams, lights, shadowy figures, mysterious bloodstains, the works.

This story can easily be found on the Internet by now: The tunnels are haunted by children killed in the tragic school-bus accident when one of the tunnels collapsed on the kids who were returning from a field trip to Cripple Creek.

It doesn't matter that this terrible tragedy never took place. The story is now so widespread that thrill seekers from come far and wide to test the paranormal properties of the Gold Camp Road tunnels. Trying to enter Tunnel No. 3 is not recommended and is illegal for a very good reason. Those rotting support timbers that didn't collapse in 1988 were destroyed or dangerously weakened by a fire in 2006. Official arson investigators have never entered for that reason. The tunnel is boarded up and fenced.

The other two tunnels can be investigated, but it's not a good idea to simply park inside either and wait for ghostly action. Each tunnel is about one hundred feet long and unlit. One is so dark that seeing the ground inside on a clear day is difficult. The other curves so that the view of oncoming traffic is limited. Other drivers could plow into you before they see you.

It should be mentioned that Gold Camp Road has a history of prankster activity that predates the collapse of Tunnel No. 3. Engineer, volunteer deputy sheriff, MUFON field investigator, and all-around Fortean researcher Chuck Zukowski of Colorado Springs learned a story that might explain the ghostly train whistle.

I was talking at work, not long ago, to a couple of other engineers about Gold Camp Road and my own recent visit to check it out. And one of the contractors who happened to overhear me spoke up. He says, "My dad and his best friend got hold of an old-time locomotive whistle when they were teenagers, and they installed it on my dad's car. My dad told me they'd drive up and down at night on the dirt road that goes around the tunnels and blow that thing." That must been around the late '50s, early '60s, I'm thinking. Maybe the ghost of this guy's dad is reliving his youth.

Casey May, a young machinist and documentary film-maker from Indiana, was living near Colorado Springs in 2006 when he first heard about the infamous Gold Camp Road.

I was intrigued by the stories and decided to check it out. I consider myself a scientist. I really think there is a logical explanation for everything; we just don't always know what it is.

The third tunnel is actually a little tricky to find if you don't know exactly where to look, as it was on old Gold Camp Road. Now, Gold Camp Road takes a different route. At the trailhead above Helen Hunt Falls

there is a closed road that takes you about a mile to the tunnel. It is closed off with a large iron gate on both sides. The park department and I personally suggest that you do not climb the fence and go into the tunnel. In 2006, there was a fire inside the tunnel that destroyed all of the remaining supports. It is considered dangerous enough that they did not even investigate. But even before that, in 1987, the third tunnel was closed to traffic due to rotting timbers and fear of collapse; therefore, it would be highly unlikely that a school bus full of children would be driving through a closed tunnel.

The "blood spots" that are found in all the tunnels, and especially the third, are actually rust formed because of how iron-rich the rocks are in this area. To prove it, I took a rock from the third tunnel and gave it optimum conditions to rust. Within a day or two it looked just like the "blood spots."

I spent countless hours day and night exploring Gold Camp Road and did not see or even hear anything [other] than a lot of teenagers either looking for a scare or trying to scare someone else.

This gave him and a few like-minded friends the idea to see just how much people were ready to believe.

As an experiment, we played a little joke on some people that were parked in a tunnel. I was dressed in a white suit and had a rope tied around my neck. After [we made] some noises with a walkie-talkie we had planted in the tunnel earlier, they exited the tunnel very frightened. As they were exiting they were being followed—by a tree limb tied to a fishing line that was looped to our side. By this time, they were running and screaming. Just as they came out of the dark tunnel they saw me, dressed in complete white, jump off the side of

the cliff. Well, the jumping off the cliff was not really part of the original plan. After screaming and running and scaring them pretty badly, I just had the idea to jump off the edge of the road. At the time, I assumed there was a steady slope down but it turned out to be a small cliff, and I fell a pretty good distance before hitting some trees and stopping. Luckily, I was not seriously injured and was able to climb back up.

They were hysterically screaming and jumped into their car and left very promptly. I am sure they had a great story to tell when they got home. We also put lots of fingerprints on their windows to add some effect. We usually did that when people would park their car and walk through the tunnels. . . . The point of this whole joke, besides being very funny, is that sometimes what we think is happening is something completely different—whether it be someone else messing with you,

you imagining things, or misinterpretation. I really do not believe that any of these tunnels are haunted, just creepy.

This is not to say May isn't still fascinated with the legend. He has a Web site devoted to Gold Camp Road (www.goldcamproad.com) on which he has posted the stories people send him. A couple are reproduced here with his permission.

Whatever the myths about the tunnels, the area around Gold Camp Road has a verifiable, unsettling truth. It's a body dump.

"People use Gold Camp Road and the adjacent road, Old Stage, to get here. It's got the perfect combination of being minutes away from an urban center but out where there aren't a lot a witnesses, if you pick the right time," says Tom Healy, law enforcement officer for the U.S. Forest Service.

"Stolen property gets dumped here. Stolen cars, stolen safes, and bodies. The last one was a couple of months ago. And, in every national forest, there are suicides. People come out here because it's close, and they can find solitude. Maybe because they have some good memories of the place. At least it's pleasant."

Healy grew up in the Colorado Springs area and, at the time of this writing, has worked for the Pikes Peak Ranger District for five years.

"I don't know where the haunted-tunnel story came from, but Gold Camp Road has always been what we call a 'trouble point.' In the 1970s to early '80s, there wasn't as much law-enforcement presence out here as there is now. Used to be you'd run into people having huge parties with live bands and forty to fifty kegs of beer. Lots of biker gangs, many assaults. Wasn't too long ago some people brought a guy up here in a car trunk. Thought he was dead, but he wasn't. His captors tried three times to kill him, but they got caught before they could finish him off."

Gold Camp Road's wilder days may have passed, but the tunnels' paranormal legend has not made Healy's job any easier.

"It's a constant headache," he admits.

Gold Camp Tunnel Visions

Myself and a group of eight (nine if you include the sleeping child) went up to Gold Camp Road in Colorado Springs last night (June 31, 2008). We got up there around 12:00 A.M.

We went all the way through the first two tunnels and up to the area where you have to hike to the third tunnel. Nothing was really going on just a scenic drive to me. Although I had heard all the stories, I am a little skeptical that they are just that, stories.

Well, we had three cars in the group and most of the time we were parked right outside the second tunnel in between the first and second. I sat in the car a lot of the time being that the guys in the group are mostly pranksters and I wouldn't really believe most of their idiocy.

Well, they took a video camera into the second tunnel with them. The first time me and my cousin watched it was about 1:30 A.M. By this time, the boys had gone in and come out two-three times each time saying rocks were being thrown at them, and my brother and his friend both had gashes on their arms when they had long sleeves on.

While watching the video it became static and the voices kinda drowned out like a slowing down record player. We rewound it and watched it again about three times. Well, apparently it is no longer on the video, and I know her and I saw it.

Also shortly after I got up the courage to walk into the tunnel with them. That didn't last long. Instead, my cousin and I drove her car into the tunnel with the boys standing outside the driver's window. We stopped and turned off the lights and killed the engine. I kept my one hand on the light switch and one on the key to turn on the car.

About twenty seconds later, we heard a rock or something hit the car. I instantly flipped on the lights and looked at the boys who all were standing away from the car with their hands in the air. I was staring them down, thinking they were just trying to scare us when tons of heavy/rocky sand slammed into the top of our car. There was no one else around except the boys who I had my eyes on.

Then we all got out of the tunnels, and we were scanning over the car looking at all the handprints and weird stuff on the car when I looked up at everyone standing behind the car and saw one of them (or what I thought was one of them) walking off the road and down the hillside.

I asked which one left, and they instantly told me they were all present. I didn't believe them so I asked more, demanding (to know) which one left. None had left, but when they went over there to see what it was (in) the bushes that were rustling like someone had quickly walked down there. Again, here was no one but us there. We all decided it was time to leave (and time was also getting close to the witching hour, 3:00 A.M.).

We were in the lead with a jeep behind us and my brother's car in the rear. After passing through the first tunnel we noticed the jeep flashing its lights so we pulled over by the first parking lot and they informed us the last car with my brother in it had died in the tunnel. The lights flickered out, and you could tell that they were just dimming and brightening.

My cousin's husband jumped out of our car and ran back to help them. Me and her could have sworn we saw Tim pushing the car down from the tunnel and then jump in our car. But everyone else says that he jumped in their car and jumped out of the backseat when they pulled up next to us.

Then when we got home and we watched more of the video tape. There is a part where it is pitch black, you hear the boys all talking about something that wasn't there before, and then you see a very quick and very bright flash of light and this weird, sizzling noise.

They instantly ran out (of the tunnel) of course. —*Missy*

Gold Camp Road

Legend has it that a lot of weird things happen up near the third tunnel—like witchery and cult activity—so a few of my friends and I decided to go one night. It was near midnight when we drove through the first tunnel without anything special occurring. We drove into the second tunnel, went about halfway through, and stopped the car to get out. We were dead quiet, and when we heard weird noises emanating from throughout the tunnel, we got a bit spooked and ran back to our car, which had inexplicably moved several feet forward while we were out.

We continued up the narrow road to the third tunnel, and then walked the remaining distance to the tunnel. The moment we got out of the car, we all had the weird feeling we were being watched.

Using only a small key-chain penlight, we climbed over the fences and onto the footpath. We heard rustling and things running in the forests on both sides of us. At one point, we even thought we saw a small human watching us. We freaked out and took off back to the car and sped back down to the bottom of Gold Camp Road.

We've never made it to the collapsed tunnel, but rumor has it that it's covered in pentagrams and the remains of sacrificed animals. We still drop by Gold Camp Road for a good thrill and a fun night. —*Wade Shaw*

Kings Crown Road

In a small residential area on the very edge of Woodland Park, there's a road called Kings Crown. It circles the neighborhood, but at several points, it branches into cul-de-sacs that serve as trailheads for several hiking paths. One of these is a secluded cul-de-sac that's quite popular among local teens. A narrow road leads into the cul-de-sac, and tall dead trees circle the perimeter.

A lot of kids started talking about weird experiences happening up there at night, and being the rowdy bunch we were, my friends and I decided to test the legends. We drove up to the cul-de-sac and parked. A fresh coat of snow had fallen, and we could see the only prints on the ground were our tire tracks.

We turned off the car's lights and waited. For about half an hour nothing happened, so we turned on music, talked, joked, and just continued to wait.

Then, one friend saw a figure pass by in the rearview mirror, so we turned down the music and looked around. We saw four or five black silhouettes circling the car, and then they approached the car and began shaking it violently. We all waited the shaking out, assuming it was a few other friends playing a prank on us. After a minute, the shaking stopped, and the silhouettes left. We got out of the car, still skeptical and laughing, but when we looked around, we saw there was no one visible. The only tracks in the snow were still those left by our car. —*Wade Shaw*

Oh My Gawd Road

Officially, this is Virginia Canyon Road, a scenic mountain route that invite oohs, aahs, and the occasional, "Oh, my Gawd!" which is how it got its second and most popular name—Oh My Gawd Road. (The Idaho Springs Chamber of Commerce says that is how the unofficial name is spelled.)

Once an essential toll road between Idaho Springs and Central City, it was built in 1861 before the railroad arrived. Miners and merchants used it for transporting supplies, and stagecoaches brought people through a treacherous area bristling with bandits. President Ulysses S. Grant, his wife Julia, and his daughter, Nellie, took this route in 1873 on their way from Central City to Idaho Springs. At the reins was the legendary character Hiram "Hy" Washburn, who treated them to a thrilling example of hell-for-leather driving prowess.

According to Ethel Morrow Gillette's *Idaho Springs: Saratoga of the Rockies*, the president's daughter was in white-knuckle mode when Washburn assured her that he wasn't suicidal and knew what he was doing. Fortunately, Washburn was as good as his word, because Nellie's daddy signed the bill that made Colorado a state in 1876.

Oh My Gawd Road is high, narrow, well maintained, and mostly dirt. The view is breathtaking, in every sense of the word. It is exceptionally scenic, but drivers are advised not to be distracted by the beauty. There are plenty of steep grades, switchbacks, blind curves, and eroded shoulders, but no guardrails and no passing. If you meet a car coming in the opposite direction, etiquette decrees that the vehicle on the downslope must back up to a place where the uphill car can safely pass.

Oh, and watch out for the bicyclists.

Schofield Pass and the Devil's Punchbowl

Miners created this narrow, scrabbly "shelf road" in the 1800s as a route between the towns of Marble and Crested Butte. Along the way was the settlement of Schofield that is today a neat little ghost town. The road hugs soaring canyon walls in an area marked by aspen trees and a series of waterfalls. It overlooks—a long, long way down—the Devil's Punchbowl (see inset), a deep pool of water.

Local legend from pioneer days says that a tethered horse's skeleton was found on a narrow path. It was thought the owner had fallen to his death, and his mount couldn't free itself.

As challenging as the road is for the intrepid hiker or bicyclist, Schofield Pass can be a white-knuckle adventure for even experienced four-wheeling drivers. A Hummer did make it through once (as reported on a Hummer Web site called Flash Off-Road, http://flashoffroad. com/Articles/schofieldPass/schofield_pass.html), but the drivers were highly experienced and prepared.

Schofield Pass is not passable until mid-July, if at all, and even then, the folks at the Aspen-Sopris Ranger District are not especially encouraging if one calls to check on conditions. Besides being unpaved, narrow, and uneven, the road has few turnouts, plenty of blind curves, and no guardrails. In addition, in some places, the unpaved road crosses a creek. Wet brakes have been the undoing of more than one driver before a steep descent.

If you look down into a gully, you might see a few wrecks. Besides the fatal accidents, the worst stories are about vehicles encountering each other in areas where passing is so hazardous, forest rangers have to be called in to direct maneuvers.

 Colorado's worst four-wheeling accident, so far, occurred here in 1970 when a driver parked his vehicle full of passengers on a slope and left it to take a picture. The driver had just made a wet crossing, which caused the parking brake to fail. The vehicle rolled into deep, icy water more than one hundred feet below, killing nine people, including a young boy whose body has never been found. At least five other known fatalities have also occurred on the pass.

As infamous as Schofield Pass is, at the time of this writing, it has inexplicably wound up as one of those "shortest routes" recommended on some Internet mapping sites and global positioning devices. Well, it *is* a shortcut, which is why the miners and railroad men put it there in the first place. However, just getting to the road can be a challenge, as the officers of a small police station at the ski resort of nearby Mount Crested Butte can tell you.

"I've called MapQuest about this, and they said they'd get right back to me. They never did," says Officer Brad Phelps. Phelps has seen the number of stranded motorists increase in recent years. "People who have never driven our mountain roads, who don't have four-wheel

Manitou and Vicinity—No. 47. Devil's Punch Bowl—Glen Eyrie.

drive, let alone high clearance, for some reason, they trust the maps, these GPS devices, and directional things more they do then the signs we've got posted.

"The worst incident was recently—early December. This seventeen-year-old girl was driving from Marble to meet with her parents in Crested Butte. She headed for Schofield Pass because that was the way her GPS device told her to take, and her car got stuck. Her parents called us, hours later, frantic, no idea she took that route. She was walking down the road [in the dark] using her cell phone for a flashlight and got lucky. Some elk hunters found her, and she stayed overnight in their camp. They helped her get her car out. She might have died otherwise."

If you consider yourself a very experienced driver and have a four-wheel-drive, high-clearance, narrow-wheel-base vehicle with good brakes and plenty of power, then by all means, says Ted Hart, consider giving it a try. He recommends bringing someone along who can get out the car and walk ahead to "spot" the driver through the trickier parts.

Hart is the leader of the Blue Mesa 4 Wheelers club out of Gunnison. He remembers heading for the excellent trout fishing areas of the Devil's Punchbowl with his dad in a 1946 Jeep when he was a youngster.

"Back then, the road was pretty well maintained by the county," he says. "It was a regular shortcut for a lot of people. Then, sometime in the late 1960s [or] '70s, whatever business interests that were served by this road disappeared, and the county stopped keeping it up. Erosion, avalanches, and rockslides took out a lot of it. Our club agreed to adopt the road with the Forest Service; sometime in the '80s I think it was. We go out about once a year to do some clean up and make sure the hazard signs are still up."

The "clean up" is, necessarily, minimal and can't really start until at least August anyway. The canyon is narrow and deep and easily blocked with snow and debris for a good part of each year.

"I don't think there's [ever] not been snow down in the canyon," says Hart. "The sun doesn't get to all of it."

Without heavy equipment, club members can only move fallen trees, rockslides, and other obstacles up to a point. They have to let the Forest Service do anything more difficult, and that's an expensive proposition the service is more reluctant to undertake these days. If you don't have the right experience and vehicle to drive the most dangerous road in Colorado, Hart says, this spectacular area can easily be enjoyed by other means.

"I've seen all modes of travel through it. On foot, bicycles, ATVs. Seen people kayak through the Devil's Punchbowl. Don't think horse riding would be a good idea, though."

It may strike you that, even with all the warnings and cautions, no one is advising that you not visit the Devil's Punchbowl.

"It's worth seeing," says Hart. "But you've got to respect it."

Ominous Place Names

Looking at a map of Colorado, it might strike you that the Devil gets more than his due in the number of place names reflective of some satanic quality. These names came from nineteenth-century settlers, prospectors, railroad workers, and adventurers with a penchant for giving fanciful labels to distinctive natural landmarks. The more risk in getting around, through, under, or over the landmarks, the more likely they'd wind up with *Devil* or *hell* in their names. Some of the names repeat or are pretty near alike.

For instance, there are at least three Hell's Holes (not to be confused with Devil's Hole Mountain), at least two Hell Canyons and a Devil's Canyon, a couple of Devil's Slides, three Devil's Kitchens plus a Hell's Kitchen.

Saguache County has a Hellgate, and Eagle County has a Hell's Gate. There are a Devil's Chair (San Miguel County), a Devil's Rocking Chair (Animas County), and Devil's Armchair (Chaffee County). Archuleta County claims Devil Creek, Little Devil Creek, and Hell Creek. In addition, there are Devil's Staircase (Gunnison County), Devil's Stairsteps (Huerfano County), and Hell Roaring Creek (Pitkin County).

A number of Satan's body parts are scattered about too—Devil's Head (mountain in Douglas County), Devil's Nose (mountain in Clear Creek County), Devil's Backbone (rambling rock formation in Larimer County), and Devil's Elbow (cliff in Baca County). In Boulder County stands the Devil's Thumb, an upright, curving rock spire that locals have long maintained looks like a much more rakish appendage.

His Wickedness has some rather more singular hangouts and personal effects here and there: Brimstone Road, Devil's Causeway, Devil's Curve, Devil's Den, Devil's Gap, Devil's Gate, Devil's Kettle, Devil's Knob, Devil's Lake, Devil's Lookout, Devil's Park, Devil's Playground, Devil's Point, Devil's Rockpile, Hell's Half Acre, Hell's Half Mile, and Hell's Hip Pocket. Colorado seems like it was the Devil's backyard at one time!

Devil's Grave, on a mesa in Routt County, is a pile of sandstone rocks that supposedly resembles a large tomb. A profile-like formation—Sorrowful Satan—is found in Cheyenne Canyon, El Paso County.

The Colorado landscape is riddled with other striking names indicative of some horrific events that are, unfortunately, now lost to history.

Devil's Curve, Thompson Canyon

At least, they seem to be lost to local written records. You just have to wonder about places named Upper Disaster Falls (Moffat County), Scare Mountain and Spooky Mountain Summit (Rio Blanco County), Spook Point (Dolores County), Phantom Canyon (Teller County), Terrible Mountain (Gunnison County), and Terror Creek and Terror Trail (Delta County).

Cannibal Plateau in Hinsdale County is one exception. It's where the unlucky members of Alfred Packer's prospecting group were found and buried. (See Local Heroes and Villains.)

We have several places named Dead Man's this or that, but Dead Man's Canyon between Colorado Springs and Cañon City is the only one I could track to an identifiable person—William Henry Harkens, a victim of the Terrible Espinosas. (See Local Heroes and Villains.)

Nonetheless, if you buy into the old folk belief that places with devilish or ominous names attract supernatural activity, then Colorado's wilderness is ripe with possibilities.

Devil's Kitchen, Colorado National Monument

Sorrowful Satan, Cheyenne Canyon

The River of Lost Souls in Purgatory

Probably the most romantically misnamed river in Colorado is the River of Lost Souls in Purgatory. Its official name is Purgatory. This legendary whitewater beauty is associated with treachery, a murder, a mysterious disappearance, ghostly voices, and a fabulous lost fortune in Spanish gold.

According to Charles Skinner in his nine-volume *Myths and Legends of Our Own Lands*, in 1896 Spain ordered an regiment from Santa Fe, New Mexico, to carry a chest of gold for the payment of soldiers in St. Augustine, Florida. After wintering in southern Colorado the troops set off through a canyon with a river, never to be seen by white men again.

Many years afterward a Native American told a priest in Santa Fe that the regiment had been attacked by Indians. Seeing that escape was hopeless, the colonel—so said the narrator—buried the gold that he was transporting. No Spaniards survived. Thousands of doubloons are believed to be hidden in the canyon, and thousands of dollars have been spent in searching for them.

The echoing of the water as it tumbled through the canyon was said to be the lamentation of the infantrymen, and so the Spaniards called the place El Rio de las Animas Perdidas—the River of Lost Souls.

The longer version of this story has the added drama of treachery and mutinous murder. According to this version, a Spanish expedition set out from Mexico in 1539, led by the Portuguese Don Humana. The second-in-command was a Spaniard named Bonilla. The group came to a halt alongside a river in Colorado when the troops discovered that the jealous Lieutenant Bonilla had slain his commander. The accompanying monks

demanded that the expedition return to Mexico. However, the lethal lieutenant and the men who supported him insisted they would continue the mission.

The monks then declared they would abandon the expedition—a serious threat for that time, as the soldiers would be left without those who could perform the required Catholic rites of confession and absolution before death. (According to Catholic tradition, a good person who dies without confessing his sins finds his soul detoured into purgatory, heaven's waiting room. On the other hand, the soul of a murderer who received no absolution is condemned to hell.) So the monks departed with those soldiers unwilling to stand with Bonilla, and the monkless troops were never heard from again. The river was named for these "lost souls."

This story seems to be confused with real events you can read about on the Internet. According to the New Mexico Office of the State Historian (www.newmexicohistory.org), Francisco Leyva de Bonilla was a captain from Nueva Vizcaya, now the Mexican province of Chihuahua. In 1593, he was ordered to lead troops in the recapture of stolen cattle, but when they came close to the New Mexico border, Bonilla decided to divert his troops in search of fortune to the north.

Despite admonitions to turn back, Bonilla and the more reckless fortune hunters pressed on. They camped by a Colorado waterway that the local Native Americans supposedly called the River of Ghosts, which translated into Spanish as El Rio de las Animas Perdidas. Tales of a fabled city of gold called Quivira drew the adventurers to eastern Kansas. Quivira turned out to be a large village of grass huts populated by Wichita Indians. There was no treasure.

Bonilla's enraged lieutenant, Antonio Gutierrez de Humana, killed his captain. The next day, the citizens of Quivira slew every invader except an Indian slave, who

escaped and related the story back in New Mexico in 1598.

Over time, the river acquired the unofficial, longer name that actually contradicts Catholic theology—souls are not "lost" in purgatory, only detained. It was French trappers who first called the river "Purgatoire"; the English speakers who came later mangled that as "Picketwire." At some point, it finally came to be known as Purgatory.

The area still draws fortune hunters looking for traces of Spanish gold. A skeleton in Spanish armor, bits of antique weaponry, and even gold coins are rumored to have been found along the banks and in a cave near the river. There are tales of people who have camped and fished along the Purgatory and heard wails over the sounds of the rushing waters—when no one else was around.

If it's true that the Indians called it the "River of Ghosts," then it's also possible that people have been hearing—and will continue to hear—disembodied voices from Purgatory for a long time.

A Night of Hell on Earth: The Big Thompson Canyon Flood

In 1976, the biggest regional flood in ten thousand years hit the Big Thompson Canyon between Estes Park and Loveland. It was Colorado's deadliest natural disaster to date, one of the worst floods in U.S. history—and it could happen again.

Intense summer storms are nothing unusual in Colorado, especially in the high country. Strong winds usually ensure that storms move out as quickly as they move in. When floods occur, they generally rage through in short order. That's why they're called flash floods—they can be lethal for people caught in the wrong place.

Knowing the local geography is key to understanding why this particular flash flood was such a massive tragedy. The twenty-five-mile-long Big Thompson Canyon is about an hour's drive northwest of Denver. The Big Thompson River (and yes, there is a Little Thompson River elsewhere) starts high in the Rockies near Estes Park. The Big Thompson flows gently downward east through the narrow canyon and to the plains west of Loveland. It's usually fairly shallow, at two to three feet deep.

Highway 34, a two-lane paved road, winds through the canyon between meadows, rocky slopes, and towering walls of sheer rock. The only development then, as now, was limited to small businesses that cater to tourists, cabins, recreational campsites, and modest retirement homes.

On July 31, 1976, Colorado was celebrating its centennial. Thousands headed to the Big Thompson Canyon on that Saturday to beat the heat and enjoy the scenic beauty. Estimates put between 2,000 and 3,500 people in the canyon on that day. Around 6 p.m., a thunderstorm moved in at the upper end of the canyon. For some reason, the usual strong mountain winds never showed. So the storm parked itself for more than three hours—and rained.

The upper part of the canyon quickly went from summer twilight to pitch-black night except for flashes of lightning. The other end of the canyon looked fine,

and people continued to enter despite later warnings. During the first hour alone, eight inches of rain fell. Unfortunately, a previous storm had left the ground unable to absorb any more water.

Around 7 P.M., the first flash flood warnings were broadcast. Highway 34 at the dark upper end was awash in places, and boulders had crashed into the road. However, many people were camped outdoors or in places without radio, television, or even a telephone. No warning sirens existed in the area in those days. Larimer County sheriff's deputies, Colorado state patrol officers, and other local law enforcement personnel tried to warn as many people

as they could. Some of the officers went into the canyon as far as possible to warn those there; others stayed near the mouth of the canyon at the lower end and tried to convince skeptical motorists to turn back.

It didn't take long for the water to spread and fill the gap between the canyon walls and then move downhill all the debris it had picked up. As the flood approached narrow points in the canyon, this debris would pile up and create a temporary dam until the water swelled enough to burst through. Then, the river became a boiling wall of trees, rocks, boulders, buildings, furniture, propane tanks, cars, campers, and other rubbish.

People caught in buildings in its path or who tried to outrun the flood in vehicles were the most likely to die. Those who managed to climb to areas above the raging waters survived. An ambulance from Loveland was smashed into rocks, and the crew barely escaped. Michael Conley, an off-duty Estes Park police officer, and Sgt. Hugh Purdy of the Colorado State Patrol lost their lives while leading people to safety. Both were killed when their cars were engulfed.

Many Web sites, newspaper articles, and books are available in which survivors have recorded their memories. Their accounts describe a night of hell.

People clung to slippery surfaces in the pouring rain, in darkness relieved only by lightning, flashlight beams, and the occasional flare from a floating propane tank. The air was filled with the odors of gas, sewage, and diesel fuel. Screams were heard between cannon peals of thunder and the cacophony of the debris-laden water that rushed by with cars and camping trailers in which flashlights waved frantically inside.

The flood crest was nearly twenty feet by 9:40 P.M., when it tore through the mouth of the canyon, took an enormous reservoir pipe off its supports, and spread out over the plains, which helped to dilute its power. However, it still had enough force to destroy Loveland's main waterline and everything at the hydroelectric plant except the turbines.

The entire episode took was less than three hours.

Rescue of the thousands of survivors stranded in the canyon took the better part of two days. Some of the bodies weren't found until three months later. The number of confirmed dead is 139, from a toddler to a ninety-four-year-old. Five people are still listed as missing, their bodies never found.

The U.S. Geological Survey said that while the big, stalled storm was a meteorological rarity, it could happen again. Hydrologists, geologists, meteorologists, municipal governments, emergency responders, and a lot of other folks around the country have studied this uber flash flood. As a result, there are many more rules for building near rivers like the Big Thompson, better flash-flood warning systems, posting of signs, and so forth.

Still, when visiting Colorado there's one important thing to remember: Outrunning a flash flood is a terrible gamble. Make for higher ground.

Colorful Colorado Ghosts

Trying *to pare down* Colorado's hauntings is a lot like choosing the proverbial short list of books you'd take if you were exiled to a deserted island.

This is a state that, aside from the Native Americans, drew hordes of the greedy, the desperate, and the dogmatically impractical into situations of high danger for many decades.

That's just before the twentieth century.

As a result, Colorado has a rich lode of ghost stories that has been mined for years—enough to fill a library shelf with books.

The stories chosen here are still remarkable, but from the lesser-known veins of ghostly ore—personal experiences, tales from a distant time and location, those with a limited impact within a limited area or lack of definite origin. And one in Denver with a shadow of shame across it that has kept it in the back pages of history.

There's even a list of preferred sites if you're looking to experience a ghostly happening. Happy hunting!

Flossie McGrew's, Denver

Known as "Grandma Goth" (see the Local Heroes and Villains chapter), Suelynn Gustafson operated a quirky thrift and costume store called Flossie McGrew's in Denver for about twenty years before relocating a few blocks away next to her family's longtime business, Grandpa Snazzy's Hardware.

The two previous businesses in that location had no reports of anomalies. But after a few months of settling in, Gustafson and her employees began noticing strange goings-on.

One area gave off a cold, oppressive feeling that came and went.

"Over where the prom dresses are," says store manager Jeana Crum. "It's away from the front of the store and feels creepy. I felt someone touch my arm over in another area."

As comfortable as she is with the idea of the quick and the dead, there are times when the atmosphere encourages even Grandma Goth to give up the idea of spending a peaceful late night working in the store.

"I just don't feel welcome sometimes," she says. "Then I know it's time to go."

Anomalies don't appear to be linked to the building's history, which seems to have been uneventful. Given that much of the used merchandise currently sold is culled from dead folks' estates, defunct insane asylums, and such, perhaps the store's spookiness has been imported.

A clerk named Dan would occasionally spy a shadowy figure that seemed to slip away when approached. A baby stroller that was not known to be in the inventory was found hidden in the middle of a rack of clothing.

Dan spent the night in the store a couple of times—on an antique iron-frame bed reputed to be from the old Bellevue Hospital in New York City. Quite alone in the building, he nonetheless heard someone going through the metal racks of clothing. On another night, the stereo in the office switched on at full blast.

Crum says the copy machine in the office also suddenly turns itself on, and objects reputed to have very stable bases or attachments—such as the store's neon OPEN sign—have abruptly fallen down with no apparent cause.

A plumber, called after the store was flooded by a plumbing problem, was using a device to track old buried pipes when he said his metal-detection equipment went haywire for no reason he could tell.

On the front door of Flossie McGrew's there is a sign that reads NOT CELL PHONE FRIENDLY. The warning has more to do with strange doin's rather than poor reception.

Crum's cell phone rang at the store one day with an operator inquiring as to why she had called Information.

"[The phone] was over on the counter, not even within my reach at the time she insisted I called," says Crum. "And my daughter has been at home when she got two calls in a row from my cell phone with no one on the line."

On a Personal Note

As soon as I finished interviewing Grandma Goth and had walked away from her office to explore the rest of the store, my husband received five quick calls in succession from my cell phone. My phone was on, but stowed in my purse. I hadn't yet put any numbers on speed dial, nor had I accidentally redialed, which requires pushing more than one button.

Cheesman Park, Denver

Tragedy is the stuff of our spookiest legends, but it's not the fact that so many people were buried here that was the tragedy but what happened to many of them afterward.

By 1890, the city of Denver had grown to swallow the acres around an old cemetery called Prospect Hill at the intersection of Franklin Street and East Eighth Avenue. As fine new houses went up in the area, folks complained about the graveyard's weedy neglect. Cows were seen to graze there.

Most people preferred to bury their dead in the newer, better-kept cemeteries.

With the pressing needs of residential real estate to think of, the city of Denver decided that the bodies should be moved elsewhere and called on families and religious groups who maintained various portions of the cemetery to transfer their dead. But the largest portion of the cemetery, called "the Bone Yard" or "Boot Hill," was largely unaffiliated, and along with "Potter's Field," where the poor were buried, there were many graves left unclaimed.

So Denver hired an undertaker named E. P. McGovern to remove the caskets to Riverside and Fairmount cemeteries. That's when a dignified removal process quickly degenerated into crass commercial chaos.

There may have been a shortage of cheap adult coffins, which meant McGovern had to make due with child-sized coffins. Or not. McGovern was paid $1.90 for each coffin transferred so, whatever the excuse, it was a lucrative practice to use as many boxes as possible. McGovern's workers may have decided to compensate themselves for the gruesome job when they helped themselves to any valuables buried with the dead.

McGovern hadn't been paid to refill the gravesites, so gaping holes were everywhere. All this and general carelessness resulted in an unsightly and malodorous clutter. Denver newspapers took note and made an outcry.

As public indignation rose, local spiritualists (the period equivalent of today's "psychics") warned that if the bodies weren't reburied with a prayer said over every one, there would be hell to pay. One of McGovern's workers had already been nearly scared out of his wits by what was believed to be a spectral attack (he claimed a ghost had jumped on his back).

The embarrassed city government tore up McGovern's contract and moved to literally cover up the scandal quickly.

An estimated one thousand graves and countless scattered human remains were left where they were. The earth was graded and leveled over them, and the area eventually transformed into the beautiful attractions today known as Cheesman Park, City Park, and the Denver Botanic Gardens.

The grounds are landscaped and have structures. That requires gardening and other occasional earth moving, and that means once in a while a human jawbone or something equally disturbing surfaces. Once that comes to the attention of the news media, the old story of Prospect Hill gets a new airing. Otherwise, it's a largely forgotten scandal.

On a moonlit night, the stories say, you can see the telltale rectangles in the manicured grass that indicate back-filled empty graves or collapsed wooden caskets.

"Actually, you can see 'em better on a fall afternoon just before sunset," says Bryan Bonner, co-founder of the Rocky Mountain Paranormal Research Society (RMPRS). "But moonlight sounds better."

Bonner and the other members of RMPRS have been researching not only the anomalies, but the history behind the Southwest's allegedly haunted sites since 1999. Cheesman Park is a favorite.

The organization has been collecting stories about the park for some time. Because, as Denver's spiritualists warned, apparently there was hell to pay when the dead were left in a disturbed state.

It started early, with the residents of the fine new houses around the cemetery. As the desecration went on, alarmed neighbors shared reports of doorbells summoning them to empty doorsteps, strange faces appearing in mirrors, disembodied voices, and even vaporous visitors vanishing within homes as mysteriously as they had arrived.

Odd activity in the surrounding neighborhood continues to be reported to this day. People who have simply walked through the grounds of the transformed cemetery, without knowing the history of the park, have long commented on the feeling of sadness that seems to permeate the air.

But the number and quality of overall paranormal incidents are what's given the area, particularly Cheesman Park, its reputation for being the most haunted place in Denver. RMPRS granted permission for *Weird Colorado* to reprint two of the stories they collected here.

A Voice in the Moonlight

My cousin took an apartment near the park, and one night in 2002 we were walking through the dark to get to his place from King Soopers pharmacy. As we got near the pavilion, the moonlight was full and you could see anything in the bright light, including the dew on the outline of the graves on the grassy areas.

We were walking and heard a voice come at us from behind a tree or something, saying, "What are you doing here, please leave me in thy peace!"

It was audible from about two feet away.

Both stunned, we looked for the person and didn't see anybody. We heard the voice again asking us, "What are you doing here, please leave me in thy peace!" and followed it to a big tree, but there was nobody there or up in it.

It was not language from the twenty-first century, as people don't talk like that anymore. It kind of freaked us out. I made a joke saying if it was some dead person, they are probably pissed that people are in his space.

I do feel a sense of sadness in the park, especially driving near the south side, and up near the crest of the hill. There are also bad vibes from the botanical garden, where it seems the plants are not that lively there. It is like people are sad that they are forgotten about or lost, or something terrible happened there.

I am not keen at picking up spirits, but sense there are people who have had their graves desecrated and some who are just forgotten about. I feel women and children here who are very sad—perhaps some that have died from diseases. —*Jim*

It's Always the Graveyard Shift

I actually work right next to Cheesman Park at Denver Botanic Gardens. I am a security officer there and I have almost two years of tenure. During those two years I have worked day, swing, and graveyard shifts. I have experienced a multitude of things during that time.

Seeing "mists" of human figures. Seeing discernable human figures, color of clothing, skin, and hair were clearly visible. And I could not see through them, which is what usually happens.

Hearing my name being whispered. Hearing screaming in my ear. Women screaming inside the building and out in the gardens. Hearing doors slam. Hearing footsteps. Hearing the crinkle of someone sitting on a leather couch and no one was there. My keys fell out of a door and landed several feet away from the door.

Not to mention the countless times of overwhelming feelings of sadness, anger, and fear.

. . . [In addition] I have several witnesses to the following events.

A chair rolled across the room. Something grabbed my friend's ankle, and she literally jumped into my arms. Something grabbed my other friend's shoulder and tried to pull him into a boiler room.

The emergency phone from inside the elevator has rung on more than one occasion.

Something grabbed my friend's necklace, which had a "moon crystal" where the pendant would normally be. It lifted it, looked at it for a second, then dropped it back on her chest.

We have videotape of what appears to be a boy peeking out from behind a file cabinet in a secret staircase from the library to the master bedroom (which have now both been converted to offices) in the Waring House, which is an old mansion that was donated to the gardens.

We have pictures of "orbs" in some very haunted places in the main building. The white figment of a boy allowed us to touch him, put our hands through him, which sort of changed the color of our hands and we could still feel something, but there was no temperature change.

That about sums it up as far as the paranormal activity that I've seen, but the other security officers and employees of this facility have given countless other stories of paranormal events.

In addition, gardeners have found coffin handles, finger bones, and countless other items while digging and planting their plants. —*Anonymous*

Mackey Auditorium, CU Boulder

Organ music coming from a room long after the organ was removed and the room turned into an office. Blood stains reappearing on the walls. The screams of an invisible woman. The pale figures of two people that fade in and out.

Ghost stories about murders in old school buildings are not uncommon. Unfortunately, the story behind Mackey Auditorium at University of Colorado, Boulder is true, and it may be one of the granddaddies of its kind in America.

Since it opened in 1877, the campus northwest of Denver has been called one of the most beautiful universities in the United States. Mackey Auditorium, added in 1923, is one of the most attractive and best known of the buildings. As with the rest of CU, the auditorium's architecture—sandstone, brick, and neo-Gothic towers—suggests medieval Europe.

On July 6, 1966, a twenty-year-old zoology major named Elaura Jaquette was having her lunch and bird watching on the grass near Mackey while she waited for a couple of children she babysat to get out of a nearby movie theater. The remains of her lunch, her binoculars, and her wallet were found there, near the little irrigation channel that runs between the Guggenheim and Hale buildings.

A couple students discovered her body later that afternoon in the isolated organ recital room, in Mackey Auditorium's west tower. Jaquette had been raped and beaten to death so ferociously that several of her teeth were knocked out. Someone had tried to set her face on fire, possibly to hide her identity, but the volume of blood had thwarted the attempt.

A police investigation concluded Jaquette had tried to crawl away from her attacker, who had swung her by her feet so that her blood splattered as high as seven feet on most of the room's walls.

More than a thousand people were interviewed, and thirty days later a campus janitor named Joseph Dyre Morse was arrested. Morse, thirty-seven, had two teenage daughters who had seen their dad on the day of the murder carrying a bucket of bloody clothing. The print on a plywood board found at the crime scene also matched one of Morse's hands.

It turned out the normally placid and unremarkable janitor had a raging inner beast that was unleashed by alcohol. Witnesses saw him drinking at a bar near the campus that day, and stories of drunken passes at women and incidents of violence later came to light.

Morse was sentenced to 888 years in prison. He claimed innocence until 1980, when he finally made a terse confession: He'd met Jaquette when she worked at the CU admissions office. He never said how he lured her up the winding stairs of the west tower and into the organ recital room, but Jaquette had been an accomplished singer and pianist and loved music. He may have made some excuse based on that.

Once he had her in Mackey, Morse said, he made sexual advances that she rejected. And then, he said, "Things got out of hand." He refused to say anything more and died in prison in 2005 at age seventy-seven.

Alan Cass, the now retired theater manager of Mackey Auditorium, says he practically "grew up in Mackey," as his father was the building director. Alan was a student at CU and was employed at Mackey as a stage manager when the murder happened. He was vacationing out of town with his family when he heard of the news on his car radio, and drove all night to get back to Boulder.

Cass never met Jaquette, but he has helped keep her memory alive on the campus. On October 14, 2006, he and

the Jaquette family had the satisfaction of seeing a sandstone memorial installed on the grassy area where Jaquette was last seen. It was her birthday, and had she lived, she would have been sixty-one.

Stories about ghosts at Mackey Auditorium and other campus spots have floated around for decades. Cass says he's never had any spectral encounters there, although he's open to the possibility others may have seen specters—of a woman, and a man in a brown suit. But long familiarity with Mackey's workings has taught him that strange noises can be made by antique steam pipes and the creaking of an old building. Those noises could be mistaken for distant cries and organ chords. Odd shadows, fleeting images, and weird echoes, particularly in the service tunnels, could easily be the product of architecture and wonky lighting.

But those familiar with Jaquette's case and her family say the murdered student would not be the type to haunt the scene of her death. Jaquette was a devout Christian, they say. She would have forgiven her killer and been eager to be with her Lord.

A family friend who wished to remain anonymous says, "If ghosts are supposed to haunt the scenes of their demise because of the horrific nature of the crime that happened there, or their inability to accept their death, then that wouldn't have been her."

Of course, that might not be the case with her killer.

And the reappearing bloodstains in the former organ room?

"The whole room was cleaned up and painted over," says Cass. "I saw it soon after, and you'd never know what had happened there. Later, it was turned into an office for a retired professor, and he's put the place off-limits because he wants to keep his privacy. But plenty of people have had keys to the place, and probably looked in or gave looks to others. I think I know why they thought bloodstains kept reappearing on the walls."

The tower room has large, Renaissance-style, stained-glass windows. The windows are set in lead, and they leak.

"That room doesn't get cleaned a lot, and it's dusty," says Cass. "Water runs off the wet lead into the room, mixes with the dust and leaves grubby stains on the walls. We can clean it off, but every time the lead gets wet it happens again."

It was a long time ago, but out in western Colorado, a family still grieves for a daughter buried in a Grand Junction cemetery. Whatever odd and unexplained things might be happening in Mackey Auditorium, the friends and kin of Elaura Jaquette want you to know her spirit has graduated and moved on.

Morrison, near Denver

Seventeen miles from downtown Denver, drive off Highway C470 onto a road that slopes down to Morrison and you'll know why locals call it "The Nearest Faraway Place."

Morrison has the feel of an isolated mountain town because it rests in a small canyon-like area west of the Hogsback rock formation, with Bear Creek running through it.

It's best known for the famous Red Rocks Park and Amphitheater, a spectacular natural setting in sandstone used for everything from rock concerts to Easter sunrise services. But the restaurants, antiques shops, museum with dinosaur fossils, and the scenic locale make the town a tourist magnet all year round.

Morrison has about 430 permanent residents and, as some like to say, more ghosts per capita than any other American town.

That's according to Joel Chirhart and Renee Nellis, partners in a Morrison walking tour business called Colorado Haunted History. But they can point to plenty of people in town, as well as patrons of the tour, who bear their words out.

"We do about fifteen stories, ghostly and historical, in a one-and-a-half-hour tour," says Chirhart. "I don't have a real total of how many ghosts there are because there's something strange reported in just about every building in town. People tell us things all the time."

Some of the stories date from 1874, when the town was first founded by settlers who worked in the nearby rock quarries. A few of the best stories are from that early pioneer period. The Hanging Tree, for instance.

Well, actually, it's a stump now. At the edge of a parking lot. Seems it still carries a sinister aura.

"Supposed to have been a tree where people were hung right after their trial," says Chirhart. "We say that the amount of time it took to walk from the courtroom to this tree, that's how long they had to appeal! We've heard of sightings of 'shadow people' around it, black corners, weird smells, and photos that show orbs and mists with faces."

Over at the nearby Lacey Gate Antiques, the odors of sweet tobacco and baking have been reported—with no activities going on that would account for them. Visiting psychics claimed to have seen misty faces in the windows of the Horton House Bed and Breakfast (http://hortonhousebnb.com) and the Cliff House Lodge (www.cliffhouselodge.net).

There's the place called Tony Rigatoni's Italian Kitchen (www.tonyrigatonis.com).

"People sitting at the bar have seen the figure of a little girl descending the stairs," says Chirhart. "Dressed like she was from the 1800s. She doesn't seem to like men. The male chefs have had frying pans tossed at 'em, and there's a gate that will swing suddenly and hit 'em where guys don't like to be hit. Just the men. A manager came in one morning to do prep and was using the men's room. He couldn't get the bathroom door open. Stuck there for two hours. Somebody finally came and found a high chair wedged under the door knob."

Then there's the venerable Morrison Inn, now a bar that specializes in margaritas served in beer mugs.

"Few years back, there was a bartender who refused to believe the stories," says Chirhart. "One night, she's alone and decides to call on the resident ghost to show itself. All the televisions turned on by themselves. She runs upstairs at some point and sees a little old woman wearing ragged clothes and semi-transparent. They just stare at each other until the old lady vanishes."

Then there's the legend of the Hatchet Lady of Red Rocks.

"We've had people on the tour who remember the

Hatchet Lady," says Chirhart. "They admit to being among the teenagers in the 1950s who used to tease her. Nobody seems to know her name. She was homeless, but she lived in a cave among the Red Rocks. She'd come into town with this hatchet, I guess for chopping firewood or for protection. She got teased a lot. She finally passed away in her cave. Which nobody seems to know where it is these days.

"Maybe there was a rock slide, or the park maintenance staff just decided to seal it off, destroy it so it couldn't be used again. You can really hurt yourself climbing around the Rocks. Anyway, there's been several stories that says she suddenly appears, waving that hatchet. Little kids and teenagers, especially, they're warned to be careful when they're out among Red Rocks."

Helen Hunt Falls, near Colorado Springs

8407. Helen Hunt's Grave, Cheyenne Mountain, So. Cheyenne Canon, Colorado Springs, Colo.

Helen Fiske Hunt Jackson (1830–1885) was a passionate advocate for the rights of Native Americans and in 1881 wrote *A Century of Dishonor* about their mistreatment by the U.S. government. But she is best known for her 1884 novel *Ramona*, set in Spanish-ruled California with a Native American heroine.

After she moved to Colorado Springs for health reasons, Hunt fell in love with the city's North Cheyenne Cañon Park. She was buried on Cheyenne Mountain, and one of the waterfalls was named for her.

After a few years, her family grew disgusted with the toll gates that kept people from free access, and the vandalism that went on at her burial site, and transferred her body to Evergreen Cemetery in Colorado Springs. The original memorial plaque remains on her former burial site near Helen Hunt Falls.

The lovely waterfalls draw plenty of visitors, but the slippery, sloping trails around them are treacherous. Some people claim the souls of unlucky accident victims haunt the area.

An Occurrence at Helen Hunt Falls

At first, it started out great. We arrived at the investigation site and split into two groups of three girls and three guys.

We girls went up to "Helen's" area and walked around for a couple hours, doing EVP work, taking pictures and video. The guys stayed below and did their own EVP work and tried to provoke the "spirits" into moving something. They thought they heard something humming behind them.

When I reviewed the footage, it wasn't humming they heard. It was a little boy's voice that said, "I don't want to move anything." That was pretty cool.

We girls came back down from our hike, regrouped, discussed what had happened, and chatted for a bit when Becki (our founder) got the urge to check out a path that we hadn't noticed before. Then it all went to hell. . . .

She went down to check out the path and was leaning on a very large rock. She stared out on the other side of the creek for a while and seemed to be in some sort of trance. We stayed up top around the fence and took pictures. Then all of a sudden Becki just collapsed. Apparently she called out and asked someone to come get her and the only person who heard her was Travis (my husband), so he went down to get her and swore he felt something rush past him.

He brought her back up, and she recovered and said, "Don't let me back down there." We hung out on the benches around the building for a little bit, letting her rest. Fifteen minutes later, she started running back down the hill to the path, so Jen (a fairly new member of our group), Travis, and I ran after her.

Finally, Becki stopped in front of a drainpipe. She was staring at it and pointing at it. Jen and I dragged Becki up the hill, kicking and screaming. I couldn't think of anything else but getting her away from that path. When we got her back onto the road, she collapsed again and came to a few minutes later. She was very confused and couldn't remember where we were or what had happened.

Apparently while we were on the path with Becki, Travis blacked out after having a vision of two people being gutted on the rock by a creature with a sunken-in face and long sharp claws.

We were going back to the cars when Becki leaned against the car with the same weird look on her face and made a growling noise I had heard in the woods earlier. (There is *no* possible way for a human to make that noise . . . . We all tried it later and couldn't.) After a couple minutes Becki was herself again. We got into the cars and got the hell out of there.

Before all of this happened, we decided to turn off all of our equipment for some reason. All cameras and voice recorders were off, and I don't know why. We usually leave them all on until we get into the cars to leave, especially the digital cameras. When we started walking along the path, I had my digital around my neck. Yet I remember when we started walking, I said, "I don't need this, I don't know why it's on," and then I turned it off.

Before Becki went down the path the first time, she took the voice recorder out of her pocket and said, "I'm not feeling anything, I'm going to turn this off now."

Something *did not* want us having proof of this. . . .

I know, the story seems absolutely ridiculous, but I swear it all to be true and have four other people who will back me up on it who were all there that night. This experience was truly frightening for all of us. We haven't been anywhere near this location since, and I doubt we will ever go back.

—*Stacey, co-founder of P.I.G. (Paranormal Investigating Group of Colorado Springs and Victor, Colorado)*

Dead Man's Canyon, between Colorado Springs and Cañon City

William Henry Harkens, sometimes known as Henry Harkins, was one of the earliest known victims of the "Terrible Espinosas" (see the Local Heroes and Villains chapter) murdered on March 19, 1863, in southern Colorado. He was found dead outside the cabin he was building near Little Fountain Creek off the Cheyenne Mountain Road between Colorado Springs and Cañon City.

Harkens, then about fifty-five, had an ax sunk in his forehead. His white horse had been stolen, the cabin vandalized. His friends and neighbors buried him nearby.

The area became known as Dead Man's Canyon. Travelers in the area almost immediately began to report the horrific vision of a bearded man with an ax in his forehead. Sometimes he rode a white horse. Always he charged at people, laughing maniacally, sometimes for miles, sometimes just for a few minutes.

According to the book *Twilight Dwellers: Ghosts, Ghouls, and Goblins of Colorado* by MaryJoy Martin: In the fall of 1874, a man named J. P. Galloway reported being swooped on by the ghost on Cheyenne Mountain Road. Two men who rode at a distance behind Galloway saw him chased by a strange figure wearing what they thought was odd headgear.

The two men, Lawrence Poole and Adam Baker, shot wildly at Galloway's pursuer, who laughed at them and vanished. When the dust cleared, Poole discovered he had winged his horse in one ear and Baker had grazed his own toes. All three reported the experience to a doctor in Colorado Springs.

Then in July 1884, Mrs. Clark Wyatt of Colorado Springs reported that she slashed the ghost with her buggy whip and scolded it for scaring her grandchild. The ghost vanished, and did not reappear on her return trip.

Cheyenne Mountain Road is now Highway 115. Little Fountain Creek still burbles quietly near rocks and cottonwoods, but the remains of Harkens's cabin are gone. According to the Cemetery Project in Pikes Peak, Harkens's grave is about 5.8 miles south of the main entrance to Fort Carson, southwest of Colorado Springs, on the east side of Highway 115. It is supposed to be visible from the road, on a little wooded mound with a white fence around it. The original grave marker is now encased in a bigger one.

Pine Creek High's Auditorium Phantom

My old high school, Pine Creek High School, had a very tragic school year in 2003–2004. Three students died that year: Huston Bossler had a heart attack, another guy fell through some ice on a lake and drowned, and another hung himself on a children's play set at an elementary school. Soon after, rumors that Pine Creek was haunted began to circulate.

The rumors said that a ghost lived in the auditorium. The students who saw it said it walked the rafters or hung around in the corners of the auditorium. One or two saw it on the stage. Some students say that the auditorium is where the first boy died (the heart attack victim, Huston Bossler), but I am unsure of the accuracy of this statement. The students who made it public knowledge that they had seen the ghost were teased and mocked mercilessly, and so many chose to tell only their closest friends. The teachers tried to dispel the rumors, but then one had a brush with the Auditorium Phantom.

Mr. Bill Dykshorn, the band director, had just finished recording some of the band's music, and had put the CD in the computer in the auditorium to listen to it. As he did, he heard very clearly on the CD a deep voice saying, "Get out." At first, Mr. D was angry because he thought a bunch of the students had been messing with the recording, so he tried to eject the CD to dispose of it. The CD refused to eject, and instead, the hardware of Mr. D's computer melted. The Pine Creek administration replaced the computer and said it was an electrical problem.

I was skeptical of these stories, so I agreed to look for the ghost with one of my friends who'd been doing research on ghost hunting.

We got to the auditorium and decided to use six dice to communicate with the ghost on certain questions. We began the séance and my friend asked how old the ghost was. The dice read 18. He asked again, and again the dice came up 18. He asked once more. The answer? 18. By now, we were all authentically freaked out, and even I, the group skeptic, found it difficult to think it was coincidence. The probability of the dice coming up 18 three times in a row was not high at all. But it happened.

My friend asked the ghost if it wanted us to get out. The answer was yes. He asked the ghost if we wanted to stay. The answer was no, and then we all simultaneously felt a chilly draft. Panicked, we packed up and hurried out of there as fast as possible.

The next day, I went back to look for a vent that must have caused our draft. I couldn't find one. In the entire auditorium, there wasn't a single vent positioned at the angle it would have needed to hit us with the draft.

Reports of cold spots and ghostly sightings in the

We were all authentically freaked out.

auditorium are still whispered about, and they became more public, since Pine Creek now had a teacher who had witnessed these odd events. Teachers still try to disprove the rumors, and have taken to banning students from the auditorium during free time. Mr. D was called a liar. Even I still have trouble believing in the phantom. But always in the back of my mind is the memory of those six die coming up 18 three times in a row. —*Emily J. Misciagna*

Odd Fellows' Lodge, Boulder

Boulder Lodge No. 9 of The Independent Order of Odd Fellows and its auxiliary, Ivy Rebekah Lodge No. 51, has continued to hold ritual and revelry in their handsome old building at the corner of Sixteenth and Pearl Streets in Boulder since 1899.

By 2000, however, the structure needed a lot of updating and restoration and, fortunately, the lodge was able to get a grant for historic preservation to do it. Over the next few years, restoration work involved many of the lodge members, who noticed strange things were afoot.

The thing that really tended to shiver people's timbers was the footsteps that would come up or down the old wooden staircase inside the building and to the threshold of whatever room someone was working in. And there they'd stop, as if something was looking.

It happened several times to Betty Chronic. She recalls a perfect example:

I was in a room by myself, and I could have sworn I was alone in the building. Then I heard the footsteps, which I assumed were Bill's (her husband). And those footsteps came right up to the room's doorway and paused. I had my back turned and I was busy and finally I said, "Bill, what are you doing just standing there? I need you." nd after another minute I turned and there was nothing there. Well, I looked all around the building for whoever that was. The doors were still locked.

When the outspoken Chronic brought the incident up, it unleashed a flood of relief for members who had experienced similar events but were afraid to speak. They were mystified. The building didn't have a history of ghosts or other anomalies. At least one person has privately claimed to have heard billiard balls smacking around on the elegant antique pool tables in the recreation room. But no one was actually in the room, and the equipment was still sitting innocently in its rightful places.

In the lodge's heyday of thousands of people coming and going, one member was notable for taking on repairs and any necessary construction work himself. He and his wife were childless, and the lodge was their life.

This member died sometime in the last century at the Odd Fellows' home for aged members in Cañon City. But his strong involvement and proprietary attitude toward the lodge made him the perfect candidate if anyone were to come back to check on the old place.

His name was Wilbur. So that's what lodge members have named the manifestations as a single entity. Footsteps pausing outside the door? Wilbur's just checking in. Doorbell ringing without reason? Wilbur's making sure someone's on duty. Scent of tobacco mysteriously lingering in the air? Wilbur's having a smoke.

After all, the Odd Fellows' motto is "Friendship, Love and Truth." And that, apparently, goes beyond the grave.

The Beast in the Basement of the Stanley Hotel

The Stanley Hotel in Estes Park is a well-known landmark for locals and [was] the inspiration for Stephen King's classic novel *The Shining*.

This place is very haunted. The hotel is very old and just underwent a complete remodeling. There are three buildings on the property, which is perched high above Estes Park, giving King good reason to name the hotel in his book. The Overlook Hotel. The main building isn't very creepy and is a nice place to stay, but every building is haunted in one way or another. The building I'll focus on here is the theater.

I already knew the main building quite well but had never explored the theater, which is adjacent to the main building. The site was buzzing with activity in the middle of the day, with tons of construction going on and workmen and equipment everywhere.

After I entered the theater, the whole mood of my visit changed. All of the hustle and bustle of a busy construction site went away. I was now in a dark theater that hadn't been used for many years. The windows were boarded, the seating was tipped over, and there was dust everywhere. Spray paint and vandalism decorated the inside, and there was a thick, musty smell to the air.

I slowly crept in toward the stage, which was littered with old props and seemed still set up for the show that once played there. I made my way up on stage and saw two narrow corridors on either side of the backstage area. The hall on the right led to an old wardrobe and make-up area, still filled with clothes and props.

The hall on the left would change me forever.

Slowly making my way towards the backstage left hall, I noticed a strange, awful smell. I peeked around the corner, expecting to see another makeup or wardrobe area, but instead saw very old, very rotted steps that went straight down into the basement. The entrance was boarded up and spray-painted GO

AWAY. The shoddy construction of the wall left places where you could see through to the other side, and I saw a moving light source gleaming through the cracks.

I stood silent, listening for anything that would clue me in to who was down there. I said "Hello?" down into the dank basement, and the light immediately stopped moving. I heard a small rustle from below, and said it again: "Hello?"

I really didn't think too much of this situation, considering there was a $300 million construction project going on not five feet outside the front door. I wasn't alone here, and how much danger could I really be in, surrounded by huge concrete workers?

After my second attempt to confirm if someone was in the basement, I stood painfully still, listening for anything. The light moved again, but only slightly. I thought maybe there was a construction worker down there, and he was trapped or stuck.

I made my way down to the wall that was blocking entrance to the basement and peeked through the cracks in the plywood. There was an empty, dirt-floored room, with a single lightbulb swinging from the cord attached to the ceiling.

I said for a third and final time, "Hello?"

I heard breathing, seemingly right on the other side of the wall. Then it happened. As I peered from left to right through the crack in the plywood, I saw another eyeball staring directly back at me through quarter-inch plywood. I froze for a second, not sure I was even seeing what my brain thought I was seeing. The eye was bright green and staring unamused straight through me. I also could now smell the horrible stench of his/her/its breath through the crack.

I couldn't move, couldn't breathe, and couldn't do anything. The figure in the basement didn't speak, didn't break the stare into my eyes, and only let out an animal-like grunt. I ran as fast as I could back up the stairs, off the stage, and out the door. I never returned to the Stanley Hotel. I don't know what was down there, and I don't want to know. —*Jeff Bittner*

Haunted Inns and Watering Holes

It makes sense that long-established lodgings, restaurants, and bars in old buildings are almost like ATMs for ghost stories. Ask a bartender, housekeeping manager, or waitperson who's been around awhile and you'll generally get a few stories about strange, even spooky incidents on the premises.

The Stanley Hotel

When you mention ghosts in Colorado, the Stanley Hotel comes up the most often. It's a magnificent old building with 138 rooms set against the background of the Rockies in the town of Estes Park.

Author Stephen King was inspired to use it as a model for his murderously haunted, winter-shuttered resort in *The Shining*. Although the Stanley was not used as the location to film the movie version, it's in the 1995 television miniseries and has served as a movie location in other films.

Freeland Oscar Stanley, inventor of an early automobile called the Stanley Steamer, opened the hotel in 1908. It had everything but heat, as it was intended to operate only during the summer. Famous guests of the past include President Teddy Roosevelt, Margaret "the Unsinkable Molly Brown" Tobin, and John Philip Sousa.

Stanley sold the hotel in 1926, and it went through several changes of ownership until it was refurbished and reopened in 2002.

There's a long history of hauntings at the Stanley reported by both staff and guests, including Stephen King. One of the best-known ghosts is supposed to be that of an Irish peer, Windham Thomas-Quin, the fourth Earl of Dunraven.

Lord Dunraven did his best to grab up the whole of Estes Park for his own private game preserve. The locals put up so much opposition to the fraud and strong-arm tactics his agents used that Dunraven eventually gave up on the idea and sold some of the land to Stanley, where the hotel is built.

Dunraven's spirit is associated with Room 407, where he has reportedly been seen standing. The lights in the bathroom turn on and off independently, and a face has been seen peering out of one of the windows

In season or out, the hotel seems to be continually operating on another plane. Sounds of children playing are heard both inside and outside Room 418 when there are no children booked at the hotel. Doors open and shut on their own, elevators move independently, invisible footsteps are heard, music by unseen bands plays, and various ghostly figures of men, women, and children, including Mr. and Mrs. Stanley, are seen fairly regularly.

The Peck House

Less well known as a haunted hotel is The Peck House in Empire, thirty-five miles west of Denver. It was built in 1862 and is Colorado's oldest hotel. Some of its most notable guests include P. T. Barnum and the Civil War generals Ulysses S. Grant and William Tecumseh Sherman. In more recent years, it's been a bed-and-breakfast.

Among the ghosts believed present here is that of the founder, James Peck, who was killed in a buggy accident at age seventy-nine, and Gracie Peck, who died of pneumonia at age thirteen (her coughing can occasionally be heard).

The Lumber Baron Inn

The Lumber Baron Inn in northwest Denver is also a nineteenth-century bed-and-breakfast. It's a redbrick mansion in the Queen Anne style surrounded by a lush garden planned by John Moat, the original owner, who made a fortune in the lumber business.

Its fortunes declined with a succession of owners and, like many old, big houses in Colorado, it was cobbled into several apartments. In 1970, it was the scene of one of Denver's most notorious unsolved crimes, a double homicide.

The bodies of two young women were discovered on October 12, 1970, by a man who was looking for a friend, Marianne Weaver, eighteen, a college student. He found her dead in the cheap studio rented by a runaway named Cara Lee Knoche, seventeen. Weaver was laid out neatly on the bed with arms crossed and a bullet hole in her forehead. Knoche was found stripped, strangled, and stuffed under the bed.

Their killer has never been found. Investigations, both police and of a paranormal nature, never turned up enough evidence on which to base an arrest.

Walter Keller bought the old house in 1991, when it could diplomatically be called a "fixer-upper." He spent years, sweat, and money restoring the house and garden to their original splendor. It's now a popular site for wedding parties, meetings, and other special events.

According to a 2003 interview in the *Denver Post*, Keller, his family, and various guests have experienced a number of strange incidents—seeing or simply sensing a presence that would evaporate in a gust of cold air, smelling pipe smoke or women's toilet powder, hearing someone come down the stairs as the treads moved, feeling something invisible brush past, and more. Keller's small son claimed the ghost of a teenage boy in his bedroom greeted him pleasantly every morning.

The Hotel Jerome

When the Hotel Jerome opened in 1899, it was the swankiest place the silver-mining boomtown of Aspen had seen, a grand hotel compared to the fabulous Ritz of Paris.

As Aspen went from boomtown to ski town to millionaire's playground, the hotel definitely aged well, kept up with the need to modernize, and continues to be one of Colorado's premier's lodgings.

Any place over a hundred years old is bound to rack up some ghost tales, but there's one story that tends to be the most enduring. Roz Brown and Ann Alexander Leggett tell it best in *Haunted Boulder 2*:

> *After a long day of sightseeing in Aspen, the woman staying in room 310 returned to find a little boy standing in the middle of her room, dripping wet and shivering. After leaving to find a hotel attendant, she returned to find only damp footprints on the floor. The hotel register was checked again and again in hopes of finding the parents of the lost boy, but to no avail. As a matter of fact, no children were registered in the hotel at the time. Further research would prove that room 310, located in the newer addition of the hotel, was situated directly over the old hotel pool, since covered over, where a young boy had reportedly drowned many, many years ago. Sightings of the boy throughout the hotel have continued over the years.*

The Old Louisville Inn

The Old Louisville Inn in Louisville is just what it says, and once it was a lot more. The back room once functioned as a brothel, and a prostitute named Samantha is said to have been stabbed to death there.

This, after all, was the heart of the Red Light District that served the farming, railroad, and mining men of the Louisville area with twenty-two saloons and many brothels.

The Inn boasts one of Colorado's oldest bars, a beauty built in the 1880s from three kinds of cherry, birch, and mahogany, cut to fit without nails, and graced with a copper spit trough that used to have running water. That trough was necessary as flammable gases from the Acme Coal Mine below the inn continually seeped upward. Bar patrons mindful of mortality chewed tobacco rather than risk explosion with a lighted match.

Louisville has always been known for its community spirit, and that was never as evident as during Prohibition in the 1920s. This being a mining town, there was no lack of skilled volunteers to rise—make that descend—to the occasion and dig tunnels in short order that connected all the saloons. At the first sign of the sheriff's approach, all the customers would vanish with their libations.

In 1994, Garrett and Martha McCarthy bought this last surviving saloon of Louisville's Red Light District and soon learned that more came along with the place than a lot of colorful history.

Again, we're indebted to Roz Brown and Ann Alexander Leggett for the research and interviews they did on the old bar for their *Haunted Boulder 2*.

Garrett McCarthy entered the basement one day and walked into a "cylinder of freezing cold air" that literally froze him to the spot for a brief, unforgettable moment. Staff members have heard footsteps when no one else was about and, once, the unmistakable sound of a rack of pots and pans crashing. Of course, nothing had actually happened.

After hours, the security monitors give little reassurance to people working elsewhere in the building who happen to glance at them. McCarthy once dropped his paperwork and bolted up the basement stairs to find that there was no man sitting calmly in the back booth, as the monitors had shown.

When he bought the inn from previous owners, McCarthy heard about a female ghost dubbed Samantha, after the murdered prostitute. He was personally introduced to her after hours one night when the spring-loaded kitchen door swung open on its own. McCarthy was sitting at the bar with his brother-in-law and asked Samantha to give them a sign that it was she who had opened the door.

After closing up and leaving the building, they noticed that the inn's unlit neon sign had turned itself back on.

Since McCarthy is originally from Ireland, that country's best athlete for more than eleven years and a World Championship Triathlon gold medalist, it's a given that the inn hosts a blow-out party every St. Patrick's Day.

For years, sudden problems with the heating, plumbing, computers, etc., would threaten to shut things down right before the event. Apparently, Samantha didn't care for big crowds.

McCarthy is careful now to do preventative maintenance in the week leading up to his party and give Samantha a little sweet talk as he does so.

It must be working. The party is on for this year.

The Buckhorn Exchange

The Buckhorn Exchange in Denver may be the one place in the world that advertises itself as a combination of museum, restaurant, and saloon.

It was founded in 1893 by Henry H. "Shorty Scout" Zietz, who was issued the state's first liquor license. "Old West fare" has been offered in the same location ever since, including rattlesnake and the infamous Rocky Mountain

oysters. Plus it's got a cocktail created at the Buckhorn's elaborate white oak bar by no less than William "Buffalo Bill" Cody.

On the walls are 575 examples of taxidermy, from buffalo to the mythic jackalope. Oh, and a two-headed calf, the real thing. The establishment's gun collection carries about twelve pieces.

So many colorful folks have bellied up to the bar here for so long that it's no wonder stories of odd goings-on abound. Voices, laughter, snatches of music, invisible footsteps, elusive faces in mirrors, lights going on and off by themselves. And sometimes the tables move, without visible assistance and rather suddenly. Witnessed without the benefit of having Cody's cocktail first.

University of Denver

Some institutions don't like to acknowledge the paranormal anomalies that are reported about their buildings, but the University of Denver is quite open about them, and even mentions on its Web site that it's supposed to be one of Colorado's most haunted spots.

The school is the oldest and largest private university in the Rocky Mountain area. Its first buildings went up in the 1890s.

Mary Reed was a Denver women's rights activist and philanthropist who donated generously to the university.

The school named a building for her in 1931 and another for her daughter, Margery, a University of Denver grad who died at thirty-one of an illness contracted in Peru. Reed herself died in 1945. The Mary Reed Building today serves as the campus's secondary library, providing overflow library storage and administrative offices.

Staff, students, and visitors have reported odd things happening in the building for years—doors quietly shut by themselves, lights and elevators operate independently, fresh lightbulbs burn out too soon, and rattling noises no one can trace are heard after dark.

Sometimes people see the transparent figure of a woman on the staircase. Because of Mary Reed's close involvement with the building, it's generally believed that it is her spirit, or Margery's, watching over the place.

There is a small library room in the Mary Reed Building's tower that rises over the campus called the DuPont Room. This was named for Marcella Miller Du Pont, a poet and socialite, who donated money for a separate study in the library in memory of her parents in 1966. She died in 1985.

Marcella Du Pont had a close and affectionate relationship with the school and, in a letter to a faculty member in 1967, wrote, "Remember that when I am far away, I am always thinking . . . of the Room."

Perhaps it was harder to leave it behind than anyone could imagine. People walking in have been greeted by an elderly woman reading in a chair before vanishing. There are reports of cold spots in the room, lights that turn on and off by themselves, and books that suddenly fly off the shelves.

Otherwise, the room has stayed pretty peaceful, even after a recent renovation. The little room is still much the way it was when she spent time there, with high-backed leather chairs and glass-front bookcases.

Less pleasant stories tell of students and employees being shoved by invisible hands, sometimes while on the staircases.

That doesn't seem to fit in with the known characters of the Mesdames Reed and Du Pont. Given the thousands of people who have come and gone on the campus over many years, it may very well be that there are other, less thoughtful, spirits making themselves felt in the Mary Reed Building.

RMPRS's Best Places to Experience Ghosts in Colorado

The Rocky Mountain Paranormal Research Society (RMPRS) has been investigating places alleged to be haunted in the Southwest since 1999.

It is a deliberately small group—eight people with various technical skills and areas of expertise—that doesn't claim to have "certified ghost hunters," "demonologists," or even "psychics." The focus is to help people who have been disturbed by paranormal activity and advance legitimate research in an area historically dismissed by scientists.

Here are a few of the group's favorite haunts for those who'd like the possibility of a paranormal peek.

Brook Forest Inn and Spa, Evergreen

Built in 1919, thirty-five miles west of Denver, this Alpine-style hotel and spa has a history that includes outlaws and Nazis. The management gladly shares a number of ghost encounters reported by guests and occasionally offers paranormal lecture tours, assisted by the RMPRS.

The Elk Horn Lodge, Estes Park

Built in the 1870s, it's the oldest dude ranch in the Rocky Mountain region and the oldest continuously operating hotel in Colorado. It's located at the base of Man Mountain, sacred to Native Americans. It's been alleged that the nearby Stanley Hotel has taken credit for many of the ghostly sightings and other encounters actually reported here.

Melting Pot Restaurant, Littleton

A fondue eatery is housed in the former Carnegie Library just south of Denver. Previously it was a jail, and an escaping inmate was killed here. Restaurant staff and patrons have reported poltergeist activity and disembodied voices.

Cemetery Safari

Whether crowded old churchyards, aboveground crypts, or spacious parklike grounds, cemeteries are the mute repositories of our history and testimony to our social changes.

What's surprising is what occurs in so many cemeteries: clandestine meetings, theft and vandalism, monument repair, paranormal investigation and genealogy searches, picnics and competitions. It's almost enough to wake the dead.

And if you look around you might find memorials to the departed in odd places—dedicated to some unlikely local characters. Reminding us that in the midst of Life, the dead truly are still with us.

Evergreen Cemetery, Colorado Springs

One of two pioneer cemeteries in Colorado Springs (the other is the smaller Fairview Cemetery), Evergreen offers an interesting look at some bygone customs. The Arts and Crafts–style nondenominational chapel, built in 1900, was an ivy-overgrown derelict when cemetery manager Will DeBoer started restoration efforts in 1992.

"The roof was shot, half the stained-glass windows were broken or missing, and the woodwork was a disaster," he says. "We got it listed on the National Register of Historic Places and that enabled us to get grants for restoration work. But, there's still a lot to be done—as yet, there's no heating, no plumbing, and no permanent seating. Sales from our book, *Here Sleeps Colorado Springs*, and fund-raising like our annual walking tours help, but we've had to put those things on hold for now."

When open for a rare tour, a chapel visit is a must to see the original mechanical casket lifter that transported coffins from the vaults below to the first floor. The vaults were meant to store bodies when the ground was too frozen for digging. Huge, arched, wooden double doors open

to reveal stark brick rooms with stacked slate slabs on which the bodies rested in their caskets. It's definitely cool and dark down here, even in the middle of August, but that wasn't enough to deter some of nature's least aesthetic processes, so "bloat balls" were sometimes employed.

At least that's what a "half-blind, eighty-year-old carpenter from Lithuania told us they were during the restoration," says DeBoer. "I've researched the subject all over, but I haven't ever found another reference to 'bloat balls.' I don't have another explanation for what these things are, though, so it's good enough for me."

A bloat ball, if that's what they are, resembles a concrete bowling ball with a single finger hole. Supposedly, one was put on top of a corpse's torso to deter the accumulation of gases that might otherwise cause a body to swell right out of its coffin. The chapel has three of the bloat balls on display.

If that's more information then you'd like to know, you can still enjoy Evergreen for its beautiful landscaping, handsome old crypts, interesting grave markers, and colorful stories.

Possibly the best-known grave marker here is one that's been featured several times over the years by Ripley's Believe It or Not! in its long-running newspaper feature. It's the headstone of a couple named Gunn and is inscribed, "Papa, have you wound your watch?" Addie, wife of Charles B. Gunn, a railroad worker, would ask her husband this question daily so that his pocket watch would keep him punctual. Addie died in 1909; Charles, in 1935.

From about the 1930s to the 1950s, Evergreen Cemetery was famous for its many rose trellises over individual headstones.

"It was said when the roses were in bloom you could smell the place for miles," says Dianne Hartshorn, director of the Evergreen Cemetery Benevolent Society.

Roses need lots of water—a challenge in the Rockies' arid climate. Today, just keeping the grass green in Evergreen and its smaller sister, Fairview, costs about $150,000 annually. While the cemetery is owned by the city of Colorado Springs, the individual graves and crypts are supposed to be the responsibility of the plot owners, and without survivors to keep the graves tended, the roses died off. The bulky, weed-sheltering metal trellises are being phased out, but many remain.

A lack of survivors to tend the plots also creates a problem when grave markers are broken or stolen. DeBoer says he's had to do some grave dowsing a few times to locate a lost grave. (Dowsing has been called a form of divination, produced by involuntary muscle movement or ideomotor action. It's been used for everything from finding water to locating bodies.)

"I can always tell where the earth's been disturbed," he says.

Fortunately, the Evergreen Cemetery Benevolent Society volunteers address the needs of the older, orphaned plots.

"The society has just been a gift from heaven," says DeBoer. "The members take care of the graves that don't have a family to care for 'em, and they help us with the fund-raising. They dress up like some of the folks buried here and do the annual walking tour, which gets a great turnout."

"We're trying to raise awareness of Evergreen," says Ingrid McDonald, a volunteer who is also a police officer. "When there's a community that cares about its cemetery and takes care of it, you won't have a lot of the problems of vandalism and theft. You preserve the history that literally goes into this place, the people who built this city and gave us so much. People used to groom and decorate graves all the time, bring in a picnic lunch and just enjoy the beauty and quiet and the memories. We want to see that kind of respect for it again."

Fund-raising efforts have helped raise the level of public awareness and appreciation. The chapel is still occasionally used and has even been the site of a costumed Halloween wedding—the bride made her appearance via the casket lifter.

"And, that couple is still married and has a couple of kids," says DeBoer, who counts that as among his favorite Evergreen stories.

Another is the biker funeral that took place not long ago.

"Real, hard-core bikers," he says. "Their sergeant-at-arms died, and the whole club wanted to participate in his funeral here. There I was in my white sport coat, tie, and white minivan leading all these Harleys and a sea of leather. They brought a whole flatbed truck full of flowers. They wanted to dig the grave and fill it in themselves.

"There must have been seven hundred to eight hundred attendees, and even after they passed around quite a few bottles, it was one of the most respectful and orderly crowds I've ever dealt with. All they left behind were the flowers and trampled grass."

Besides the walking tour, the cemetery also shows classic horror movies in the chapel at Halloween.

"You gotta get creative with the fund-raisers . . ." says DeBoer.

The "Olympics" of Cemetery Skills

Since 1988, Colorado has played host to a biannual contest that showcases the very particular talents of cemetery workers. Cemetery skills are about much more than just digging a final resting place. This competition puts them all to the test: funeral setup, backhoe skills, a backhoe obstacle course, mower operation, trailer backing, backpack blower skills, and weed-whackin'—the backstage sort of things that many people do not notice.

"Our skills are every bit a serious service for the public," says Tom Van Buskirk, manager of the Linn Grove Cemetery in Greeley. "And, our competition is just as meaningful and purposeful as competitions between firefighter stations or police teams or something."

Van Buskirk's been a bit put out at the jocular tone that dominates most news media coverage of this event. Sure, when he first proposed it at the convention of the Colorado Association of Cemeteries in the late 1980s, he thought a contest would be something fun. It was never meant to be an event just for morbid yuks though.

"The Summer Olympics were going on, or maybe it was the Olympics trials; I don't remember which," he says. "But, anyway, I think I was president of the Colorado Association of Cemeteries, and we were having our convention at the same time. And, I proposed to the rest of the board at the closing banquet that we, as professionals, have our own kind of Olympics. I thought it would be a great way for our line workers to demonstrate their skill levels, have a day off and a little fun among their peers. And, I'll admit I'm a fairly competitive guy. I liked the idea of exposing the excellence of my staff and property."

Van Buskirk proposed that the first competition be held at the cemetery he managed in Greeley (sans the "Olympics" title to avoid a clash with the official athletic events).

"Our property was so symmetrical I knew it would provide a pretty fair and evenly projective competition," he says. He wouldn't have a home-team advantage, in other words. Still, the Lynn Grove team has most often taken home the first place trophy, as awarded by a panel of judges. Participation averages twelve teams from different cemeteries, and Van Buskirk would like to see more.

"The smaller properties, I think they're a little bit intimidated," he says. "Some of them only have one or two guys."

The point system should make it possible for even the smallest teams to win, he says. In August 2008, the competition was begun on a warm Saturday morning in Evergreen Cemetery in Colorado Springs.

A yellow backhoe lumbered up to a row of rectangles sprayed onto bare earth, and competitors demonstrated how to wield the digging bucket as if it were a large vending machine claw. Soil to a certain depth was brought up—without straying outside the painted rectangle—and transferred to the back of a dump truck.

Other backhoe operators picked up automobile tires and dropped them over a tetherball pole. Rather surprisingly, this appeared harder than digging a grave. Another backhoe was used to test the steering (backward and forward) of this ungainly machine around a course of orange cones. There was the contest with string trimmers (maneuvering around a small field of bright little flags), demonstrations of leaf-blowing prowess (herding smallish white balls around), and the riding-lawn-mower obstacle course. Precision in a short amount of time really is an issue when trying to avoid knocking over, whacking, and dinging of the cemetery markers, monuments, floral tributes, and other mementos.

The crowd-pleaser event may have been the funeral setup. Two-person teams raced against the clock to drape an open grave with decorative cloths, set up the rack on which the coffin would rest before being lowered into the ground, and put the seating for the mourners into place. Judges watched all the action intently, and while there was some sweating on the part of the participants, camaraderie between all parties was high.

Everyone broke for lunch—a fine catered affair with plenty of barbecue—and then the competition resumed for a couple of hours, and ended around three in the afternoon with a medal-awarding ceremony. What's impressive to an outside observer is the quiet dignity these cemetery workers show. They don't horse around, and they take an interest in new technology, such as the casket a manufacturer's representative brought to the event to demonstrate its resistance to years of soil weight.

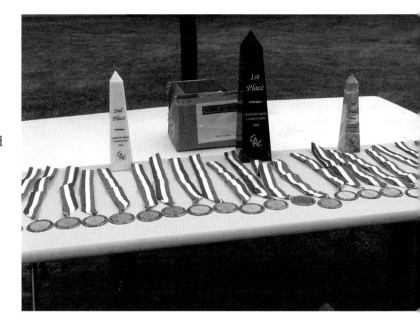

"I don't know how much longer some of us will be in this business," says one man who gives his name only as Jim. "There are places where the owners are talking about how it's too expensive to have a regular staff. They want to outsource—bring in guys who'll come in once a week or less to just do a mow and blow. You can't keep a cemetery looking as good as we do with that kind of thing. The mow-and-blow guys won't have a stake in the place. They won't know the people buried there, and they won't much care, either. And, if there aren't people around all the time, well, forget about keeping the vandals out. That's how you see gravestones pushed over and broken or stolen, crap spray-painted everywhere, monuments used for target practice."

Van Buskirk received a lot of back slapping when the event was over and looked like a very happy man. "This may be the year I retire as a cemetery manager, but the competition will keep on. It's been a real success and a lot of fun, too."

The Dancing Lights of Cross of the Assumption and Silver Cliff Cemeteries

Local lore in the tiny neighboring towns of Silver Cliff and Westcliffe says that the mystery lights are more often seen in the Catholic cemetery than in the neighboring Protestant Silver Cliff Cemetery. In addition, the lights are best seen well after sunset when the moon and stars are dimmed by clouds—not foggy or misty, just cloudy enough to darken the skies.

Ever since folks returning from a party in 1882 first reported the strange dancing lights, skeptics have said the lights were reflections of the moon and stars off the surfaces of polished stone gravestones and other markers. They said perhaps the lights were from Saint Elmo's fire.

However, that would require a storm coming in, and none was reported the night the lights were seen. Another thought was that the lights came from fox fire, the glow of decay in rotting wooden grave markers—despite the fact that the cemeteries were barely two years old when the lights were first reported. Bioluminescence doesn't explain,

though, why the lights were moving and seen in areas where no wooden markers stood.

The tale was laughed at in town. Some people speculated that the lights came from lanterns used by pranksters. On the following night, a small party went out to see for itself. The two women in the group eventually grew bored and left. The men were on the verge of leaving when the lights appeared. What they saw were not astral reflections or bioluminescence but blue orbs or flames that darted and floated mostly in small clusters of three and four. There are few appearance of fireflies in Colorado, and none has been reported in this region. The men were so spooked by this disembodied behavior that they hightailed it back to town.

Many more people made the trek out to the cemeteries over the years, and the sightings are varied. The lights were said to be blue, white, or gray. They danced, darted, hovered, and, at times, seemed to flicker in a coded sequence. Sometimes the lights appeared to focus on one grave; other times on a whole row. In 1956, reports said a number of the lights were the size of basketballs, and they appeared to pulsate and vanish if approached.

In later years, skeptics said the town's electric lighting caused reflections off the polished stone grave markers. On a given night in 1963, all the townsfolk of the larger community of Silver Cliff turned off their street lamps and house lights for the evening. Yes, people still saw moving lights.

These days, seeing the mysterious lights on a trip to either cemetery on the dirt road known as Mill Street seems to be more difficult. Fewer people reside in the region than in the boom mining days of the 1880s, but there is a lot more light pollution from houses, ranches, and passing cars and trucks.

As with many of Colorado's oldest cemeteries, Silver Cliff and Cross of the Assumption are small, quaint, and lack most of the wooden markers they once had in abundance. Even the oldest graves look well tended, however, and a few of the newer ones are decorated with a kind of loving eccentricity.

The place is surrounded by ranchland, so curious cattle sometimes peer through the barbed-wire fencing. Their lowing at night when they are nearly invisible probably scares the heck out of unaware visitors.

People I talked to in Silver Cliff and Westcliffe had heard the stories about the lights for years, and while I didn't meet an actual witness, many of them said they knew those who had. So I wish I could say I saw these mysterious cemetery lights for myself because it was a wondrous, if long, drive into the beautiful area known as the Wet Mountains.

Alas, the weather made the region live up to its name for most of the time I was there. So, you'll just have to go there on a cloudy, not rainy, night, and try to see for yourself.

WHERE SHIPS OF PURPLE
— GENTLY TOSS —
ON SEAS OF DAFFODIL —
FANTASTIC SAILORS — MINGLE —
AND THEN —
THE WHARF IS STILL!

Buffalo Bill's Grave

William F. "Buffalo Bill" Cody's exploits—both true and fantasy—made him a folk hero during his lifetime, and his famous traveling Wild West Show allowed thousands of people to catch a glimpse of a legendary American past in the United States as well as abroad. When he died in 1917, the king of England, the kaiser of Germany, and President Woodrow Wilson all offered personal tributes to the man. And during the throes of World War I, it was rare to find anything those three leaders could all agree upon.

An early will stated that he wanted to be buried in Cody, Wyoming, a frontier town that he helped found. A later version left the choice of a gravesite to his wife, Louisa.

After Cody died in Denver, local journalists campaigned to have the frontier superstar interred in Colorado. They allegedly pressured the widow into agreeing. The top of Lookout Mountain in nearby Golden was chosen, with a view over the Great Plains. Cody was buried here on June 3.

The American Legion of Cody, Wyoming, never forgot. Buffalo Bill built a number of hotels there and established a huge ranch where he entertained many famous guests. Cody had encouraged the townspeople to embrace the resulting tourism, which declined after his burial elsewhere.

In 1948, Cody, Wyoming's American Legion offered a cash reward for anyone who could return their patron. The Denver branch of the Legion was forced to post guards while a more secure grave was dug to ensure that Cody's resting place would remain his final resting place.

As a result, visitors to Golden can still visit Cody's grave on Lookout Mountain—the large assemblage of stones make a grand monument for the man. The Buffalo Bill Museum has also been built on the site, so you can make a day out of a visit.

Linn Grove Cemetery

This is Tom Van Buskirk's stomping grounds (see "Cemetery Skills" in this chapter). Linn Grove has managed to keep its records and its historical character intact, no small effort for a cemetery established in 1874. It has always been owned by the city of Greeley and is still open for burials today (my father-in-law is buried here).

A regard for the dead goes beyond keeping the grass clipped and the grave markers upright. The lawn is lush, the graves are groomed, and the attractive office on the premises provides visitors with maps, directions, and other services. Only a few unrecorded burials have unmarked graves. Linn Grove makes free temporary headstones for the survivors who can't afford a marker and regularly replaces old markers that have deteriorated.

With caretaking like this, the colorful stories you'd expect to find in an old cemetery have a better chance of being remembered and passed on. Take the demise of William and Rosalia Humphrey, killed by lightning in July 1876. Perhaps they were newcomers to the area—not much else is known about them but the unusual manner of their death. The Humphreys were found locked in a cindery embrace and had to be buried in one coffin. They have a combined headstone; it's one of Linn Grove's periodically replaced temporary markers.

A mass grave was made for circus roustabouts killed about ten miles west of Greeley on August 29, 1884, when the train car they were sleeping in blew up. According to newspaper reports of the time, the managers of Orton's Anglo-American Circus kept two barrels of gasoline or naphtha in the same car for lighting the circus grounds at night. The only door to this car was blocked with heavy luggage. Six badly burned men managed to escape through a window; ten others were trapped inside. All the train crew could do was separate the burning car from the rest and tow it to a safe distance. Then the locomotive took off for Greeley to bring back doctors. ROASTED ALIVE! screamed one newspaper headline.

Circuses have always been places for escape—as much for the people who work in them as for the audience. The full names and hometowns of only three of the dead men were reported. The rest were known only by names such as Andy, Frenchy, and Smithy, and one was never identified at all. The marker has no names, but it's been replaced three times over the decades.

One of Linn Grove's best-known citizens is a man who never lived in Greeley but had founded another town. Oliver Toussaint Jackson, the man who established the African American settlement of Dearfield (see the Abandoned Colorado chapter) about twenty-five miles east, was buried here by his wife, Minerva.

Carnero Creek Cementerio

La Capilla de San Juan Bautista (Chapel of Saint John the Baptist) was first established in La Garita (The Lookout) in 1872, but it's believed that the settlement goes back to 1858. To outside visitors, the area about fifteen miles north of Del Norte may be best known for that little place passed on the way to Penitente Canon where there are ancient pictographs, a portrait of the Virgin Mary on a cliff wall, and the legend of the mysterious Penitentes (see the Local Legends chapter).

Today, most of the residents of La Garita appear to be interred in Carnero Creek Cementerio (the Spanish spelling on the arch over the entrance is misspelled). It's one of Colorado's rare survivors of the old Spanish-colonial culture, with a time line of history that one can follow by studying the grave markers.

The oldest graves begin in the right corner near the entrance, and some are marked with nothing but a small stone with a Spanish-style cross etched into it. Headstones were inscribed in Spanish until about the 1920s, when more non-Hispanics moved into the area and English became the required common language.

One group of graves indicates membership in the oldest known and still active Hispanic mutual aid society in the United States, the Sociedad Protección Mutua de Trabajadores Unidos, usually abbreviated as SPMDTU (Society of Mutual Protection of United Workers, see the Abandoned Colorado chapter).

One of the more striking SPMDTU gravestones is for a gentleman who apparently lived up to his name: Perfecto Bueno, 1890–1932, "beloved by God and man."

Another group of graves is represented in two sad little rows totaling thirty-two small wooden crosses. These are the children of La Garita who died in the 1918 flu pandemic. If there were names on the crosses, they have long since worn away.

No one is truly forgotten here. The graves show

CARNERO CREEK · CEMETARIO

plenty of individuality, with many homemade markers, mementos, and quirky decorations. The grounds are maintained by volunteers headed by Rich Garcia and his father, people still tied to the land by farming and cattle ranching. It's a way of nurturing their roots though they no longer live in La Garita. They organized funding for a new fence around the cemetery in recent years and fought successfully to regain once-lost water rights.

"Now we can green things up," says Garcia. "Every Memorial Day, we get a bunch of people together and go in and do a big cleanup. We want a nice place for people to visit."

The most unusual tombstone here is a replica of the Mount of the Holy Cross (see the Local Legends chapter) installed in the memory of a couple named Atencio, according to Ben Gallegos, who now lives in nearby Center but comes out to the cemetery frequently. Gallegos remembers when as many as forty families were living in La Garita. A retired farmer, Gallegos is proud to still be a member of the SPMDTU and as active a member of the
La Garita community as he can be these days.

"I'm eighty-seven, I can't do as much as I used to, but my father, my wife, and some of my grandkids are buried over there, so I help keep the weeds down, and I stay out of the way of people who can do more," says Gallegos. "I collect money for those who need help with the burial, and I measure the plot."

Yes, even with very few year-round people on the other side of the grass, the cemetery is still the place for former residents of La Garita and their descendants to come "home." Unlike many pioneer cemeteries in Colorado, this one is still tied to a nearby church, and June 24 is a big day to celebrate the feast of the church's namesake, San Juan Bautista. Church and cemetery are owned by the San Juan Catholic Community, part of the Diocese of Pueblo. When the original church burned down in the early 1900s, a replacement in a similar style was finished in 1923.

It's a simple adobe building with a bell tower topped by an old Spanish six-armed cross. Abandoned in 1957, it was a folk arts studio for a few years but has since been reclaimed as a "mission chapel," open for special occasions and infrequent Masses.

"People saved much of the old furnishings in their own homes when the chapel wasn't being used as such," says Father Joseph Vigil, the area's presiding priest and church affairs administrator. "Otherwise, we might have seen a lot of it stolen or damaged by vandals. When we restored it as a mission, they brought everything back."

A few yards away from the church is an adobe wall with a doorway—all that's left of the old convent that used to be here.

"We hope to preserve it with plaster," Father Joseph says. "Maybe put some tile up, and make it a place of meditation. But, we have to put a new roof on the church, too. We've had a lot of wonderful help from the people to restore the inside of the church, but now we need to raise more funds for these other concerns."

Across the fence that separates the cemetery from a pasture a small herd of llamas graze. The llamas look oddly at home with a backdrop of the Rockies.

Riverside Cemetery

At the time of this writing, the landscape is more dirt than grass. Imposing Victorian crypts are crumbling, while many of the oldest grave markers are losing their legibility. Paint is peeling off the old buildings, and grafitti is beginning to cover the boarded-up chapel. It's a great setting for a horror flick, but this not a movie set and neither is it an abandoned graveyard.

Step outside the cemetery entrance, where trains rumble past, and you can see the tall towers of downtown Denver. Here on the banks of the South Platte River is the once-posh final resting place for Colorado's four territorial governors among the notables of the sixty-seven thousand people buried there. It's on the National Register of Historic Places, no less.

When opened in 1876, the organizers boasted that Riverside Cemetery would be a grand park rather than the traditional rambling graveyard. Carriages and pedestrians moved on the pathways between beautiful landscaping, well-tended gravesites, many grand monuments, and a few handsome crypts. Frank E. Edbrooke, the same architect who designed Denver's fabulous Brown Palace hotel, designed the administration building.

As it happened, Denver grew in the opposite direction from Riverside Cemetery. The train tracks right outside the front gate came in around 1900. Industrial businesses closed in, and Riverside was no longer the last parking place for the elite and notable. Yet, for a long time, this was still a place where families would come for a picnic on holidays and to bring flowers to graves. That all changed sometime in 2003.

The Fairmount Heritage Foundation, which manages the perpetual endowment fund, says it costs more to run the place than the fund allots annually. They say the cemetery lost its water rights and had to turn off the irrigation, so they then cut the custodial staff and halted the sale of burial sites.

Nonsense, say some Riverside supporters, angry about the state of their loved ones' final resting place. They believe it's really about poor management of the available money and resources.

As you might guess, lawyers have entered the picture and at the time of this writing are peeling back the charges and claims like the layers of an onion. Meanwhile Friends of Historic Riverside Cemetery, a nonprofit organization, is trying to find practical ways to save the place.

In the meantime, Riverside remains a fascinating place for local history buffs and has some of the best examples of funereal art in Colorado.

The best written history about it is *Denver Riverside Cemetery: Where History Lies* by Annette L. Student. For instance, any visitor to Riverside wants to know what's the scoop on the amazing miniature stone-cabin monument. That's the grave of Lester Eugene Drake Sr., a miner who helped found the town of Black Hawk.

Drake made good in Black Hawk and purchased a farm near Denver in 1879. When he died in 1889, his family commissioned a monument that recalled his pioneer days. Denver sculptor M. Rauh turned out a three-foot-high limestone replica of Drake's log cabin, complete with miner's pickax and shovel, flowers, and mule droppings.

Cliff Dougal of Denver, longtime manager of Riverside, was one of those let go in 2005. Get him to reminiscing and he might share some of the many strange experiences he had with the cemetery during his tenure.

He recalled one gentleman who made regular visits to his late wife's grave in Block 13. He told Dougal about the three nice girls who always seemed to be nearby at the same time. So sweet and polite.

"I looked right at him while he was at the grave a couple of times, and I never saw who he was talking to," says Dougal. "But the man seemed perfectly reasonable."

His strangest story is about tomb robbers and the head of Ovando Hollister, a Colorado journalist who died in 1892.

Twice, he said, "a bunch of college kids" broke into the red-brick crypt and took Hollister's head. They ignored the body of Hollister's wife, Carrie, who died in 1917. Both times the theft was thwarted by police officers who correctly assumed that people exiting a cemetery late at night with a duffel bag were up to no good. Each time, they called Dougal to return the head to its appropriate location.

"After that second time we welded the crypt gates shut," says Dougal.

When Dougal says Riverside Cemetery was like a second home, he's obviously, affectionately sincere. No one at Riverside was forgotten under Dougal's watch. Among other things, he created programs to provide headstones for the unmarked graves of early Colorado pioneers.

Twenty-one children from the old Denver Orphans' Home (in operation since 1876 and renamed the Denver Children's Home in 1962) are buried in Block 28. Only three orphans had headstones until Dougal and other compassionate citizens raised enough funds to put up a granite monument with all the dead children's names on it in 2002.

Dougal joined Friends of Historic Riverside Cemetery, and Annette Student dedicated her book to him in 2006.

The Cemetery Dowser

As Tom Monaco walks toward a grave in small, slow steps, the thin copper rods in his hands that were parallel suddenly form a cross. He stops.

"That indicates where the earth was disturbed and the magnetic field broken. So, that's the grave," he says.

He moves forward. The rods go parallel. "Here's the body." He lowers his left hand, and the rod in his right swings clockwise and points to the right. "It's a man."

He raises both rods and moves closer to the headstone. Both rods swing inward toward his chest. "There's the head."

Monaco moves toward another grave. This one is covered with a layer of cement and has a Union soldier's marker. The copper rods do the same thing as at the first man's grave except that the rods never move toward Monaco.

"Well, look at that," Monaco says. "No head. Haven't seen that before."

It's a warm August morning. We're standing at Alfred Packer's final resting place in Littleton Cemetery, south of Denver. We know that Colorado's most famous cannibal is buried here. What we're trying to find out—in what is admittedly a highly unscientific, unofficial experiment—is whether his corpse is intact. Ripley's Believe It or Not! claims to have Packer's preserved noggin on display at its facility in San Antonio, Texas.

Monaco says his copper dowsing rods have always behaved in the same way when held near an intact corpse. This is a definite anomaly. It's enough to convince Monaco that desecration to Packer's body was, indeed, done.

"That's not right," he says, with a head shake. He is a member of Sons of Confederate Veterans and has a keen sense of what's fitting.

Monaco is also on the volunteer cemetery committee at Greenwood Pioneer Cemetery in Cañon City, the older of two operating city cemeteries. The first recorded burial was in 1865. Today, only descendants of those interred in this hillside acreage can be buried there. As far as Monaco knows, that does not include Monaco or his wife, Melody, both originally from Texas. Nonetheless, Greenwood, he says, is home. It's where he learned from a veteran dowser how to find graves and where he honed his sensitivity to the presence of restless spirits.

"I feel like I know these people buried here," he says.

Sometimes called doodlebugging or water witching, dowsing also been used to look for oil, minerals, buried treasure, and even golf balls.

"I don't know why it works," Monaco says. "I don't know why I'm able to do this. I'm not a psychic, but I think I've been sensitive to spirits all my life. It's gotten stronger over the years—the more I've done it. Maybe it's a gift, but plenty of people can do it with practice."

Erratic results, he said, led him to look up the records of those buried. If the death was violent, the psychic resonance of that trauma seemed to make an impression on the dowsing rods. The rods acted differently depending on the gender and age of the dead.

When the cemetery volunteers performed a systemic inventory of the graves, Monaco was able to help in the identification of unmarked burials.

His most gratifying find, he says, was the unmarked graves of two little girls who died in a house fire on an American Indian reservation in New Mexico in 1930. Because the sisters were not Native Americans, they could not be buried locally. So, their remains were shipped to Colorado where, at the time, their grandfather Claude Rogers was mayor of South Cañon (now part of Cañon City). The burials of fifteen-month-old Claudine and two-year-old Beulah Blanche Polhemus could only be guessed for years as somewhere near the family plot in Greenwood. Their three sisters, who were born after the deaths,

contacted Cañon City's history center for help in tracking down their kin.

Monaco dowsed for the Polhemus girls. His rods spin around over a child's grave. "The faster they spin, the younger the child," he says. The rods picked up the presence of two very young female children buried near their kin. A little investigation revealed the metal boxes the two badly burned little bodies were buried in.

Greenwood has several unmarked mass graves. Two are where victims of the 1918 influenza panemic lie. One large plot has a mystery attached to the cement object in its center.

"Looks like an old school bell, doesn't it?" says Monaco. "I've never seen another grave marker like it."

The engraving is hard to read, but the name Fanny Clark can be made out.

"There's a woman buried there. And, there're about ten kids buried around her. All girls on one side of her; all boys on the other. We think Fanny was a schoolteacher and something happened that killed her and the children together. Fire, avalanche, we don't know."

Woodpecker Hill

As we walk over the hard-packed, rocky soil, it's not hard to imagine Greenwood Cemetery as it looked in its earlier days, because little has changed.

The view is magnificent: mountains loom over Cañon City in the valley below us. The old Colorado Territorial Prison (see "Prison Museum" in the Roadside Attractions chapter) is the most prominent human-made feature in the landscape—an inescapable reminder of a significant portion of Greenwood's population.

Woodpecker Hill is the informal name of the section of deceased convicts from the prison. Approximately six hundred prisoners were buried here from 1872 to 1971, but only 350 of their graves are marked. Many of the unmarked graves lie just outside Greenwood's fences on private land. The other graves originally had cheap wooden slabs that harbored insects highly attractive to woodpeckers—hence the moniker for this section. Eventually, the wooden markers were replaced with small metal plaques on stakes that have rusted to a flaking brown.

The vast majority of dead inmates' families couldn't afford better grave markers or perhaps washed their hands of their incarcerated relatives. Today, unclaimed dead convicts are cremated.

Monaco points to one marker.

"We think this is James Armstrong. That guy always boasted that once he was dead he'd finally be free of the prison. He was a real pain to everybody, and when he finally did die, he was buried with a cell door on top of him."

One mass grave is part of this section. In 1929, five prisoners whose escape attempt was thwarted set off a three-day riot that killed eight guards and destroyed several buildings.

One ringleader died in the melee; the remaining convicts finally killed themselves and a jailhouse informant. All but one of the riot instigators are buried together in an unmarked plot. No one seems to know what happened to the fifth man; perhaps his was the lone corpse claimed by relatives.

Joe Arridy's large granite marker stands out against a fence. He was convicted of participating in the assaults of two teenage Pueblo sisters that resulted in the death of one of them. Arridy was a homeless man who had been in and out of institutions most his life and had the mind of a child. At one point, his IQ was measured at forty-six. He couldn't tell the same story of the crimes twice. No real connection could be made between Arridy and the confessed murderer, who had been fired by the girls' father and who never implicated Arridy. However, Arridy was convicted anyway.

Possibly for the only time in his life, Arridy was treated well and assured of three meals a day. He was the "happiest man on death row," said the warden, Roy Best, who gave Arridy a toy train for Christmas. Despite efforts to change Arridy's sentence to life, the Colorado State Supreme Court voted to continue the execution by electrocution, which was carried out in 1939. A campaign to have Arridy pardoned was started in recent years. In 2007, supporters replaced the old prison marker on his grave with a new tombstone. It has a photo of Arridy playing with his train.

Monaco points to a tiny model train placed on the stone.

"I was up here with a paranormal research group from Denver when they put that there and filmed it to see if it would move," he says. "It didn't. But, look at this."

He takes out his copper dowsing rods and edges slowly across Arridy's grave. The rod in his right hand spins clockwise briskly, indicating the body of a small boy lies here.

Joe Arridy was twenty-three years old when he died.

Goin' in Style

If you didn't own a Harley motorcycle in life, you can still get a ride on the way to your ultimate destination.

In Colorado, this last ride is offered by the Horan & McConaty funeral home, based in the Denver area. A customized, three-wheeled 2005 Harley-Davidson Road King pulls a Victorian-styled, black-and-chrome hearse tricked out with maroon curtains, brass lanterns, and decoratively etched safety glass. John Horan, president, CEO, and descendant of five generations of funeral home directors, heard about this idea from a couple of friends in the funeral business back east.

"People define themselves in so many ways," he says. "Catholic, Republican, architect, whatever. The baby boomers, especially, have a way of wanting to define themselves in death as well as in life as different from their parents and grandparents. We have so many bikers in Colorado I just could not think of a better way to appeal to that community."

Besides its conversion to a three-wheeled model, the Road King has a reverse gear and a heavy-duty fan to keep the motor from overheating during a funeral procession's slow pace. Tombstone Hearse & Trike Company of Bedford, Pennsylvania, has been producing and selling the Harley-drawn hearse since 2002 and reckons it's being used by eighteen funeral homes around the world, mostly in the United States. The president of the company, Jack Feather, was a long-time biker when he saw a photo of the nineteenth-century hearse used to transport Billy Clanton (of the OK Corral shootout fame). He instantly knew that would be just the thing for a Harley-driven hearse.

"I was in a completely different business before I got into this," he says. "Never designed anything for a motorcycle before. Call it my midlife crisis."

Horan paid approximately $75,000 for the unit in 2008, and charges $500 for its funereal use. For this last ride, he and his funeral director, Daren Forbes, will don black helmet, black vest and pants, and a bolo tie.

The Harley hearse is generally transported on a trailer when not actually in procession to the final resting place. Sometimes Horan will take it to a motorcycle rally, such as Colorado's annual Thunder in the Rockies, or a special event, such as the Colorado State Parade of Honor, commemorating veterans, law enforcement officers, and firefighters.

"About half of its value has been the public relations effect with bikers," he says.

Yes, it's elegant and unusual but also, as John Horan sums it up, "It puts the fun back in *funeral*."

Annie the Railroad Dog

A very rare historical landmark can be found on Mason Street in Fort Collins: the grave of the dog Annie. In front of the town's library stands a statue of the dog that serves as a memorial. Fort Collins, it would seem, is obsessed with the memory of this collie—those who know the history of Annie know that it is for good reason.

In the early 1930s, railroad worker Chris Demuth came across a starving and pregnant collie wandering around at a stop along a train line he was working. Sympathy for the lonely animal led him to bring her back to the Colorado and Southern Railroad Depot in Fort Collins, despite the depot's strict no-dogs policy. Everyone who met her fell in love, and an exception was made for Annie. She became the mascot of the yard, and the lovable pooch showed such an appreciation and enthusiasm for her new home that she became a local icon.

Annie would hurry out to the yard when trains pulled into the station. Perhaps out of gratitude for the hospitality

of the town, Annie seemed to take it upon herself to be a warm presence for all of those who entered it. She would sit patiently and happily against a wall, and if any visitors waved to her, she would run over to them for petting. Her behavior became famous, and legend has it that many Fort Collins residents would say hello to Annie immediately after departing from trains—keeping their families waiting as they played with the pooch in the train yard.

The most legendary tales of Annie involve her behavior toward the end of World War II. By that time, Annie had been greeting guests in Fort Collins for more than a decade, and she represented home for the many hundreds of GIs who came back to Colorado through the town's train station. Many soldiers who had endured unspeakable horrors became overwhelmed with emotion as they stepped off of their trains. Annie would run up to greet these soldiers, and as they kneeled to pet her, she licked the tears off their faces.

Annie died in 1948. Railroad workers buried her in the yard and put up a headstone in tribute. The dog was well remembered and her legend endured in the years after her passing. As the depot underwent a massive renovation decades later, officials planned to remove the grave to clear way for construction. An enormous outcry rose among locals who loved Annie and what she represented, even though many had never met the pooch. They rallied together and managed to have Annie's grave dedicated as a historical monument. Annie had gone from a mangy mutt wandering the rails to a bona fide historical icon in just a few short decades.

Loveland sculptor Dawn Weimer was struck with inspiration upon hearing the story of Annie. She has created more than thirty statues of the famous dog, the most famous of which stands in front of the Fort Collins library. Some older residents of the town who remember Annie were said to burst into tears and hug the statues upon their creation.

As the old saying goes, "Dog is man's best friend." In Annie's case, that friendship extended to an entire community. The friendship she offered to all who crossed her path has made Annie representative of the community of Fort Collins in many ways. The annual Annie Walk & Pet Fest is a popular event in Ft. Collins. Pet lovers bring their dogs from far and wide to celebrate the bond between dog and human, and to participate in a one-and-a-half-mile dog walk held in Annie's honor that embarks from the statue of the dog on the library's lawn. —*Chris Gethard*

The Tombstone Fixer

Jayne Uhlir has an addiction to stones, such as the kinds of splendid marbles and handsome granites she finds in old cemeteries with their wealth of "one of" monuments that are true works of art. She soothes her itch with a rather unique form of volunteer work—preserving and restoring aged and damaged stone grave markers.

"I've always loved stone, even as a kid, loved old walls and buildings," says Uhlir. "I liked cemeteries where there is so much wonderful stone art. I was in Fairmount Cemetery (in Denver) around 2005, when I noticed the large number of old headstones that seemed to be dumped in Block 17. I asked about them, and it turned out they were transferred from the cemetery in Denver that is now City Park. Hundreds of these markers were brought here, too. Some of them without their bases so they were just lying there or even sunk into the ground. We did an assessment and found about twenty that could be repaired. Some of them had snapped in two, or they had laminate sheets that broke off."

Uhlir took a class in cemetery-monument conservation offered through the National Center for Preservation Technology and Training, which is run by the National Park Service under the U.S. Department of the Interior. She learned how to assess what needed to be done: how to clean properly, reset a leaning marker, patch, and make repairs with the right adhesives and reinforcement materials. Among other things, she learned to use "historic mortars" that are specially designed to work with stone.

Then, she went on to take other workshops to advance her knowledge and skills.

"Each training course takes two to three days, and the frustration is that they're all offered outside Colorado," Uhlir says. "You have to go out of state."

A self-described "information tech geek" by profession, Uhlir soon found herself in a world of conservationists, historians, stonemasons, artists, individuals, and organizations such as Colorado Preservation, Inc.

"I grew up in an artistic family," she says. "But I sort of thought the art streak passed me up. This just tells me you never leave off learning."

Uhlir learned that her best resources were people who could guide her through unknown territory and a supportive family that didn't mind meeting some unusual needs.

"I've known some really talented and bizarre people all my life, but now I've got a network I rely on to meet needs and problems I never dreamed of—colleagues around the world. And, my husband and kids have been great about those odd Christmas gifts I asked for, like steel-toed boots and an engine lifter."

An automobile engine lifter?

"You need something to pick up some of those big ol' stone pieces."

Fairmount Cemetery gives Uhlir studio space to work on monument repair, and she has only six markers that still need help, down from the original twenty. Uhlir has taught basic assessment and cleaning of cemetery monuments to members of Friends of Historic Riverside Cemetery and says she'd like to teach more. Repairing cemetery monuments has become more than a hobby but, at least at the moment, less than a vocation.

"My only regret is that I can't do it often enough," Uhlir says. "When I'm in the flow, I lose all track of time. This fills up the center in me."

Prunes, Shorty, and Bum

In the nineteenth century, mining was at the center of many Colorado residents' lives. A good donkey was a commodity that could help keep a mine running and, in turn, could help keep a community thriving.

Fairplay, the seat of Park County, probably takes donkeys more seriously than any other town in the United States. Each July, the town hosts Burro Days, a festival that celebrates donkeys and features a twenty-nine-mile donkey race considered the world championship of burro racing. If any town in the world appreciates a donkey, it's this one—and that appreciation is notably shown through memorials that honor the memories of two very special burros.

According to legend, Prunes was perhaps the most dependable donkey in Colorado history. Miners were known to trust him to do his job even without a human escort. While entrenched atop mountains, miners would tie shopping lists to Prunes's collar and send him into nearby towns. Shopkeepers would load him with the requested supplies, and Prunes would unfailingly return to camp with all the goods. Prunes became something of a local celebrity in the area. There wasn't a local mine Prunes hadn't worked before he was retired.

Even after retirement, the residents of Fairplay embraced and took care of Prunes. He was free to wander the streets of town, and when he approached homes, he was graciously fed in tribute to his years of service.

In 1930, tragedy struck when a sudden blizzard made its way into downtown Fairplay. Once the weather calmed down, residents found Prunes holed up in a small shed, freezing and on the brink of death. For a few sad weeks, the town rallied around Prunes, attempting to nurse him back to health, but their efforts were useless. The ass passed.

Prunes wasn't just a donkey. He was part of the backbone of a mining community and a beloved resident of the town. Close to eight decades after his death, his memorial is still well maintained, and he is rightfully well remembered.

In 1949, a scraggly, down-on-his-luck stray dog, known throughout Fairplay as Bum, was wandering through town looking for respite from a cold night. While he didn't find shelter, he found another animal outcast in the same boat—a blind burro named Shorty, who was equally legendary around town.

Shorty, as he was known among miners due to his short legs, had worked gold mines in the area from a young age. When mining began to dry up, his owner abandoned him, and he had become famous for wandering around town and begging for food. As he grew older, he lost his sight and was no longer able to find his way. It was a sad end for an animal that had served his owner well.

On that night in 1949, two lost animals found each other. Bum saw Shorty huddled on the ground, desperately trying to stay warm and sidled up next to the burro. They stayed next to each other throughout the night, surviving on each other's body heat.

In the morning, the animals didn't leave each other's side, and they never did so again. Something clicked between the two beasts—maybe Bum saw Shorty's blindness and knew he had to help. Maybe Shorty sensed that Bum was a kindred soul and trusted him. Somehow, the two animals of different species were able to communicate to each other that they should stay together, and they did.

Bum would lead Shorty through town, walking slowly so that the blind burro could follow his scent. They would travel from door to door, to beg food from townsfolk. They became legendary—there was something irresistible about seeing these two former hard-luck cases work together to improve their fates. A town employee made them a straw bed to sleep on behind a town building, and on particularly cold nights the animals were even allowed to sleep in empty cells in the town jail.

Sadly, the same allegiance toward each other that helped Shorty and Bum survive ultimately led to their demise. One morning while walking through town, Bum gave in to the temptation of chasing a small animal he saw on the other side of a street. He darted across the road in pursuit. Shorty didn't understand that Bum had gone off to have some fun. As always, he followed his friend's scent. He was hit and killed by a passing car.

Sanitation workers took Shorty's body to the local dump. Everyone who heard the tale felt awful about how Shorty had died. Some concerned townsfolk tried to track down Bum to care from him in what was sure to be a sad time for the dog. No one could find the canine. Eventually, someone checked the town dump, where Bum was found sitting faithfully at the side of his best friend.

Some residents put money together and had Shorty's body cremated so that Bum might be able to move on. When they tried to remove Shorty, Bum had to be physically dragged away before anyone could touch Shorty's body. After the cremation, Bum went back to wandering around town.

For a few weeks, townspeople saw Bum sadly sauntering through his old stomping grounds. To most, it seemed strange to see Bum without Shorty. Apparently, Bum felt the same way. Three weeks

after Shorty passed away, Bum jumped into the middle of a busy street and was also killed by a car. Many have sworn that the dog committed suicide because of the depression he felt at accidentally leading his pal to his demise.

Bum and Shorty's remains are now both buried on the courthouse lawn in downtown Fairplay. An image of Shorty is etched into their gravestone, and fittingly, Bum's name is listed along with the phrase "his beloved pal." In life and death, Shorty and Bum stuck together.

—*Chris Gethard*

Abandoned Colorado

We lose many things in Colorado not because they are abandoned, but because too many people think that something that looks abandoned is something of no value to the community at large. These are the people who think it doesn't matter if they burn down some strange old building that's been sitting vacant for years, who let wondrous and unique things be stolen and vandalized because they see value only in the grand, the perfect, and the celebrity-connected.

If we're lucky, we have people who can show us the stories beyond the gaping doorways, collapsed roofs, and weathered surfaces. People who saved abandoned things that deserve to be preserved because of the role they once played.

Abandoned Commerce
Forsaken Mines

Colorado has twenty-three thousand abandoned and inactive mines. Yep, they've been counted. The Colorado Division of Reclamation, Mining, and Safety has been in charge of these sites since 1980. Out of all those, 6,127 are now safe for visiting, and you can find out which ones on the DRMS Web site: http://mining.state.co.us/Tourist Mine Links.htm.

Exploring a mine *not* on this list is most emphatically not recommended. People are killed or injured every year while ignoring the DON'T TRESPASS signs (twenty-two people in one recent year). The site has a selection of these unfortunate trespassers' deaths listed, and their ends ain't pretty.

Trespassers have died not just from the usual dangers you might expect—cave-ins or falling through rotted flooring—but lesser-known hazards such as deadly, odorless gases or hidden pits of deep, freezing water.

Lost Resorts

If you happen to come across remnants of old lodges, tourist cabins, chair lifts, etc., know that you're not just looking at signs of a failed business, but part of Colorado's long history of skiing. While Colorado is famous for its ski resorts, more than 145 sites have been abandoned or are no longer used. There are fewer than 30 surviving resorts today.

Immigrants of Nordic ancestry brought skiing to Colorado with the prospecting and mining rushes that began in the mid-1800s. Ordinary webbed snowshoes couldn't cope with deep snows, which made the long "Norwegian snowshoes" the only practical way to get around on foot. According to the Colorado Ski and Snowboard Museum and Hall of Fame, some historians say the use of skis advanced settlement of Colorado by at least a decade.

The U.S. Army's Tenth Mountain Division that famously made skiing a technique of war during World War II trained at Camp Hale (unfortunately, torn down long ago), thirty miles south of Vail.

Ski resorts have come and gone but are not totally forgotten. ColoradoSkiHistory.com keeps track and celebrates the memories of these lost sites. You can get a poster listing a number of these resorts and their locations through the Colorado Ski and Snowboard Museum and Hall of Fame in Vail: www.skimuseum.net, (970) 476-1876.

Ridge Home

In Arvada, Colorado, there used to be an abandoned asylum named Ridge Home. It was closed in the 1980s, as were so many others, and left to fall apart. In high school, a friend of mine and I visited it many times. Although we never discovered the underground tunnels that so many people talked about, we did have some weird experiences of our own.

I once borrowed a camera from another friend in a photography class and we went to take pictures. We mostly drove around the site, snapping shots of the main building. I hopped the fence to take a couple of close-ups of staff housing, but then noticed a patrolling police officer and ran back to the car. We snapped a few more and then returned to school.

We continued to explore the buildings, although many teenagers had ruined much with nightly paintballing and graffiti. I did, however, find a reel of audio tape with a patient's file. I was so afraid to listen to it and after a while forgot about it and it was lost in the rest of the junk in my house.

I later spoke with a woman who used to be a nurse at Ridge Home. She told me that the home was mostly live-in care for sufferers of Down syndrome and other such illnesses. She also said it was shut down from a lack of funding, and the patients were either shipped off to group homes and families or left to the streets. All I know is that I was always rendered instantly sad when entering the grounds.

I'm pretty sure Ridge Home has been demolished by now, due to constant vandalizing and new development.

—*Lauren Lautenschlager*

Tara in the Rockies

If you happen to stop at the rest area off Interstate 70 East near the little town of Arriba, you might notice a rather odd sight for Colorado—what looks like a shabby antebellum mansion reigning over acres of barren fields. A large, peeling sign nearby proclaims WELCOME TO TARADO and promises FOOD. There is also a tall billboard with a colorful picture of a woman cooking up a lavish feast and the words RESTAURANT HOMESTYLE COOKING.

Tarado won't show up on any map, and at this time of this writing nothing has been cooking recently in this faux version of Tara (and, yes, *Tarado* is a combination of *Tara* and *Colorado*).

A semicircular driveway curls in front of the building, and a cupola on the roof resembles an overgrown birdcage. There is a carriage house to the rear and a cottage nearby that looks like servants' quarters. The only thing that speaks of a more modern age is a series of tall cement rectangles holding up the mansion's porch overhang instead of the Grecian-style pillars one might expect. There is a smaller, two-story house next door that has two garage doors on the bottom floor and a circular staircase out front.

The locked mansion shows shabby, empty rooms through the windows. The rear of the main building has a glassed-in atrium through which a double staircase can be seen. Here and there are glimpses of old moldings, a handsome floral carpet, and the hints of a mural on one wall.

In the field in back of the mansion is what looks like an old wooden speedboat. It's been gutted and the interior filled with junk, but it's still sitting on a trailer.

Despite the modern touches, it's clear this old house really is old, and so are the small buildings around it. A placard in one dusty window advises the reader to call a caretaking service to report any problems, but there are no FOR SALE or NO TRESPASSING signs. A real estate sign in a nearby field had a name and phone number that I wrote down.

A call to the Arriba Museum owners netted a bonanza of information. Local historians Shirley and Bob Coulson remembered the old Tarado Mansion well. Shirley used to work there as a docent. The mansion had been an old hotel in Arriba before the whole building was moved across the highway by an antiques dealer in the 1970s. The dealer opened a restaurant there, and filled the house with antiques for sale. Docents gave tours.

"Whenever they needed me I'd throw on a white apron and run right over there. Oh, that used to be the most wonderful place—you wouldn't believe it to see it now!" says Shirley. "The restaurant served gourmet food, and the rest of the house was furnished with antiques. . . . It was absolutely beautiful, especially when they decorated for Christmas. It was like another world!" It was the showplace of the area. "Even the governor dined there."

The antiques dealer's name was Sterling Shull. He built the smaller house for his parents, and had an elevator installed. A tunnel connects the house and the mansion. His mother was a partner in the Tarado enterprise. By the early 1980s, Sterling Shull and his mother had moved out (the senior Mr. Shull had died in the meantime) and left the property with a former business partner. The place went downhill rapidly after that, Shirley said.

I reached Sterling Shull at his home near Yuma. His mother had long passed on, and he was still exhibiting wares at a few antiques shows a year. Tarado Mansion he recalled with pride and some sadness.

"It was the Adams Hotel, built in the early part of the century by Minnie Adams, about a mile away in Arriba," he said. "It wasn't in the best shape when I bought in 1971 or '72. Even after we gutted it for the move, it weighed a hundred tons. We turned it so the side became the front and put a couple of wings on it.

"The carpeting on the first floor was very expensive. Each room was decorated with antiques in a specific style—a French Room, an Oriental Room, a Victorian Room. And I had the best cooks for the restaurant. Just excellent."

Shull spent more time on the road in those days, doing thirty to fifty antiques shows a year while his mother managed Tarado. They eventually decided to take on a third partner.

"He was fine when he just worked for us, but when he was made partner he turned into a piece of crap," Shull said. "One day, I finally said, 'You can have it. Lock, stock, and barrel,' and mother and I moved out. I never looked back, never went back. I heard it was foreclosed on him, and it's been all sorts of things with different owners."

A call to the number on the real estate sign got a response from Matt Morgan, who said he was the son of the last owners of Tarado before the business failed and the bank foreclosed again. Fred and Thongthet Fairchild purchased the property around 1999 and created a bed-and-breakfast/restaurant. But they were forced to give up about eight years later.

"My parents put a lot of money and sweat into that place to fix it up again," Morgan said. "I heard it was a brothel a long time ago. I stayed in the mansion a few times, and I tell you I'm not crazy but that place was haunted. My mother is very sensitive to this kind of thing, and she told me the house was haunted by the spirits of a couple of teenagers who

had been killed nearby on the highway in a wreck.

"One night my wife and I were sleeping in one of the downstairs rooms, and I swear I saw a shadow enter the room and hover over us. It went real, real cold. I just pulled the covers over my head. And there's a room you enter just before you reach that little tower on the roof that always felt creepy as hell."

Next door in the smaller house, his sister-in-law had a nearly fatal accident while in the elevator with a number of children.

"A cable snapped just as the door opened," he says. "She managed to throw the baby she was holding into the hall before she was trapped between the doors, and we had to pry them off her. The baby was OK, but my sister-in-law was nearly crushed, and she was scalped. She was in the hospital for months.

"She said later maybe the spirits wanted her to join them."

Cursed or merely unlucky, haunted by spirits or perhaps just bad judgment, the Tarado Mansion remains at this time in a state of suspended decay, brooding over lost dreams and awaiting its next chapter.

Windsor Hotel

If the population of Del Norte remains about the same as in the 2000 census, you could fit all 1,705 townspeople into the old Windsor Hotel. That might just happen when the long restoration of the building is finally completed. The Windsor Restoration and Historical Association has been at it since the wrecking ball was halted in 1993. Built in 1874, the hotel had twenty-two lodging rooms and two dining rooms, a parlor and other features. It's actually a business complex, with retail space on the first floor. Altogether, it occupies 22,500 square feet, almost half a city block in Del Norte.

The hotel declined steadily into the 1970s after multiple owners and changes, yet somehow managed to remain one of the community's social hubs. Its last use was as the Old West Hotel, made kitschy with barn-wood paneling and other "western" touches. But by 1993, the hotel had been vacant and derelict for nine years. Plans were to raze the whole thing and put up a hamburger restaurant.

When the wrecking ball broke into the fake log portico, wails literally rang out from horrified locals. Barbara Culp persuaded her husband, Dr. Raymond Culp, to step up and make the building's owner an offer. A few private and public meetings later, Del Norte found itself in the middle of a feud. The town split between the preservationists who wanted the old Windsor restored and those who felt it was a white elephant blocking the area's economic development.

In the end, the hotel's owner agreed to take the Culps' offer, and the preservationists put a support group together. By 1994, the long process for historical designation, assessment, and grants and other funding was underway. Meanwhile, volunteer cleanup of the old hotel began. Among the surprises uncovered was a stone addition believed to have been used for a slaughterhouse and winter storage for bodies awaiting burial.

You can look at the Windsor Hotel today and see why so many people saw beauty in an abandoned hulk and wouldn't let it die. Plans at this writing are to reopen the hotel with the addition of a restaurant, and to lease the storefronts.

Colorado historical preservation funds put up the bulk of the grant, totaling $685,000. A number of local contractors also bid low and stuck to their earlier estimates even after the cost of steel and other materials skyrocketed. But it was the citizens themselves who put $545,000 of their own money and a priceless amount of volunteer labor into this project. Quite a feat for a small, self-described "economically challenged" town.

Walsenburg Electric Plant

If you're a fan of interesting old buildings, a glimpse of this one as you're traveling Interstate 25 near U.S. 160 will make you want to do a U-turn. It's a tall and imposing redbrick structure sitting in a field outside the town of Walsenburg, population 4,182 by the 2000 census. The building has been gutted of its enormous steel doors, ornamental ironwork over the windows, and other metal, but it's still a magnificent sight. This is a former electric plant built in 1873. It was first built to power the camp that housed workers at the Walsen Coal Mine owned by Fred Walsen, a German immigrant.

The mine suffered flooding in 1931, which eventually forced the business to close. Walsen Camp soon closed up also, but the plant continued to power the nearby town of Walsenburg until 1965, when the cost of bringing fuel in to feed the enormous coal-fired boilers became too expensive. The San Isabel Electric Association built a substation next door to the old plant—which makes a heck of a visual contrast—and sold the antique structure. It's changed hands a number of times and suffered a slow death.

"Every time the prices of metals went up, somebody went in and ripped out more old equipment to sell for scrap—copper, brass, you name it," says Rebecca Goodwin, a cultural historian. She's a volunteer member of the review board for Colorado Preservation Inc.'s program for listing endangered places.

At the time of this writing, the former plant is owned by brothers Guillermo and Nicolas Sanchez, who work in law enforcement and sales, respectively. They like old buildings.

"We have family in Texas. Driving back and forth on I-25, we used to see that old electric plant and stop and admire it," says Guillermo. "One day, we noticed it was for sale. We thought we'd be the ones to save the place from being destroyed. I've restored my own hundred-year-old house. Figured maybe it'd be our retirement project. Get it fixed up and get a new business in there someday."

"It's structurally sound. That was kind of amazing given its age and all. But the cost of making it usable again—well. It's just not practical for us. We've got it up for sale now. I kinda figure if it doesn't sell, that's cool; it'll still be my retirement project."

For sale: One elegant but derelict former electric plant. Metal mostly gone. Seven weedy acres between railroad tracks and an interstate included.

Railroad-Related

Trains don't figure in America's consciousness today as they did before the invention of the automobile and the airplane.

Miles of railroad track, thousands of rail cars, and hundreds of railroad buildings were abandoned in Colorado as highways and air cargo routes took a chunk out of the transport business. Fortunately, before the last remnants could wind up on the literal scrap heaps of history, some people set out to rescue them for our present and future education and enjoyment.

At the Colorado Railroad Museum (www.coloradorailroadmuseum.org) in Golden, there's no shortage of the past presented here. There's what looks like a nice old train depot, a roadhouse, a wide variety of railroad cars and related vehicles, even one of those massive old turntables. It's actually a mix of the authentic and the replicated. The depot and roundhouse are re-creations. Most of these original buildings have been lost in Colorado. (Glenwood Springs opened another rail museum in its 1904-built station in 2003.) The train cars and locomotives are real, however. A good thing, as reproducing them these days would cost a fortune.

"Most of them were rescued from scrap dealers," says Rex Thrash, purchasing agent at the museum gift shop. "We paid $863 for Number 346 back in 1950. We paid $1500 for Number 318 a couple of years later. The rest of the collection was either donated or bought for a buck. . . . Buying 'em is cheap. Getting 'em here is expensive."

For instance, moving one defunct car that a railroad no longer wanted took two construction cranes, a flatbed truck, a road tractor, and eight hours of labor. The total cost was $20,000 to move it three-quarters of a mile.

With the invention of the modern

locomotive that could go in reverse, the roundhouse went from an essential feature of rail transportation to a white elephant in pretty short order. Roundhouses were torn down all over, if they weren't converted to other uses. Colorado is fortunate to have three of these structures that have survived abandonment. One of them found a new life when Van Briggle Pottery bought a Midland Terminal Railroad roundhouse in Colorado Springs in 1949 and remodeled it into its new facility in 1955. The remaining two roundhouses are awaiting their next incarnation.

Como Roundhouse

The near–ghost town of Como has a roundhouse that is fairly unique because it was built with stone. The masons were from Como, Italy, hence the settlement's moniker. It operated until 1939, when the small railroad fell on hard times and sold it to the Coulee Sand & Gravel Company. The building was remodeled to fit new needs, and the turntable pit was filled with sawdust. The next owners couldn't come up with a doable plan for the roundhouse and put it up for sale around 1982.

This was when Bill Kazel, a mining contractor, saw it on his regular journeys to and from his job as manager of the reopened Mary Murphy gold mine.

"I liked neat old stone buildings," he said. "And one day I noticed that the vent stacks on the roof had fallen down, endangering the building. I thought, 'Somebody needs to do something to save that place.'"

With encouragement from others, including the Colorado Historical Society, "somebody" turned out to be Kazel.

"I thought it'd take about a couple of years and maybe $10,000 to save it," says Kazel. "Turned out it was more like thirty years and $2.5 million."

"We" consisted of Kazel, his son, Greg, occasionally the crew of the Mary Murphy mine, sundry workmen, and all the volunteers he could corral. Stone mason Charlie Womack spent fourteen summers on site restoring the structure's walls.

"So we got the walls fixed and the roof repaired and we put in the doors and windows and got the roundhouse sound again," said Kazel. "And then we looked at each other and said, 'Now what?' I wanted to save this neat old stone structure, and I had. It was for someone else to take it from there."

"Someone" this time was Dr. Charles "Chuck" Brantigan, a vascular surgeon in Denver. He and his wife, Kathy, are historic preservation fans and had done quite a bit in that area previously. They both play tuba in the Denver Brass ensemble.

"I wasn't a rail fan," Chuck says. "But I love unique, historic old buildings like this. We were tired of being landlords of a rental property we owned in Denver so we contacted Bill Kazel and swapped. But we kept him on as a kind of a caretaker, because he really knows the place."

> **"I wasn't a rail fan," Chuck says. "But I love unique, historic old buildings like this."**

The Brantigans are now trying to find a secure future for the Como roundhouse. There has been talk of making it a regional heritage center, or a Forest Service interpretive park that features the history of the area. Funding, as always, is the stickler.

They've had a very determined booster in Gary Nichols, director of the Park County Office of Tourism and Community Development. He's been working with the Como Civic Association, a small group of merchants, artists,

ranchers, and property owners in establishing an economic base for places like Como that will preserve the local way of life and a historical heritage visitors can enjoy, too.

Hugo Roundhouse

It takes money to make more money, and that's been true for another small town in its efforts to restore the last surviving Union Pacific roundhouse in Colorado.

Hugo, population 885 in 2000, has been working at it for a number of years and has put a lot into the vision of a historically significant tourist attraction. The town, like most on the sparsely settled Eastern Plains, is based on farming and ranching. Now that the railroad is gone, Hugo could use an economic boost.

The town hasn't had much attention outside Lincoln County since President Teddy Roosevelt got off the train here in 1903 and had breakfast with the local cowboys. The Hugo roundhouse was on the state's Register of Historic Properties by 1997, and in 2001 was nominated as one of Colorado Preservation Inc.'s Most Endangered Places. The commissioners of Lincoln County decided at that point to step in and make the effort to save the roundhouse official.

If this was a Hollywood movie, the feisty little town of Hugo would have come up with the money for the roundhouse by holding hoedowns, rodeos, and bake sales, culminating in every able-bodied soul picking up a hammer. Maybe some wealthy local curmudgeon would have stepped in, too.

Of course, it takes way more than that to restore a large, historically significant building these days. In 2002, citizens took on the more realistic route of forming a nonprofit agency, Roundhouse Preservation, Inc. It's been soliciting grants from the state, charitable foundations, corporations such as Wal-Mart, individuals, and anything else the board could come up with. Funds have come in fits and starts.

"We don't have city staff to work on this," says Dee Ann Blevins, treasurer for the RPI board. "We're amateurs and volunteers, and we do this on our own time. We don't get much guidance, and we somehow always seem to be dealing with a different official in the same organization. So it's disheartening when some required paperwork is turned down on a technicality with the comment, 'You need to do a better job,' and that's it, we have to start all over."

Nonetheless, Hugo has managed to forge on despite these and other setbacks. The north wall was in the process of being rebuilt at the roundhouse when a sizeable windstorm came through in late May 2008. Without a roof, part of the wall collapsed back into a pile of bricks.

"Turned out to be a blessing in disguise," says Kate Piskorski, who's in charge of the membership for the RPI. "Because the project was covered under county insurance, and that paid for the wall's rebuilding, and this time they insisted on adding rebar so it wasn't likely this would happen again."

Why, yes, they are accepting donations, nice of you to ask! Check with their Web site to see how they're doing: www.hugoroundhouse.com.

Small towns and sparsely populated counties in Colorado have realized that these orphans of railroad history are interesting to a lot of people, not just rail fans. Like The Little Engine That Could, these citizens are determined to chug along even if it's uphill all the way.

Ghost Towns

If there's anything that Colorado has a lot of, it's ghost towns. All those mining booms and efforts to carve out a Utopia, or just a new town, resulted in a bunch of settlements that thrived for a brief period and then dwindled into a clutch of boarded-up buildings.

In Colorado, *ghost town* doesn't necessarily mean deserted, let alone forgotten. Some of these towns are, in fact, places where stubborn holdouts and new residents reside, people seeking places the rest of the state has forgotten. If you drive too quickly down what's left of these Main Streets, you might miss the signs of life still there.

Some of our ghost towns are collections of old buildings removed from their original settings, gathered together, and restored, more or less, for tourism. They range from kitschy amusement park–style attractions to living history centers.

Out of their settings, they're not really like what you might imagine a ghost town is—a truly deserted community off the beaten track, still preserved enough to tell you a lot about it. Unfortunately, places like that are most in danger of being wiped out by souvenir hunters, vandals, and fire.

Here are a few examples of Colorado's ghost towns in different stages of abandonment.

Como

Como has only twenty-four year-round residents. Still, it's never been deserted, which means it's managed to keep a fair amount of the town intact from its railroad boom days. Besides an old stone railroad roundhouse, Como has its original rail freight station (awaiting restoration), an original hotel and the old Eating House on the National Historic Register, a church, couple of schools, pioneer cemetery, and other features of a more prosperous age.

You wouldn't know any of this if you're speeding by on Interstate 285 between Conifer and Fairplay. A detour is worth the effort to see this typical small railroad village from another era. It's high country out here, and that means the best time to visit is in the summer, particularly for Como's old-fashioned Fourth of July fest and its Railroad Days every August.

Dearfield

What remains of Dearfield, about thirty miles east of Greeley, north of Denver, is the last of Colorado's fifteen black pioneer settlements. Three fragile buildings are all that's left of a back-to-the-land movement for African Americans in the early 1900s.

Booker T. Washington's *Up from Slavery* encouraged a number of African Americans to found communities as homesteaders and farmers. Oliver Toussaint Jackson's claim in 1910 on 320 acres of land got Dearfield started, and other families soon followed.

It was a struggle at first, as there was little water, but dry-farming techniques brought in enough crops to keep the community going. Dearfield eventually supported two churches, a school, a restaurant, and a gas station. The Depression and drought in the 1930s hit the settlement hard, the town basically deserted by the time its founder died in 1948.

There are people now fighting to save, preserve, and keep Dearfield. They're up against time, the elements, and repeated vandalism.

After struggling for years to buy more of Dearfield's divided land from numerous property owners, the Black American West Museum in Denver got an unexpected donation of nineteen parcels of land from a local developer. The museum has been racing ever since to get what remains of Dearfield stabilized and, at least, commemorated with a historical marker. Weld County is also now working with the museum to organize a board and preservation efforts for the project.

The museum's executive director and sole staffer, La Wanna Larson, says there's been a considerable rise in public interest in Dearfield. With it come some interesting stories from former Dearfield residents, descendants, and even visitors.

"I had a lady a couple of years back call me," says Larson. "She read about Dearfield in the AAA magazine, *EnCompass*, and she thought a black ghost town would be a neat place to take her grandkids to see. When they got there, they didn't drive too close to the buildings because she wasn't sure if they were on private land or not.

"Well, her granddaughter was bored and didn't want to walk over to see the buildings, so this lady says, 'Fine, you stay by the car, and your brother and I will be back soon.' She looked back when they were a little distance away, and she saw two people walk across right where her granddaughter was.

"That concerned her because she was already worried they might be trespassing on private property, but when she hurried back those people were nowhere to be seen. And then it hit her that those folks had been wearing 1920s-style clothing. She said her grandson saw these people, too, but not her granddaughter. The lady spent quite a bit of time telling me that she wasn't crazy."

St. Elmo

This is Colorado's best-known ghost town. It's been kept in a state of arrested decay by a devoted property owners' association, although there are fewer than ten year-round residents. It's a favorite place for photographers looking for picturesque old towns that haven't been too cleaned up, and for outdoor enthusiasts who stop at the seasonally open general store.

First settled in 1878, St. Elmo was a rowdy mining and railroad town with a peak population of about two thousand. A fire in 1890 destroyed the business section, never totally rebuilt. The area mines began to shut down in the early 1900s, and the last local train took the remaining population away in 1922.

All, that is, except for the Stark family. Anton, Anna, and their three children, Roy, Tony, and Annabelle, owned and operated a general store and hotel, which also became the post office and telegraph office. They were a proud, aloof family, so sure that St. Elmo would make a comeback that they bought up a lot of the town as an investment.

Even after their parents died, the children remained. The sons ran the store and rented out cabins to tourists. Annabelle earned extra income at the Salida telegraph office, briefly married, and eventually came back, alone. Roy died in 1934, and the post office closed in 1952. Officially, St. Elmo did not exist as a town, but Tony and Annabelle stayed on and grew ever more ragged and eccentric.

After Annabelle was seen roaming her property with a shotgun to defend it, she and Tony were sent away to a mental institution. They were released after a friend convinced authorities they weren't a danger to themselves or anyone else. Tony died soon after. Annabelle died in a nursing home in 1960. They left their property to the friend who got them out of the institution.

Today, St. Elmo's buildings are privately owned, and the owners work with the Buena Vista Heritage Museum to preserve what's left of the town after fires took out more of the buildings in 2002.

Soon after Annabelle's death, people reported odd things that happened at the old hotel—doors that slammed shut without cause, inexplicable and sudden temperature changes, cleaning supplies repeatedly brought out of a locked closet when no one was around. A pretty woman in a white dress was seen in the window of the hotel from the street when no one was in the building.

Annabelle, some say, couldn't leave St. Elmo even in death. And she's still keeping an eye on the place.

Recycled Villages and Old Meeting Halls

On July 4, 1976, the town of Greeley celebrated a new settlement built from abandoned buildings once scattered around Weld County.

But no one actually lives here. Centennial Village is an outdoor museum with structures from the 1869 utopian commune of Union Colony.

Another town that corralled abandoned buildings is Burlington. In anticipation of lucrative railroad business, a man named Lowell set up the town in the late 1880s. Not only did he lack title to the land, he was off by about a mile west as to where the Chicago, Rock Island and Pacific Railroad eventually put its depot.

Those who had already built on the original Burlington site decided to transplant their buildings—a huge undertaking that involved skids, poles, and long teams of horses. When the highway and then Interstate 70 replaced the old railroad route, Burlington faced the fact that it was too easy to pass on the way to Denver and points west.

Locals in the 1980s came up with the idea of rescuing old, disused, or abandoned buildings to exhibit together as an example of a Colorado prairie town, circa 1900. There's even a general store advertising period prices.

South Park City is another reconstructed town located in the southern Colorado town of Fairplay. Colorado Springs lawyer Leon Snyder got together with a local historian and other folks to form the South Park Historical Foundation in 1957. There are now thirty-four buildings herded together, most from abandoned sites around the area.

La Sociedad Proteccion Mutua de Trabajadores Unidos (The Society of Mutual Protection of United Workers, SPMDTU) was founded in 1900 in the southern Colorado town of Antonito.

Celedonio Mondragon and six amigos organized the SPMDTU along similar lines as other ethnic fraternal groups of the day, says his grandson, Eppie Perea of Denver.

The original two-story meetinghouse in Antonito still stands, and the organization itself is the oldest surviving *mutualista* in the United States. These days, members meet in more comfortable surroundings.

Where small farming towns have shrunk or even disappeared is where you also find old meeting halls belonging to the National Grange of the Order of Patrons of Husbandry. The Grange was founded after the Civil War in 1867 as a political lobby and fraternal organization for farmers. Women and teenagers were accepted as full members, and a Grange Hall was often the center of non-church social activity.

As the number of farms has declined, so has national Grange membership—300,000 in 2005. Still, the organization tends to cling to its halls, which vary in style but are usually more substantial than the *mutualista* buildings. Denver has an active chapter, which seems odd for a city, but then Grange headquarters is in Washington, D.C.

Resurrected Amusement Ride

The crown jewel of Burlington's rescued structures is something the town wasn't all that crazy about when the county bought it for $1,200 (including delivery) in 1928. It was a carousel built by the Philadelphia Toboggan Company (PTC) in 1905 for the Elitch Gardens amusement park in Denver. It had a magnificent menagerie of hand-carved animals, hand-painted panels, and a fabulous Wurlitzer Monster Military Band Organ.

Elitch Gardens wanted to ditch this in favor of one of the new "jumper" styles where the animals move up and down.

The carousel ran until 1931, when the Great Depression suspended the county fair.

Livestock feed was stored in the carousel building, which encouraged pigeons and other wildlife to take up residence. When the fair was ready to resume six years later, the carousel was an excrement-covered mess and the organ nearly ruined.

But there were just enough locals to save it, and they kept it in business for forty more years, with records to provide music.

Kit Carson County decided in 1976 to make the carousel's restoration its special project in honor of the national bicentennial. Getting National Historic Landmark status helped, but it took twenty-five years and around $270,000 to bring it back to full splendor.

The refurbished carousel has put Burlington back on the map, and you can see why when the pavilion is opened, the lights are turned on, and the organ bursts into song. The hand-painted, hand-carved menagerie includes a half-horse, half-fish creature known as the hippocampus. Victorian panels of pastoral scenes screen the equipment, and elaborately carved wooden gingerbread provides the framework for the electric lights.

INDEX

WEIRD COLORADO

ACKNOWLEDGMENTS

This book could not have been produced without the kindness, encouragement, and support of many extraordinary people. My thanks start with Mark Moran and Mark Sceurman, who took a chance with a freelance writer who dared to tell them, "You don't know weird in Colorado!" Gratitude also knows no limit when it comes to my divine husband, Steve Winograd, and the rest of my family on both sides of our marriage circle, my friends, fellow writers (particularly those in Boulder Media Women), and members of my spiritual support group, Joyful Noise.

I sincerely hope that I have given appropriate credit in the preceding chapters to all the folks who have a particular place there. There are also a number of people and institutions not mentioned in those pages whose assistance was invaluable, or whose stories had to be eliminated for space considerations. With the fervent wish that I haven't inadvertently overlooked anyone, I am greatly indebted to: Jeff Belanger, author of *Weird Massachusetts* and other works; publisher/editor-in-chief of Ghostvillage. com; Matt Bille, author of *Shadows of Existence: Discoveries & Speculations in Zoology*, among other works; Dee Ann and Terry Blevins; Bryan Bonner and Rocky Mountain Paranormal Research Society; Judith Broeker and Jamie Donahoe of Heritage Conservation, Inc.; Linda Budzinski, director of communications and membership services, International Cemetery Cremation Funeral Association; Wayne Cornell, Caxton Press; Dorinda Dembroski, Colorado State Grange; Catherine Dold and Boulder Media Women's Alliance; Lorena Donohue, deputy director/curator of collections at the Littleton Historical Museum; Jo Downey, *Our Journey* and Prairie Development Corporation; Joe Fex, paranormal studies researcher; Peggy Ford and Nancy L. Lynch of the Greeley History Museum; Ken Frye, archaeologist, USDA Forest Service; Jackie Glavinick, Weld County Genealogical Society; Linda Godfrey, author of *Weird Michigan* among other works; Annette Gray and Johanna Harden, archivists for Douglas County History Research Center; Bill Hall, National Center for Atmospheric Research; Valerie Hamlin, Publicist, Central City Opera; Alva Hibbs, Windsor Restoration and Historical Association, Inc.; Grant Houston, editor/publisher, *Silver World*; Lake City, Ken Jesscn, author of *Colorado Gunsmoke: True Stories of Outlaws & Lawmen on the Colorado Frontier*, among other works, Deborah Méndez-Wilson, communications director, University Relations, University of Colorado, Office of the President/System Administration; Christopher O'Brien; Rayetta J. Palmer of Cheyenne Wells, Jane Penley, agricultural appraiser for Elbert County; Jan Pettit and Ute Pass Historical Society; Ed and Martha Quillen of *Colorado Central Magazine*; Rodney Sauer, early cinema historian, director of the Mont Alto Motion Picture Orchestra/Ragtime and Tango Orchestra; Jennifer Teegarden, DNR Forestry, Forestry Outreach Specialist, St. Paul, Minn.; Tom Van Buskirk, manager of Linn Grove Cemetery, Greeley; Fr. Joseph Vigil, St. Joseph's Church, Monte Vista; Lori Winblood, The Doll Lady, Lake City; Linda Wommack, author of *From the Grave: A Roadside Guide to Colorado's Pioneer Cemeteries* among other works; Della Yersin, director of the Burlington Public Library and her friend, Kay Schmidt; Colorado Division of Wildlife, Colorado Historical Society; Friends of Dinosaur Ridge; Iliff School of Theology, Denver; Ira J. Taylor Library; Pikes Peak America's Mountain; Royal Gorge Regional Museum and History Center; *SLV Dweller*, online magazine of San Luis Valley history, culture, news, and events; University of Colorado at Boulder Office of Media Relations and News Services, and the USDA Forest Service.

PHOTO CREDITS

SHOW US YOUR WEIRD!

Do you know of a weird site found somewhere in the United States, or can you tell us about a strange experience you've had? If so, we'd like to hear about it! We believe that every town has at least one great tale to tell, and we're listening. It could be a cursed road, haunted abandoned site, odd local character, or bizarre historic event. In most cases these tales are told only in the towns in which they originated. But why keep them to yourself when you could share them with all of America? So come on and fill us in on all the weirdness that's lurking in your backyard!

You can e-mail us at: Editor@WeirdUS.com,
or write to us at:
Weird U.S., P.O. Box 1346, Bloomfield, NJ 07003.

www.weirdus.com